MOMENTS OF
Cosmic Magick

The life of an intuitive in short stories—
extraordinary accounts of divine intervention,
synchronicity, encounters with Spirit, and
ordeals that test the soul

KENO M POWERS

PowersPress Publishing
INSPIRE ★ GUIDE ★ EMPOWER

Published by:

PowersPress Publishing
INSPIRE ☆ GUIDE ☆ EMPOWER

BRADENTON, FLORIDA

kenompowers.com

ISBNs: 979-8-9934913-0-1 (Softcover)
        979-8-9934913-1-8 (Hardcover)
        979-8-9934913-2-5 (Ebook)

Copyediting by Candace Johnson
Proofreading by Lori Lewis
Interior design by Gary Rosenberg
Cover design by Vesna Tišma:aleaca99design
Head shot by Michael Rischer
Feather fans and rattle photos by Thru My Eyes Productions

For the men and women who've
suffered deep pain and still rise,
to spiritual seekers in search of their
purpose, passion, and peace
who've trusted a feeling, followed a whisper,
or dared to believe there's more—
this is a journey you'll recognize.
Mystical, magickal, and deeply personal,
told with a sprinkle of humor and a
pocketful of awe and gratitude.

*There are more things in Heaven and Earth,
Horatio, than are dreamt of in your philosophy.*

—WILLIAM SHAKESPEARE, *Hamlet*, act I, scene V

Contents

CHAPTER 1
DIVINE GUIDANCE

CHAPTER 2
ENCOUNTERS FROM THE OTHER SIDE

CHAPTER 3
EPIPHANIES THAT EMPOWER

CHAPTER 4
PROFOUND BUT EMOTIONALLY INTENSE

CHAPTER 5
MORE AWE-INSPIRING MOMENTS

Definitions

Cosmic: Cosmic is the rhythm of the Universe whispering through synchronicities and divine timing. It's the invisible thread that weaves stars, souls, and serendipity into a single, unfolding dance. When something is cosmic, it feels orchestrated by an intelligence beyond logic—a gentle reminder that we are part of something infinitely greater than ourselves.

Magick: *Magick* is a term popularized by Aleister Crowley, an early twentieth-century occultist, to distinguish spiritual and ritual magic from stage magic or illusion. He defined it as "the science and art of causing change to occur in conformity with will."

Magick is about presence, intention, and co-creation with the unseen. It's the sacred act of aligning your will with the divine current. True magick lives in the quiet power of a whispered prayer, the subtle intuition that guides your next step, or the transformation that unfolds when you dare to believe in something greater. It's the art of remembering your place as both a vessel of and a spark within the sacred.

Mystical: Mystical refers to the experience of touching something sacred, vast, and beyond the limits of our understanding of reality.

It's the profound knowing that arises, not from logic, but from an alchemical encounter with Spirit—when the veil lifts and you sense the divine. To encounter the mystical is to glimpse the unseen, to feel connected to all things, and to remember that truth is sometimes felt more deeply than it can ever be explained.

Epiphany: As defined in the *Merriam-Webster Dictionary*, an epiphany is "a moment in which you suddenly see or understand something in a new or very clear way." Epiphanies arrive unexpectedly—sometimes in stillness, sometimes in chaos—cutting through confusion with quiet clarity. An epiphany doesn't just change your mind—it shifts your whole way of seeing, revealing important lessons that are applicable beyond the scenarios in which they arrive.

Introduction

Have you ever stopped to wonder when hours, minutes, and seconds were invented? The thought had never crossed my mind, but when I sat down to write this introduction, I found myself pondering the nature of time because this book is about significant moments I've experienced. Being the Curious George that I am, I decided to research their origins online.

The concept of dividing our days into twenty-four hours dates back to the ancient Babylonians around 2000 BCE, in what is now modern-day Iraq. Renowned for their contributions to mathematics and astronomy, the priests of that era tracked the sun, moon, and stars, dividing day and night into twelve equal parts. Five centuries later, the Egyptians refined this concept, formalizing the twenty-four-hour day with sundials and star charts.

Early civilizations understood the concept of dividing minutes into seconds, but they had no reliable way to measure them. That changed in 1656, when a renowned Dutch scientist named Christiaan Huygens invented the pendulum clock—allowing seconds to be tracked with precision for the first time.

Here's something interesting to think about: If you sleep eight hours a night, you're left with sixteen waking hours each day. That's

57,600 seconds in a day, 21,038,400 seconds in a year, and more than 1.6 billion seconds in a lifetime if you live to age eighty.

I realize what I'm about to say is a bit of a cliché, but it's still worth reflecting on: Each second is like a seed, teeming with potential for something amazing. That possibility lies dormant, waiting to be awakened by a thought, a feeling, an action, or a revelation—something that can lead you down a path toward the new, the unexpected, or the profound.

Speaking of profound . . . here's another interesting truth: Time (and space) aren't real. They're man-made illusions—constructs we use to organize experience. We subconsciously choose to let them define our reality. They do serve a purpose, but the truth is, reality is not bound by them.

We tend to assume that two events happening at the same time are simultaneous and of equal duration for everyone. But Einstein's theory of relativity shows that one hour for one person can literally be one decade for another, given the right circumstances. Watch the incredibly profound scene in the movie *Interstellar* with Matthew McConaughey and Anne Hathaway, where they arrive back at their spaceship after exploring the planet below, and you'll know what I mean. Time can also speed up or slow down, depending on our motion, gravity, or even perception. (A clock on a spacecraft traveling through the cosmos ticks more slowly than one on Earth.)

In the fascinating book *The Secret Life of Plants* by Peter Tompkins and Christopher Bird, plants hooked up to a polygraph machine register the thoughts from a human being 10,000 miles away at the exact moment the thoughts occur, proving that the rules of space (distance) don't always apply and that we're all connected.

In my experience with remote viewing, I was able to see places thousands of miles away in my mind's eye. Psychics can read your energy from great distances, as if you were sitting with them in the same room. Time and space work differently or don't exist outside our known reality. Given the relative nature of both, I often wonder if a hundred years on Earth passes in mere seconds on the Other Side, or if our departure from and arrival back to our home in Spirit happens instantaneously.

This book is a collection of some moments in my life—the extraordinary ones I've been honored and blessed to experience. Every story is true, though you might be tempted to believe otherwise. Only names have been changed to protect identities.

Each story stands on its own and can be read in any order, except for "The Devil Came in Four" and "The White Light," which share a continuous thread. "The Devil Came in Four" should be read first, as its events flow into the storyline of "The White Light."

This book was a lifetime in the making and took years to write. I'm excited to finally share it with you. I hope that you'll not only enjoy reading these stories as much as I've enjoyed reflecting on them, but that they will also inspire hope, healing, and wonder.

If you are moved by my memoir in any way, I would be deeply grateful if you shared your thoughts in a review on Amazon, Goodreads, BookBub, or whatever platform you used. Of course, it would be amazing if you shared it with your network too. Your support will help light the way for fellow seekers who also enjoy reading about the same kind of magick you'll find within the pages of this book.

The Meaning of Life

The purpose of life is to learn
The essence of life is to care
The secret of life is to dare
The beauty of life is to give
The nature of life is to grow
The challenge of life is to overcome
The opportunity of life is to serve
The joy of life is to love

—Inspired by William Arthur Ward

CHAPTER 1

Divine Guidance

1

Voice in a Bookstore

As a fourteen-year-old living in Brussels, Belgium, with a limited grasp of French and no understanding of Flemish, I eagerly looked forward to our trips to the US Army base PX. It was a rare chance to shop for familiar American goods—and it offered the comfort of being in a place where everyone spoke my language.

If you're wondering how I ended up in Brussels at that age, it's a simple story. My stepdad, who officially adopted me when I was ten, worked as a diplomat for the United States government. His job rotated him through US embassies all over the world on two- to four-year posts, and Brussels was one of his assignments while I was growing up.

Although my dad wasn't in the military, civilian government employees and their families were granted access to the military compound's stores. The base was an hour's drive from home, and our twice-a-month weekend shopping trips soon became a family ritual.

I don't know where I got my love for shopping, but I've always found joy in strolling through store aisles, whether browsing clothes, electronics, home décor, or even groceries. Ever since my financial wake-up call (which you can read about in this book), I consider myself a recovering shopaholic. I still feel the urge to indulge, but I've come to recognize that, for me, shopping often served as a coping mechanism known as "retail therapy"—a way to lift my mood or manage stress.

Now, I'm much more mindful about how and when I spend my money. I choose to be intentional rather than impulsive, focusing on creating long-term financial security rather than feeding my need for instant or momentary gratification.

The drive through the monotonous countryside to the base was my least favorite part of the trip. To my impatient adolescent mind, the hour-long ride always felt slow and tedious. On this particular day, our family's 1971 Volkswagen camper trudged along the two-lane highway beneath the blazing summer sun. The sun's piercing rays streamed through the side windows, cutting into the cool interior and feeling like a hot blade on my skin. The dull, dusty brown landscape offered little distraction, so I drew the curtains shut to block out the sun's relentless glare.

Bored and restless, I turned my attention to my older brother and younger sister, doing whatever we could to entertain ourselves until we finally reached the familiar guarded gates of the base.

While my dad wasn't into shopping the way I was, there was one kind of store he couldn't resist: bookstores. And luckily, the base had one. Letting my dad loose in a bookstore, however, was like letting an untrained puppy out of the house without a leash—good luck getting him to come back.

He could easily spend hours wandering the book-laden aisles. With his glasses perched on his nose, he'd scan each spine as if searching for hidden treasure. If something caught his eye, he'd pull the book from the shelf and flip through it, landing on a random page. He'd slide his glasses up onto his head, then lean in close, squinting into the book's contents, examining the words with the care of a jeweler appraising a diamond. This ritual was repeated, aisle after aisle, book after book, until he finally decided which treasures were worth bringing home.

On this particular trip, my mom gave me the task of keeping tabs on him and corralling him out of the bookstore if he stayed past his allotted time. I groaned inwardly, but out of respect as a dutiful son, I agreed.

The bookstore was housed in a makeshift structure that looked like it was hastily assembled. It had definitely seen better days. A fresh coat of cheap paint and a plain stenciled sign that read BOOK-STORE did little to conceal the wear and tear of its tired bones.

I followed my dad up the two rudimentary wooden steps and through the worn glass doors. A faint musty odor of dampness greeted us, making my nose crinkle in protest. The floorboards creaked underfoot, underscoring the building's fatigue, a sound that now lingers in my memory as a distant note of nostalgia.

I watched my dad's backside disappear down one of the long corridors flanked by tall columns of commercial-grade steel shelves, each brimming with books. There was an undeniable excitement in his stride, as if he'd stumbled upon the gates of a secret realm that beckoned only to him. He sauntered ahead, oblivious to my presence. I quickened my pace to keep up.

While my dad immersed himself in his private world, I lingered nearby, glancing at my watch, trying to figure out how to pass the time.

Reading didn't interest me the way it did him. I wish it had. It's incredible to think about how many books exist in the world and how much knowledge and insight they offer. Sometimes I feel like I'm missing out. But the act of pausing long enough to dive into a book feels like confinement. It felt that way back then, and even now, it still does. I have to force myself to start a book. Once I do, the odds of my getting far are slim unless it really captivates me.

I'm one of those people who has trouble sitting still. My legs or feet tend to sway or tap as if they're keeping time with a song only they can hear. Part of it is just how I'm wired, but there are deeper reasons why reading has never come easily for me.

One of them is that French was my native tongue. I was born in Paris, France, and lived there until I was about four, and then we moved to the Philippines. For the next year and a half, I developed a Franco-Philippine accent so thick that no one could understand me. By the time we arrived in the United States, most kids were learning to read while I was struggling to learn English.

Because I had so much trouble, my parents had me repeat first grade. And while I've never been formally diagnosed, I've long suspected I have some form of dyslexia—which only adds to the challenge.

It's not that I don't read at all, but I have to make myself slow down long enough to do it. My wife keeps suggesting I try listening to books, but that doesn't interest me. There's something appealing about holding a book and physically flipping pages.

On that warm summer day, as my dad perused the history section, I was eager to check out the latest electronics and search for a new model tank to build and add to my collection.

Before long, I realized that the stamina I had developed as a budding long-distance runner didn't translate into the patience needed to wait for my dad. Restless and bored, I ventured off to see if I could find something—anything—to pass the time.

I wandered through the silent aisles, thumbing half-heartedly through books like a child picking at a meal they didn't want to eat. I longed for something to break the monotony. Eventually, I drifted over to the books about cars and hung out there for a while. When I got tired of looking at the pictures of exotic sports cars, I went to the sports section, hoping it might offer a sliver of interest.

While browsing the small selection of books on running, my attention was drawn to the spine of an oversized paperback lying horizontally atop the row of books. It was partially hidden in the shadow of the shelf above.

To satisfy my curiosity—and my slightly compulsive urge to put it back where it belonged—I pulled it out and examined the cover. It featured a simple, almost childlike illustration: two arms and hands cradling the title in drab, earthy tones. Behind them loomed a large, burnt-orange sun, complete with a face, peering at the text from behind a stylized semicircle. The artwork was so rudimentary that it looked like a novice had drawn it. The title, printed in bold, unembellished type, confidently declared it as *The Massage Book*.

As a touchy feely kid who was a competitive runner, I was naturally inclined to rub my legs to ease their soreness after strenuous workouts or races. Until that day, I hadn't realized that squeezing muscles had a name—or that it was an actual profession called massage therapy.

Curious to learn more, I flipped through its pages, pausing now and then to study the elementary illustrations scattered among the text. I was trying to make sense of what I was reading when, all of a sudden, I heard a voice.

"You may do this one day," it announced in a calm yet cryptic tone.

Startled that someone would be standing so close to me, I instinctively turned around. No one was there. Rattled by the intrusion, I peered down both ends of the aisle, my heart beating rapidly in my chest. Not a soul was visible.

A burst of fear shot through my body, electrifying every nerve like a bolt of lightning. Visions from horror movies I was fond of watching flooded my imagination. I slapped the book back on the shelf and bolted, desperate to get away from whatever ghoul or ghost was lurking there.

Like a child pulling a bedspread over their head as if it had the power to protect them from the monster in the closet, I ran as fast as I could into the reassuring presence of my dad.

His face was buried in a book as I panted to a halt beside him. I couldn't tell if he was lost in his own world or deliberately ignoring me, hoping I wasn't there to tell him his time was up. Either way, it didn't matter—I felt safe. I didn't think my dad would have a clue about what had just happened, so I decided to keep it to myself.

The experience had shaken me so deeply that I promptly shelved it into my subconscious, forgetting it ever happened. That memory stayed locked away until almost a decade later, when another fateful moment brought it rushing back.

Eight years and several moves across the world later, I found myself living in Eugene, Oregon. I had moved there with dreams of competing for the renowned University of Oregon running team, but plans changed, as they sometimes do.

Years of training and racing had left me worn out, not just physically, but also mentally. Once I arrived in Eugene, I wasn't sure my body could handle the demands that world-class running would require, nor did I relish putting myself through the mental rigors. I ultimately decided to walk away from those childhood aspirations.

Although I chose not to pursue my competitive ambitions, running remained a constant in my life for the peace of mind it brought me and the way it helped me stay in shape. It was a form of meditation, a way to clear my thoughts and better cope with life's stresses—or so I hoped as I set out for a run one dreary winter afternoon.

Plumes of breath billowed into the cold air like steam from an old locomotive as the rhythmic cadence of my legs carried me through the final stretch of a five-mile run. Lost in thought, I didn't notice the puddle of half-frozen mud until it was too late. A cold, brown sludge splattered my legs, mirroring my mood. I cursed my luck, scolding myself for not paying better attention.

I had gone for a run, hoping it would quiet my troubled mind, but it wasn't working. I felt stressed out about my future, unsure of what it held. It was clear I was going to need more than a run to sort things out.

I was twenty-two years old, barely making ends meet, working at a fast-food restaurant. I had left college before finishing my first year, walking away from a path that felt hollow and unfulfilling. Quitting had been my choice—but now I felt stuck, unhappy with where I was in life, and unsure of what I was working toward or where I was headed.

As I neared the last quarter mile before my tiny apartment, I slowed to a walk. Whatever benefit the run might've offered was drowned out by the judgmental ruminations of my inner critic, hitting me up the side of the head as if I were a loser, undeserving of love or forgiveness. I felt like a victim of my own dissatisfied life, and I had no idea how to turn things around.

Back at home, I sought refuge in the shower. The hot spray cascading down my head and face warmed the chill in my bones and eased the tension in my mind. Showers had become my sanctuary—a place where the noise of the world receded, if only for a few moments. In that quiet, under the soothing flow of water, I leaned into the silence with a yearning—like a plant stretching toward the first light at the break of darkness—searching for even the faintest trace of calm. I clung to my affirmations and offered them as whispered prayers to whoever might be listening, hoping to find something more hopeful, something that could wash away the sins of my ineptitude.

Richard Bach, a favorite author of mine at the time, wrote about how his creative ideas often came to him in the shower. He believed his inspiration came from an external source—and even called the source "shower fairies." I don't know if I'd go that far, but I could relate. I'd had my own moments when unexpected insights arrived, seemingly out of nowhere, while standing beneath the comforting rush of water.

As I reflected on the passages from Bach's book, my thoughts turned to my future. I looked up at the ceiling as if God were there, and out of exasperation, I asked the question that had been haunting me: *What am I going to do with my life?*

Then, without warning, a brilliant burst of light popped brightly, like the flashbulbs of those large vintage cameras from the early 1900s. I should have been blinded by its intensity, but curiously, I wasn't. As I stared into the light, the words *massage therapy* slowly shimmered ethereally into view as the radiance began to fade. Bewildered, I couldn't tell if the words had appeared in front of me or inside my mind.

I mouthed them silently to myself: *massage therapy.* I was dumbstruck, as if I had just been offered an answer to a complex theory, my mind slowly absorbing the magnitude of it. The idea filled me with equal parts awe and disbelief.

Why hadn't I thought of this sooner? It made perfect sense.

As a competitive runner, I knew firsthand the benefits of massage—how it could ease sore muscles and aid recovery. I had often rubbed down my own legs after grueling workouts or races.

Before I could dwell on it further, a wave of memory crashed over me with sudden, overwhelming force, as if a dam had burst. That voice in the bookstore! The details of that long-forgotten memory flooded my senses, sending a chill racing down my spine. I stood frozen, my mind spinning as I tried to make sense of it all: the seemingly random act of pulling the book from the shelf, the strange and cryptic voice, its eerie prophecy, and the excitement and awe sparked by the mystical message I'd just received. The invisible thread connecting those moments felt surreal—like uncovering a hidden design I hadn't known was there.

I stood in stunned silence. Who, or what, had spoken to me all those years ago? How could they have known what I might do a decade later? It seemed like someone—or something—was looking at a blueprint of my life, gently steering me toward a purpose I hadn't yet recognized. The thought filled me with a deep amazement that no words could express.

Still wrapped in my reverie, I stepped out of the shower and dried off, pondering the message behind my mystical *Twilight Zone* moment.

Despite my attempt to hold onto the magickal feeling, the intensity and grandeur of the phenomenon slowly faded as I got dressed. I hated coming back to the more mundane existence of life after a brush with the rich, sacred enchantment of the spirit world. It felt like a letdown—a reluctant return to the lifeless essence of ordinary reality.

While I wasn't given any answers about the messenger, I was left with a consolation, something far more valuable: a sense of direction. For the first time in a long while, I had something I was excited to explore. I immediately researched my options, and within a couple of days (this was before the advent of the internet), I discovered a state-approved licensing program for massage therapy at the local community college.

Three years would pass before I completed the program, but in June 1988—a full decade after that fateful moment in the bookstore—I became a licensed massage therapist in Oregon.

"You may do this one day." The voice turned out to be a

harbinger of my future. Not only did I become licensed, but my career as a bodyworker would span over twenty years and include more than 25,000 appointments.

Looking back now, I can't help but marvel at how an unassuming moment in an old bookstore could shape the trajectory of my life. That voice, whoever or whatever it was, knew something about me that I didn't yet know about myself. It nudged me toward a calling I hadn't imagined.

Massage therapy didn't just become a career—it became a way to connect with others, to heal, and to be of service in a deeply personal way. Over the course of two decades, I worked with thousands of people, many of those sessions serving as reminders of how profound moments of guidance and calm can be.

The voice in the bookstore remains a mystery, one I'll likely never solve until I pass to the Other Side. But I've stopped needing to know. Because in the end, what matters isn't who delivered the message—but what I chose to do with it.

2

The Fourth Knock

I've been accused of being a dreamer, as if it's something to be concerned about. While I may have my head in the clouds (you would too if you experienced the same kinds of surreal moments I have), I also have a highly developed analytical mind with a penchant for practicality. You'd have a hard time convincing me of something if it doesn't make logical sense to me.

Our education system and its models for learning are a case in point. By the time I was a senior in high school, I had had enough. I came home one day and calmly but firmly announced to my parents that I was done with school. No argument, no debate—just a quiet declaration that landed like a grenade.

To them, leaving school meant jeopardizing my future. I didn't like disappointing them, but when it came to this decision, nothing they could say would shake my resolve.

I didn't leave school because I disliked learning. I left because I was utterly bored with what was being taught. I was tired of sitting still for hours listening to information I found irrelevant and uninspiring. It reminded me of being dragged to church as a child against my will and suffering through the stuffy sermons.

I was so despondent and disengaged that I'd literally fall asleep in class. I felt like a caged animal—pacing back and forth, watching the time with a restless eye. I couldn't understand why I was required to take classes like math, biology, or chemistry. As far as I could tell, they had no relevance to my life beyond school. I'm not knocking the subjects themselves—if you love them, more power to you. But I craved something else: learning that would prepare me for life, give me a sense of purpose, or at least spark my curiosity.

If I'd gone to a school where I had a say in what I studied, not only would I have stayed, but I would have been an A student. The same goes for college. If I'd had the chance to sink my teeth into something that felt meaningful, I would've thrived. I did eventually find something—but that's another story in this book.

My parents—especially my dad—believed that education, including a college degree, was essential for success in life. They tried repeatedly to change my mind, hoping I'd come around to see things their way, but I held firm.

While I was relieved to be done with school, it didn't solve the deeper problem. I was uninspired, bored, and depressed, with nothing to do and no sense of purpose—like a sailboat adrift without a rudder.

Getting a job wasn't an option. Since I was the son of an American diplomat living in a foreign country, I didn't have a proper visa and couldn't legally work. There wasn't much to do beyond the occasional odd job, though I did take the initiative to detail some cars on my own as a side gig to earn a bit of money.

Concerned for my well-being, my parents searched for something to help me get back on my feet. A friend of theirs suggested the Outward Bound program. After they looked into it and ran it by me, I enrolled in their monthlong program set in the rugged Blue Mountains of New South Wales, Australia.

Outward Bound originated in England in 1941 to enhance the survival skills, physical fitness, and resilience of young sailors, many of whom were dying under the harsh conditions at sea during World War II. What puzzled authorities and ultimately led to the program's creation was the significantly higher survival rate of older sailors enduring the same conditions.

Studies revealed that these older sailors fared better not because they were stronger, but because they had weathered hardship before. Their life experience gave them the mental and emotional endurance to navigate extreme circumstances more effectively. This insight underscored the power of experience in overcoming adversity, forming the foundation of Outward Bound's mission: to build resilience through demanding and formative experiences.

Today, Outward Bound is a global network offering outdoor education programs designed to foster personal development, leadership, and community through immersive wilderness challenges.

My adventure with Outward Bound was incredible, and I'm grateful my parents had the wherewithal to enroll me. But it was not easy—not by a long shot. I was pushed beyond my limits—not just physically, but mentally and emotionally. Some parts were grueling, others miserable, but that struggle was exactly what made it so meaningful. It challenged me, changed me, and made me a better person.

It also sparked something small but significant in my relationship with my dad. We had never hugged as father and son, but the first thing I did when I saw him was wrap him in a hug. He was surprised—maybe even a little thrown off—but I know he liked it. He was a good man, and he deserved my love and appreciation. From that day on, hugging became part of our connection—something we shared for the rest of his life.

To address their concerns about my future with education after I returned from Outward Bound, my parents enlisted the help of a longtime friend who had previously worked as a college guidance counselor. Mrs. Johnston was an intelligent, no-nonsense woman I'd gotten to know through my parents. I saw her as fair and wise, and I agreed to talk with her.

After our conversation—and several more with my parents—we decided the best path forward was for me to move back to the United States on my own to finish high school and earn an American diploma. I wasn't exactly eager to return to school, and I had no intention of going to college, but there was nothing for me in Australia, so I reluctantly agreed. My mom made arrangements with her best friend—someone she had known since before I was born—for me to stay with her and her family in Washington, DC, while I attended school nearby.

In January 1984, I boarded the long flight from Sydney to Washington, DC.

For the next six months, I went through the motions of high school without much fanfare. Once I graduated, however, the topic of college quickly turned into a heated debate between my parents and me. To appease them, I eventually agreed to give it a try.

Of the few places I was considering, the University of Oregon in Eugene seemed like the best fit for several reasons. First, I wanted to live somewhere surrounded by beautiful nature. Second, the school had a world-renowned running program—and as a competitive runner with the promise of greater things, I felt it was a smart choice. Last, because I had delayed my decision about college, I'd missed the application deadlines for most schools. Fortunately, the University of Oregon's enrollment period was still open.

After years of being moved around the world for my dad's work, Eugene was the first place I chose for myself. While I had doubts about going to college, I felt the enthusiasm of a young explorer, eager for a new adventure and excited at the thought of moving to Oregon.

Eugene was entirely new to me. The people were openly friendly, the city—nestled in a valley of trees—was every bit as beautiful as I'd been told, and the university campus teemed with possibility.

A few months after the move, I began settling into a rhythm. Lazy Sunday mornings quickly became a favorite. Even though I didn't live on campus, I decided to spend one Sunday relaxing in the university student union with a cream cheese bagel for breakfast. I wandered through the empty building, passing by different arrangements of tables, chairs, and couches until I found the perfect spot: a tucked-away space on an oversized, circular couch wrapped around a low wooden coffee table beside a large picture window, with a view of the grounds and rays of sunlight streaming across it.

I plopped down on the couch and took a few minutes to enjoy the silence and the warmth of the sun. I yawned, lay down, and slowly stretched out like a cat, reveling in the abundance of time with nothing scheduled. Growls from my stomach prompted me to sit up and eat my breakfast. I unfolded the crisp parchment from around my bagel and savored a big bite, smacking my lips like a young kid.

Little did I know I was about to set something in motion—planted in the stillness of an ordinary moment, destined to bloom into one of the most profound encounters of my life.

Or perhaps it had already begun.

That's the mystery of destiny and free will, isn't it? Every choice we make becomes a thread that leads us somewhere. But when did the thread of that moment at the student union begin weaving its way into my fate? Was it when I agreed to move back to the States? When I decided—quite reluctantly—to give college a try? Was it the moment I chose Oregon? Or was it a seemingly insignificant choice—my decision to walk into the student union that morning instead of spending the day somewhere else?

As I munched on my bagel, I noticed a gently used copy of the school newspaper, *The Oregon Daily Emerald*, lying on the large wooden coffee table in front of me. I grabbed it, propped my feet up, and began to flip through the paper to satisfy my penchant for browsing without commitment while I ate.

Halfway through, I was surprised to come across an article about a psychic. Finding something like that in a school paper struck me as unusual. I've long been captivated by psychics, mediums, and the world of intuition. I often wondered if I had any latent talents like the ones they expressed so freely. I'd had numerous "out of the ordinary" experiences that bordered on psychic, but they always seemed to happen to me—not because of anything I consciously did.

Intrigued, I read through the article. When I realized the psychic was local, a jolt of excitement shot through me like an electrical charge. I had often imagined what it would be like to meet a psychic—and in that moment, I made a crazy, spur-of-the-moment decision: I was going to find her.

The psychic's name was Jasmine, and the article had plenty of intriguing details about her, which heightened my desire to speak to her. Since it was Sunday, the paper's office was closed and wouldn't be open until the following day. I could hardly contain my excitement as I waited for the next day to come.

I called minutes after the office was supposed to be open.

"The article on Jasmine was written by one of our student freelance writers," the young woman on the other end of the phone remarked when I inquired about it. "Would you like her phone number?" she asked.

"Yes, please," I replied enthusiastically. I jotted it down and hung up. With a sweaty palm and my breath quickening, I dialed the writer's number. The phone rang twice, and then my call was answered.

"Hi, Rebecca," I said. "My name is Keno. I got your number from *The Daily Emerald*. I just read your article on Jasmine, the local psychic, and would love to talk to her. Could you give me her number?"

"Oh, hello," Rebecca replied. "I'm sorry, but her contact information is confidential and not for me to give out."

The wind of excitement that had pushed my sail forward suddenly dropped like a dead weight. I floundered for a moment but quickly collected myself. While I was wholeheartedly disappointed, I was not deterred. Something had stirred inside me when I read the article. Whatever it was that was motivating me, it wasn't just curiosity. I had to speak to Jasmine. I pressed the issue, telling Rebecca the story of how I happened upon the paper, how it had made me feel, and my interest in all things intuitive.

After several back-and-forth exchanges, there was a pregnant pause on her end. With an air of quiet resignation, Rebecca realized that I wasn't going to give up. While she held her ground and didn't give me Jasmine's phone number, she did offer the names of two streets in town that intersected and told me that Jasmine lived in that area.

I was ecstatic! I thanked Rebecca profusely, hung up the phone, and danced around the room like I had just won the lottery. That afternoon, I mapped out my plan. I was going to ride my moped to the intersection, scout the neighborhood, and then start systematically knocking on doors until I found her.

When I got to the intersection of the suburban neighborhood Rebecca had given me, I rode up and down each street, fanning out a few blocks in each direction. The houses were well-kept middle-class homes with neatly trimmed yards and manicured landscapes, some featuring classic white picket fences. I was hoping one of them would have a large neon arrow pointing from the heavens to her doorstep or a burning bush to indicate I was at the right place. Stranger things have happened in my life.

I parked close to the intersection, and as I got off my moped, the notion of what I was planning to do suddenly hit me. *This is nuts*, I thought. My mouth dried up like the Midwestern plains at the height of summer, and my stomach turned queasy at the thought of knocking on strangers' doors. I went from bold and resolute to questionably courageous.

I paced back and forth, mulling over whether I was going to follow through with my plan. I thought about why I was doing this and decided that it was more important for me to find Jasmine than to cave to the whims and fears of my ego—no matter how convincing its argument was that riding my moped back home was the best plan of action.

The first house off the intersection had a long walkway to the front door. As I made my way to the front stoop, I wondered if anyone in the house could see me coming. There was an ornate knocker on the door, but I rang the bell instead, thinking that would be less startling.

I could hear someone stir from inside. After a long pause, an elderly woman opened the door.

"Can I help you?" she asked, her voice frail and tentative.

"Hi. Is this the home of Jasmine ?" I asked with as much confidence as I could muster.

"No one by that name here," she replied.

I thanked her and headed to the next house. There, a middle-aged man eyed me with suspicion as he stood behind his screen door. I told him I was looking for Jasmine and asked if she lived there.

"I don't know anyone by that name" was all he said before quietly shutting the door in my face.

They say the third time's a charm, but that wasn't the case on this day.

However, on my fourth knock, a short, casually dressed woman with an unassuming face behind wide-rimmed glasses opened the door.

"Hi," I said. "Is this the home of Jasmine?" The woman peered at me from behind her glasses, with a slight quizzical gaze. "I'm Jasmine," she said, wondering who this young kid was standing at her door. I blurted out my story and asked her if she would be willing to talk to me.

"Come on in," she said with a quick smile.

I followed her into a modestly decorated living room, where

she motioned for me to sit on a couch across from her La-Z-Boy chair. I quickly glanced around the room, trying not to draw too much attention to the fact that I was checking out her place. I was half expecting to see crystal balls, spell books, and other paranormal paraphernalia, but nothing about her home seemed out of the ordinary.

In a calm, matter-of-fact way, Jasmine began to talk about me, telling me things about my life she couldn't possibly have known. I was transfixed. She confirmed what I'd long suspected—that there was far more to reality than our culture typically acknowledged. While she answered my questions, some of her answers only led to more.

Time flew by in a daze. When Jasmine was done with my reading, I looked out the window and saw that the night had quietly crept in without my notice. Not wanting to overstay my welcome, I thanked her for her time and asked if I could talk to her again. She happily gave me her number and encouraged me to call anytime.

I strode out into the clear, crisp night with a spring in my step, gazing up at the starry sky. The vastness of it filled me with awe. Every cell in my body hummed, echoing the cosmic mystery from the heavens, blurring the line between me and the divine. I felt a profound sensation that a large, invisible hand had guided me— from going to the student union to seeing the article about Jasmine to locating her home on the fourth try. I didn't realize it, but I had just experienced a spiritual awakening. All I knew in that moment was the unshakable joy radiating from my soul.

Over the following months, Jasmine and I spent more time together as promised, and she continued opening my mind to otherworldly possibilities I hadn't ever imagined. One of the most memorable events was a reading Jasmine did for a small group of friends.

"Keno," she said over the phone, "I'm having a small gathering at my house for a flower reading, and I'd like to invite you."

"A flower reading?" I asked, not knowing what that was.

She went on to elaborate. "There are nature elementals—gnomes and fairies that take care of every plant and flower in the plant kingdom. I'm asking everyone to pick a wildflower to bring to the event and I'll be talking to the fairies and gnomes of each flower."

Mesmerized by the idea, I told her I would be there.

On the day of the event, I didn't have time to go foraging for wildflowers after work, so I plucked one in the late morning before my shift and then absentmindedly left it in my backpack all day.

There were about eight people sitting in a circle that night, each holding a flower. Jasmine went around to each person and telepathically communicated with their flower's nature element.

When my turn came, I sheepishly slid down into my chair in embarrassment, trying to disappear, as I got an earful by a gnome, my flower's caretaker, for leaving it in the dark of my bag all day.

Not long after the event, Jasmine surprised me with a request.

"Keno," she said, "I want you to do a reading for a friend of mine."

"A reading?" I asked, perplexed. "What do you mean by a reading?"

Jasmine explained that everything—every object and person—was made up of energy, and that energy carried information. In the case of objects, a person could even pick up impressions about the individual the object belonged to, who had owned or worn it. The ability to "read" that energy was called psychometry. Jasmine confided that, according to her intuition, she believed I had that ability.

I was flabbergasted. I'd had intuitive moments before—some pretty amazing ones—but I seriously doubted I could do what she was suggesting. Still, after some gentle encouragement, I agreed to meet her friend Joy later that week to give it a try.

When the time came, I donned my helmet and warm jacket and rode my moped for the twenty-minute drive to Joy's house. The autumn evening felt cold against my face, but it didn't faze me. I was too preoccupied with the intoxicating mix of excitement and a sense of strange portent hanging in the air. I didn't know what was going to happen that night, and I couldn't have guessed it if I'd had a thousand tries. All I could tell as I headed to Joy's place was that the evening felt rich with hints of supernatural possibilities.

Joy was a tall, slender woman in her sixties. She was thoughtful, down-to-earth, and had a refined creative streak that expressed itself in the classy way she dressed and in the way she had decorated her cozy little home. It was no surprise to learn she had once been an interior designer.

She led me into her living room, sat me down on the couch, and walked to the kitchen to get me a glass of water. When she returned and handed it to me, she sat in an accent chair close enough to reach me with an outstretched hand. To avoid revealing details about herself and her life, we kept our conversation to a minimum and began our experiment soon after I arrived.

To start things off, Joy informed me that she was going to take me through a guided meditation to help me calm my nerves and unwind from my day. She instructed me to get comfortable and to close my eyes. When I was ready, she spoke in a soft, gentle voice, taking me through a short but effective inner journey. When she was done, I opened my eyes. I felt noticeably calmer and more relaxed.

Joy began the session by handing me a piece of jewelry and asking me to tell her whatever came to mind. I placed the trinket in the palm of my right hand and rested it on my lap. I closed my eyes, trying not to force any thoughts or impressions. I didn't expect anything to happen, so I was quite surprised when the words, "This belonged to your grandmother," came out of my mouth.

While my eyes remained shut, Joy replied, "Yes, you're right. What else can you tell me?"

"You loved your grandmother and cherished the times you spent with her. She understood you like no one else did."

Joy confirmed that everything I had said was true. "Keep going," she said with an encouraging tone.

"You were a precocious child with a vivid imagination. Your grandmother nurtured that part of you. You also had glimpses into the spirit world and felt safe sharing that with her because she was a spiritual person with those glimpses as well."

"That's amazing!" Joy exclaimed with hushed excitement. "You're doing really well. Let's try something else."

I handed her the jewelry, and she replaced it with a wispy, multi-colored pastel scarf woven with a beautiful design. I carefully folded the scarf, held it in my right hand, and then took a couple of slow, deep breaths. It wasn't long before I began picking up perceived information.

"This scarf belongs to you. In fact, I think you made this scarf a long time ago."

"You're absolutely right," Joy replied.

I continued to get impressions.

"You like to read. I'm getting an image of a book. I think it's a book you're reading right now. I sense it has a cloud on the cover."

"I have to show you something," Joy said quietly.

I opened my eyes and watched her get up and walk down a long hallway across from where I sat, past a couple of doors, and into a room to the right at the end of the hallway. She emerged a moment later holding a hardback book with a dust jacket. She strode up to where I was sitting, looked me in the eye with clear admiration, and handed me the book.

"I read every night before I go to bed. This is the book I'm reading right now."

I turned the book over to see the cover and gasped. It was a rather plain cover—a sky blue backdrop with one striking image: a single pastel-painted cloud.

"Jasmine was right about you," Joy remarked as she sat back down in her chair. "Not only can you do this, but you're amazing at it."

I blushed as the words "thank you" came shyly out of my mouth.

"Would you like to try again?" she asked. Something in her tone told me this object was particularly special.

I nodded. "Sure," I said with quiet enthusiasm. I was riding a wave of adrenaline, reveling in the amazement of what was happening. I wasn't ready for the evening to end.

Joy handed me a watch that was sitting on a little table next to her chair. It was a stylish, silver-colored watch with hands that told the time and a clinking metal wristband. It felt substantial as I held it in my hands. I spent a moment admiring it before I placed it in the palm of my right hand, as I had the other items. I closed my eyes, took a few calming breaths, and waited to see if anything popped into my mind.

"This watch belonged to your husband—your ex-husband," I added. "You got divorced a long time ago. It was hard at first, but you eventually healed your differences and became amicable, even good friends. He's passed away, and you still sometimes think of him fondly." I opened my eyes and looked at Joy. "Am I right?" I asked.

"Yes, that's exactly right," she replied.

In the periphery of my vision, a movement in the hallway caught my eye. I turned to see what it was and was shocked to catch a glimpse of a dark, shadowy figure disappear into the first room down the hallway. Chills ran up and down my whole body. Joy noticed my expression and asked me what was wrong.

"I think I just saw a spirit," I said. I had never seen anything like that before. The sight of it triggered a scary memory from my childhood.

One night when I was nine years old, as I was lying in bed waiting to fall asleep, I heard what sounded like a male voice say my name as if someone was standing right next to me. It didn't sound like a friendly voice. I don't know if my reaction was because I had seen too many horror movies or because I had an overactive imagination, but I felt like I had something to fear from whatever was speaking my name.

To say it scared the bejeebies out of me would be an understatement. Without hesitation, I scrambled out of bed and darted into my parents' bedroom across the hallway. They were reading in bed, bewildered by my behavior as I crawled into their bed, squeezing in between them. It took a while before I was willing to leave the safety of my parents' sanctuary. Nothing ever came of the incident, and while I never heard the voice again, I've never forgotten it.

So there I was, twelve years later, spooked and unsettled like I had just heard that voice again. Joy tried to calm me down and assure me I was safe, but I still felt unnerved. I suddenly felt drained of energy.

"What time is it?" I asked.

"It's 12:30 a.m.," she replied.

"It's 12:30 a.m.?!" I exclaimed. I didn't realize it until that moment, but I had been in an altered state. Like an artist lost in his work, time had passed without notice.

We made small talk for a few minutes, and then I got up off the couch, excusing myself for the night. Trembling slightly, I hugged Joy good night and walked out into the eerie silence of the moonlit night. As amazed as I was by my ability to psychically gather information from holding objects, and as much as I enjoyed the experience, I was eager to get some distance between me and whatever I had seen in Joy's house.

The roads were empty and quiet as I puttered through her neighborhood to get onto Coburg Road, one of the main arteries in town. It was a wide expanse of asphalt, a four-lane road with a narrow, low concrete divider separating the two directions. With all the shops, hotels, restaurants, and businesses lining its sides, it was a beehive of activity during the day. The speed limit was 35 mph, but most drivers drove 40 to 45 mph, making it a white-knuckle prayer of a ride on a moped with a top speed of 30. I only risked venturing out on it when I had to. That night, it was the only route from Joy's place to my house.

The night felt apocalyptic as I left the safety of Joy's neighbor-hood and merged onto Coburg Road. Barely a soul was in sight. A low-lying fog had moved in during the night, adding to my dread of the ride home. My route took me over one of the town's land-marks: a dimly lit bridge with a green-colored iron canopy spanning a river that snaked its way through the city. It was the scariest and riskiest part of my trip because the bridge created an arc in the road that bent enough to reduce visibility from one end to the other. I checked my side-view mirrors nervously as I approached the criss-crossing girders of the bridge.

My moped hummed with a loud whine as I held hard on the throttle, trying to squeeze every last ounce of power from the tiny engine.

"Come on, come on, go faster," I coaxed as if my moped were a sentient being that could increase its speed if it chose to.

A third of the way across the bridge, I caught the glare of head-lights from an upcoming car in my side-view mirror. I was in the right lane, and it was coming up right behind me. Afraid it might not see me in time, I quickly moved into the left lane to let the vehicle pass. I watched as it ambled past me. Maybe it was because I took comfort in the sight of another soul journeying through the barren night, but I kept my eye on it for too long.

Another flash of headlights behind me caught me off guard. Before I had time to think or prepare, a black muscle car with tinted windows growled menacingly as it sped past me in the right lane. Without slowing down, it darted into the left lane to pass the car in front of it. The driver of the beast misjudged the distance as he wove between us, clipping my moped.

The next thing I knew, my moped was sliding down the road on its side, my body tumbling after it. The assailant roared ahead, disappearing around a bend in the road.

When I came to a stop, I lay still. Small plumes of my ragged breath melded with the fog above me. I was immune to the cold.

My mind scrambled to make sense of what had just happened. Fear, shock, and confusion made it hard to concentrate. I forced myself to focus. The first thing I did was scan my body for injuries. *Shit!* I couldn't feel my legs. Was I paralyzed? I couldn't tell if my legs were badly hurt or just numb from the surge of adrenaline. I didn't dare move for fear of making things worse.

I looked back toward the bridge, the direction from where I'd come, and realized that a car coming down the left lane might not see me in time. My imagination conjured up some pretty ugly scenarios. I used my arms to pull my body toward the center concrete divider and got as close to it as I could. I wasn't completely out of danger, but I did lessen my chances of getting run over.

At some point, a passerby going the other direction stopped and asked if I wanted them to call an ambulance. Because I couldn't feel my legs, I yelled out a yes and waited for the EMTs to arrive. They took me to the nearby hospital, where I was relieved to hear that I had only suffered minor injuries.

My body may have escaped serious harm, but my psyche was deeply shaken. Questions about what had happened and why haunted me. Was the accident somehow connected to my spiritual exploration? Had I ventured into forbidden territory? Were malevolent spirits following me, causing the crash as a warning? These thoughts plagued my mind, casting a shadow over my newfound abilities.

Jasmine and Joy tried to comfort me, assuring me that my foray into the spiritual realm and my use of my intuitive abilities were not to blame for the accident. Yet, the fear and uncertainty were too overwhelming. I couldn't shake the sense that I had crossed an invisible line. The accident felt like a harbinger, a stark reminder of the dangers that lurk in the unseen world.

Despite their reassurances, I stopped trying to use my intuitive abilities. The experience left a scar on my psyche—a cautionary tale etched into the fabric of my being. Since that day, I continued to have profound, out-of-the-ordinary experiences—events that you'll read about in this book. Yet the memory of that night driving home from Joy's lingered, a constant reminder of the fragility of our existence and the unseen mysteries that lie beyond our understanding and the powers capable of intervening in our reality with dire consequences.

It would be twenty-five years before I dared to try psychometry again. When I finally did, it was with a renewed sense of purpose and a deeper, more mature frame of mind. Just like the older sailors from World War II who inspired the origins of Outward Bound, I had learned the ropes of my spiritual journey, cultivating wisdom and resilience.

As I look back on the series of events that led me to Jasmine and the extraordinary experiences that followed, I realize it was a pivotal time in my life—a spiritual awakening that set the stage for everything that came afterward. It affirmed a suspicion I had— there is so much more to reality than most of us acknowledge or understand—and that we are capable of far more than we realize.

The DNA of Destiny

The brisk chill of an Oregon fall hung in the air, visible in every breath as I wove my way across campus to the university bookstore. A sea of black umbrellas, dotted with brightly colored raincoats, bobbed across the grounds beneath the canopy of towering oak and maple, skirting puddles and debris from the previous night's storm. The sidewalks glistened with a wet sheen, shallow pools mirrored blurred shadows of passing students, while the splash of car tires through standing water on the nearby street punctuated the background hum of campus life.

I glanced up at the sky, grimacing at the thick, ominous gray clouds looming overhead. They bore down with a cloying sense of foreboding, deepening the melancholy and frustration weighing on my mind.

I was a twenty-two-year-old college dropout, scraping by each month with little to show for the years since I'd left school. I didn't drop out because I was reckless, rebellious, or incapable. I left because the boredom had become unbearable, and I couldn't justify paying out-of-state tuition for classes I had no passion for. Being required to take courses just to satisfy someone else's idea of what was important rubbed me the wrong way. Okay, maybe I was a bit of a rebel.

Though I believed leaving had been the right choice, it left a bruise on my ego. I wrestled with shame and guilt—not just for quitting, but also for disappointing my parents. That inner weight took a toll. Instead of a high-paying job with room for growth, I settled for low-paying, menial jobs, not because I wasn't a capable, intelligent human being, but because I was naive and carried a debilitating sense of not being good enough.

My one glimmer of hope was the pursuit of my massage therapy license. The program was affordable by most standards but still more than I could manage in one payment. Fortunately, I had the option of paying for individual classes when I could afford them, allowing me to start learning without having to wait. The downside was that the dragged-out pace prolonged the feeling that my life was stuck in limbo.

While I wasn't a student anymore, I still lived just blocks from campus and often wandered through it, drawn by its beauty, restaurants, shops, and the plethora of activities available to the public. It was a hub of activity with a slightly intoxicating buzz as hundreds of students and adults milled about like busy ants in a colony.

That day, I was dodging the occasional raindrop as I headed to the bookstore to buy a textbook for my upcoming physiology and anatomy class.

The internet hadn't been invented yet, so instead of social media, people posted flyers to get their message out to the public. Flyers were everywhere on campus, advertising everything from lost pets to upcoming events. Every lamppost on the grounds was plastered with thick layers of old and new ones, thumbtacked or taped together in a chaotic, colorful collage. Stopping to read them was an interesting way to pass the time.

As I made my way to the bookstore, a movement on one of those lampposts caught my eye. It was a flyer flapping in the wind, beckoning like an outstretched hand trying to flag down a taxi.

Before I continue the story, there's something you should know about me. I've always been the kind of person who goes out of my way to fix small wrongs. I'll pick up an item off the grocery store floor and put it back where it belongs, or knock on doors in a neighborhood until I find the owner of a car with its headlights on. I even return rogue shopping carts left out in the parking lot. My wife might tell you I'm a little obsessive. I prefer to think of it as being thoughtful and considerate.

So, when I stopped at the lamppost, my intention was to fix the flyer. I grabbed the edges of the paper, curious to see if it was just junk or something worth saving. What I read intrigued me. In big, bold letters, the top of the flyer announced an eight-week class titled "Imagine That!" Taught by a local woman, it was an experiential adult learning course focusing on goal setting, visualization, and meditation, along with exercises in self-discovery, mindfulness, and empowerment. *Cool*, I thought.

At the bottom of the flyer, slender, tearable strips of paper listed the class details in tiny print, inviting anyone interested to take one. I carefully tore off a strip, slipped it into my coat pocket, and reattached the flyer to the lamppost with a tack borrowed from an outdated post.

Later that evening as I lay on my couch mulling over my day, the memory of my run-in with the flyer popped into my head. I walked over to my coat hanging by the door, fished the crumpled strip from a pocket, and flopped back down on my couch. I unraveled the tiny piece of paper and stared at the information.

I thought back to what I had read on the flyer. Everything about the class spoke to me—offering exactly what I needed at that point in my life. I really wanted to take the class, but there was a major hurdle: the $150 cost. I was barely managing my basic expenses, along with the cost of my massage program. My practical self questioned how I could justify spending money I didn't have on another class that was more of a "nice to have" rather than a need.

Stumped but not deterred, I wondered how I could come up with the extra money. As I sat there, I had a light-bulb moment. I didn't have the money, but I did have something to offer—my skill as a massage therapist. While I wasn't licensed yet, I felt confident enough to use my talent as a bartering tool. I was already trading with my hairstylist; maybe the teacher would be open to a similar exchange? It was a long shot, but my plan was simple: I would show up on the first night of class and offer to trade massages for the course.

Several weeks later as fall waned into winter, the night of the first class finally arrived. I bundled up and stepped out the door. The brilliance of a full moon took me by surprise. I stopped for a moment, marveling at its glow. It was a welcome sight, though it did little to chase away the cold. I dug my hands deep into my coat pockets, pressing my arms against my sides in search of warmth as I made my way through the quiet night.

When I reached the campus, I followed the main artery—a pedestrian-only, tree-lined street cutting through the heart of the grounds. Normally bustling with life, tonight it felt like a ghost town. Only two distant silhouettes moved along, side by side, hurrying with deliberate strides toward someplace warmer.

Decorative streetlamps lined the way ahead, their soft glow offering comfort in the eerie stillness. The dry rustle of golden leaves scuttling across my path, carried by a stray breeze, accentuated the silence of the night. I took momentary comfort in the sound, but inside my head, a storm was brewing. With each step, doubt began to gnaw at my confidence in my plan, the feeling growing stronger with every stride.

I had no idea at the time, but I was walking up to a moment that would shape one of the most important decisions of my life—one with the power to alter my destiny in ways I couldn't yet imagine. It was what I now call a fate marker.

Moments in time are like the cells in our body. They're alive, interacting to fulfill their purpose, each programmed with its own instructions. But instead of carrying the blueprint for our physical development, a moment's DNA contains the blueprint for our destiny. This blueprint coordinates our choices and actions among infinite possibilities. Just as you can change the design of a house, so too can the details of your destiny shift—with each decision you make. Free will.

Every choice carries a consequence. Some are immediately clear; others we recognize only later—and some we may never fully understand.

I don't claim to know exactly how the world of Spirit works, but there's one thing I believe with certainty: Much like it's shown in one of my favorite films, *The Adjustment Bureau* with Matt Damon and Emily Blunt, there are beings—unseen to the naked eye—who try to influence our destiny by injecting thoughts and feelings into a moment, like a whisper in our ear, nudging us to behave a certain way or make a specific choice. At first glance, these decisions might seem insignificant. But when we look back, we often realize they were far more meaningful than our rational minds or limited perspective could grasp at the time.

If we have the awareness to hear that whisper, we can use mindfulness to process the message. Whether we choose to follow it or not is up to our free will. But making that choice isn't always as easy as it seems—as you'll soon see in my case.

My inner storm reached a crescendo—a deafening boom of thunder—as gnawing doubt erupted into a flood of judgments. I stopped in my tracks, trying to make sense of the whirlwind in my mind. Like the scene in *The Wizard of Oz* when Toto pulls back the curtain to reveal the man behind the illusion of the wizard, I recognized the entity behind the ominous threats.

It was my ego, bristling at the thought of showing up to a class without money—essentially "begging" for a trade. My plan felt beneath its grandeur. My ego launched into a barrage of criticism.

She's not going to agree to this, it sneered. *You're not even licensed. She doesn't know anything about you.* I stood there, frozen, as the inner tirade continued.

No woman is going to let some random guy give her a massage! it mocked. *That's the dumbest idea ever. What an idiot! You should turn back now before you completely embarrass yourself. Besides, you're just a kid. She's not going to take you seriously.*

I stood there, stunned and ashamed by the brutal logic. *He's right*, I thought, deflated. *This really is a stupid idea.* Feeling embarrassed for even considering such a ridiculous plan, I turned to head back home.

That's when I heard another voice in my head. It simply said, *Stop.*

I say I heard a voice, but it wasn't exactly like that. It was more like a thought—a whisper that carried the weight of a voice. It had a soothing, almost otherworldly quality. The word *stop* didn't come as a command but as something sacred—an invitation, like a calling. It cut through the storm with quiet urgency.

Once the voice had my attention, it continued: *It's important for you to go to this class.* The voice was soft, warm, and quiet, but it held an air of wisdom—one that reverberated through my soul. In the future, I would come to trust this voice more easily, but in that moment, I hadn't yet learned to put my faith in it.

My ego—ever the logical, analytical, and protective part of me—was determined to keep me from looking foolish. It heard the voice too but had no intention of letting it influence my decision. With its usual bravado, it launched a counterattack. *I know you best*, it insisted. *I'm here to prevent you from feeling embarrassed.* A flood of rationalizations followed, each one trying to discredit the whisper, erupting into an invisible battle—between my ego and higher self, between my mind and heart—raging in the debate halls of my mind.

When my ego realized it wasn't making headway, it shifted tactics, slipping into the voice of the inner critic—a clever, biting persona it used when its first strategy didn't work. It knew exactly how to keep me in line. Like an abusive parent, it hinted at consequences if I dared to listen to that voice.

Overwhelmed by the relentless barrage, I felt my courage collapse beneath the weight of doubt and fear. I started heading home, resigned, and ashamed that I had the audacity to think my plan was a good one. But just as I took my first few steps, the voice returned—gentle, steady, and unshaken. Its message pierced through the noise with quiet certainty, offering something my ego couldn't counter—a compelling promise: *There's someone at the class you need to meet.*

Those words, full of hope and profound implications, ignited a warmth in my heart that reverberated through me in a wave of invisible energy. As if by magic, the chains of my ego's control shattered—and in an instant, I was filled with courage and determination.

With that simple promise, I did a 180 and headed toward the building where the class was held. As I entered the foyer, I spotted the teacher standing behind a card table and a short line of people waiting to register for the class.

Amanda was a petite, fit woman in her early thirties, with long brown hair and soulful eyes. When it was my turn to approach the table, a frog lodged in my throat and a bowling ball spun in my stomach. I forced myself to push through my nerves. Doing my best to stay calm, I walked up to the registration table and said, "Hi, my name is Keno. I'd like to take your class, but I don't have the money to pay for it. I'm a massage student at the community college and was wondering if you'd be open to trading for massage."

When I finished speaking, Amanda took a long look at me. Her piercing gaze met mine and held. I could almost see the wheels of her mind turning as she sized me up. Then, without a word, her focus shifted inward. I watched her process my request, the silence growing unbearable as the pounding of my heart filled my ears.

Finally, as a sign that the debate had ended, her expression softened into a warm smile.

"Sure, I'd be willing to trade with you," she said with a welcoming, melodic voice. "I have to register people for the class, so head on in and let's talk details later."

I couldn't believe my ears. My body was zinging with energy—an overwhelming sense of surprise and relief at her answer, pride for having taken the courage to ask, and excitement for what lay ahead. I thanked her and practically skipped into the classroom like a little kid.

As I sat down, waiting for the class to start, I thought about the internal battle I had fought on the way here and how close I came to turning back home. It was a powerful lesson: My ego wasn't always right, no matter how convincing it sounded. And that quiet voice—the one I had almost ignored—was something I needed to listen to more often.

I've looked back on that moment many times, and I still shudder at how close I came to letting my ego make the decision for me. But, by the grace of Spirit, I didn't. Amanda and I became fast friends, but more than that, we've helped each other in countless, significant ways over the course of our decades-long friendship. Our playful spirits and shared interest in spirituality and personal growth forged a bond that lasts to this day. Even when our lives don't intersect for long stretches, we always reconnect as if the distance and lack of contact don't matter.

Sometimes, the importance of our choices is obvious, and we treat the moments around them as such—like when preparing for a job interview or a first date. And then there are those moments that appear mundane, with no outward signs of significance—like ripping the small strip of paper from the flyer for a class that looks interesting—that are actually part of a larger thread, quietly weaving a life-changing story into the tapestry of our lives. It's only in hindsight, days, months, or years later, that we understand how high the cost would have been if we hadn't taken certain actions.

How many chances slip through our fingers because we fail to recognize the hand of destiny at work? How many lives are lived on paths we settle for out of safety, a lack of courage, or simply because the opportunity to change course passes unnoticed?

But then, for those aware enough to listen, those who find the courage, there are times when something intervenes—call it fate, Spirit, or your higher self—that attempts to guide us to use our free will to make the best decision for our highest good. These are the moments when destiny isn't just written in the stars but built into time, encoded in the DNA of our existence. And if we're lucky enough to hear that whisper—to act on it—the path before us transforms in ways we never thought possible.

4

The Flying Book

"I Kissed a Girl." That's the name of a catchy song by Katy Perry, released in 2008. It was also a fantasy I was harboring about a girl I knew named Shelly.

Shelly was an employee at the upscale club where I worked, and I had a secret crush on her. It seemed like the feeling was mutual. We flirted almost every time we saw each other—furtive glances, witty banter, and the flash of pearly whites. More than once, I imagined tasting her cherry ChapStick.

There were several reasons why I was reluctant to act on my desire though. Shelly was a bit younger than me, young enough for us to be in very different stages in our lives. I also questioned whether we had enough in common. But the biggest reason for my hesitation was that we worked in the same place.

I once made the mistake of dating a coworker a few years earlier. What started out as fun and exciting eventually turned into a drama-laden nightmare that made going to work stressful and unpleasant. I had no desire to relive that mess.

Still, I couldn't get her out of my mind, especially since I saw her so often. After months of tantalizing temptation, and against my better judgment, I bit the bullet and asked her out. We hung out several times, and while I found her undeniably alluring, I kept my hands to myself. I felt like I was playing with fire.

Ever seen the cartoon of a guy with an angel on one shoulder and a devil on the other, getting an earful from both? What followed in the privacy of my mind was an all-out debate between the devil on one shoulder and the angel on the other.

Devil: *You should definitely go for a hookup. Who cares if you're not the perfect match!*

Angel: *Don't sully his soul with your garbage. He should only make love to her if he thinks it's going somewhere.*

Devil: *What? Forget that. He wants to rip her clothes off, and he should because he can. She's been waiting for him to make a move—trust me.*

Me: *I do? She is? Oh God, he's right. I do!*

Devil: *God? This ain't His department, kid.*

Angel: *You're too much. He should definitely not. It's too risky. He could really screw things up at work.*

Devil: *Screw at work? Now you're talking!*

Angel: *That's not what I said, and you know it.*

Me: *You guys are driving me crazy!*

Clearly, my own thoughts were getting me nowhere. I needed advice from someone I respected before I lost my mind. I needed to talk to Jennifer.

Jennifer was a cheerful, articulate woman with a caring heart and a keen sense of aesthetics. She owned a charming gift shop in the downtown area that catered to the spiritually minded, just a stone's throw from where I worked. I regularly stopped by to browse through all the unique and thoughtfully curated treasures she had—tasteful knickknacks, decorative home items, a small collection of books, and other intriguing odds and ends. It was the kind of place where time slipped away without you noticing.

It was also where I had some of my most enriching conversations.

Jennifer and I shared a deep interest in personal growth and spirituality. When she had time, we would dive into deep conversations about love, relationships, and aspirations—anything and everything that mattered to the soul.

More than once, I thought she could be a highly successful advice columnist, like a modern-day Dear Abby. She was full of wisdom and insight, and our talks were often stimulating and uplifting. I almost always left our visits feeling better than when I walked in.

If anyone could help me with my dilemma, it would be her. As soon as I had a long enough break between clients the following day, I ran over to see if she was available to talk.

The jangle of bells hanging on the storefront door announced my arrival. Jennifer looked up from the cash register on the opposite side of the store, where she was helping a customer. She gave me a quick hello and then focused back on her task at hand. The number of people waiting patiently in line for their turn made my prospects of getting Jennifer's ear look slim. I checked my watch and decided I had some time to wait and wander through the store.

Jennifer didn't carry many books, but the ones she did have were scattered throughout the store, mixed in with other miscellaneous items on tall, heavy, freestanding bookshelves strategically placed throughout the space. I browsed through a couple on one bookshelf before turning around and noticing a beautiful vase perched on a display table. I picked it up, admired its craftsmanship, then set it back down.

Lost in reverie, I took a few steps backward to continue gazing at the vase, completely forgetting about the bookshelf behind me. The moment my body made contact, I froze in horror as I felt the bookshelf tilt away from me.

I held my breath, bracing for a loud crash, already picturing Jennifer maxing out my credit card to cover the damages.

That long moment of expecting the worst is seared into my psyche, but by the grace of God, no crash came. The large wooden bookshelf had somehow miraculously righted itself without top-pling over.

Before I could turn around or even exhale in relief, something smacked the back of my head and tumbled to the ground a couple of feet in front of me. I flinched and turned my gaze downward just in time to see a small paperback book land face-first on the floor, splayed open.

I squatted down to take a closer look. It was a book on relation-ships by someone named Barbara De Angelis, titled *Are You the One for Me?* The subtitle read *Knowing Who's Right and Avoiding Who's Wrong.*

Out of curiosity, I flipped the book over and started reading a paragraph on one of the pages it had opened on. I inhaled slowly, then held my breath, my eyes locked on the words staring at me from the white pages. I couldn't believe what they were telling me. I read them twice, maybe three times, before finally exhaling. Goose bumps erupted all over my body.

Right there, in black and white, and in no uncertain terms, was a passage that answered my question about Shelly: Should I pursue her, taking it to the next level?

The answer was no.

Like a spiritual verdict handed down in ink, the moment I saw it, I couldn't deny the truth. It was a bittersweet moment—relief at finally having an answer to the question that had plagued me for so long, and disappointment that my attraction (or lust) wouldn't get to play out.

I stood there stunned, absorbing the weight of what had just transpired—and the fateful, serendipitous journey that had brought me there. The flirting and doubt that sparked the question. The impulse to seek Jennifer's advice. The circumstances that led me to linger and browse. The careless, absent-minded step backward into the bookshelf. The flying book that struck me like a cosmic tap on the head—landing open to the exact message I needed.

All of it was like a movie directed by silent, invisible calls for action—and cut.

Jennifer was still busy behind the counter, but I no longer needed her help. Spirit had given me my answer in a way no human counsel ever could.

I waved goodbye and stepped out into the sunlit afternoon, my heart lighter and my mind clearer. I marveled at the thread of events that led me to my resolution. Not just for the burden that had been lifted, but for the deep, unshakable sense that my life was being guided—answering even my most private struggles, like what to do about Shelly.

I made my way slowly back to work, smiling as I reflected on the karmic clarity I'd been given. I was disappointed not to be frolicking with Shelly, but I sensed a bullet had been dodged—and was grateful for a gentle tap on the head now rather than a cosmic two-by-four later on.

I went to Jennifer's store looking for advice, but what I got was exactly what I needed—a moment of divine intervention.

5

Friend on a Flight

The Christmas decorations still hanging after the holidays at the San Francisco International Airport had lost their charm as I lugged my overstuffed carry-ons through the terminal in the early morning hours of the new year. I was heading back home to Eugene, Oregon, from my annual pilgrimage to Washington, DC, to visit my parents and the siblings who could make it in for the holidays. Christmas with family, in the house that held many fond memories, was always a highlight of the year. I'll forever cherish those times, but after two weeks, I was eager to be home, living my own life, sleeping in my own bed.

I grumbled as I rushed through the busy airport. Why do booking companies plan connections with barely enough time to switch planes? Don't they bother checking how far one gate is from the next? My mood wasn't helped by the fact that I had to get up at 3:30 a.m. to catch the first leg of my trip. This wasn't the first time I'd scheduled a sunrise flight, and I silently cursed myself for scheduling yet another one.

Why did you book such an early flight? I muttered silently to myself. It was a rhetorical question, but I heard more responses than I bargained for. I was about to have a Snoopy comic strip moment, mimicking the ones Charles M. Shulz created for the Peanuts series, where some of Snoopy's body parts make comments while he's out for a jog.

My pragmatic side spoke up first: *Early morning flights are cheaper, and you'll get home at a reasonable hour. That way, you can settle in before your first week back at work.*

Making sure he was heard too, my inner child whined, *I'm tired! I hate getting up so early. Let's never do this again!*

Then my GI tract chimed in: *Early flights mess with our pooping schedule!* (Did I really just write that?)

My bladder jumped in next: *We hate sitting still until the seat belt sign turns off. It's torture!*

And no matter how much water you drink, the GI tract added indignantly, *we're always getting constipated on trips!*

I shook my head at the internal drama and refocused outward, scanning for signs I was heading in the right direction. Throngs of people milled about the wide walkways between shops, eateries, and gates—some hurrying to their own flights, others staring blankly as they wait to board, and a few with headphones, oblivious to the world around them.

I threaded my way through the crowds, the heavy weight of my bags pulling at my shoulders and the pressure of making my flight exacerbating my strained mood. Despite all that, I made it to my gate with minutes to spare.

Though flying can be stressful and tiring, there are two things I genuinely enjoy about it. One is the opportunity to get dressed up. I'm one of those rare guys who would rather go shopping for clothes than watch sports. While some people save their best outfits for a play or a concert, I like to look sharp at 30,000 feet.

I think it's a crime, but men generally have it easier in our patriarchal world. With that said, and I hate to admit it, I'm glad to be a man. Still, if there's ever a reason to be a woman, or at the very least, to envy them, it's for their clothing options and accessories.

My go-to travel outfit is simple yet polished: a pair of chic jeans, a stylish long-sleeve shirt, and my favorite square-toed designer boots. If I'm traveling in colder weather, I top it off with a long black wool overcoat that makes me feel both suave and snug.

The other aspect of flying I enjoy is the chance to engage in witty banter with strangers. Catching a plane feels like an adventure into the world of possibilities. I always wonder if I'll meet interesting people or have unexpected, cool experiences.

You know the phrase "Chatty Cathy"? My wife loves to laugh and roll her eyes at me because I'll often strike up conversations with strangers and talk up a storm. So now, she's nicknamed me Chatty Keno.

My favorite flying experience was a Christmas season flight from Washington, DC, to Eugene, Oregon, when I was in my midforties.

As a side note, I've had a very youthful-looking face for most of my life, especially in my twenties. I was once carded at a nightclub when I was twenty-eight years old. The bouncer looked at my driver's license, then at my face, and then back down at my ID with an air of disbelief. Finally, as he handed me my license, he exclaimed, "Damn, man, you look good!"

For this particular trip, I had hoped to book a nonstop flight, but there weren't any, so I opted for a short layover in Chicago, where I didn't have to get off the plane.

The window seat was my first choice as a kid, but now when I fly, I always grab an aisle seat. That way, I don't have to ask anyone to get up when I want to use the bathroom, stretch, or mingle with the flight attendants in the back of the plane, and it gives me the opportunity to talk to more than just the person I'm sitting next to.

On the first leg of my journey, I sat across from two young women, one of whom was celebrating her twenty-first birthday. We struck up a conversation early on and exchanged witty banter the entire way. When the lead flight attendant heard that one of the girls was celebrating her twenty-first birthday, she gave them free booze and even crafted a crown out of peanut bags stuck together with coffee stirrers. By then, the four of us had developed a fun, festive rapport.

Have you ever seen those flight attendants who make everyone laugh with their zany, over-the-top intercom announcements? Ours was exactly that—fun, boisterous, and brimming with personality.

When I headed to the back of the plane midflight to use the restroom, the charismatic flight attendant and two of her coworkers were gathered nearby. As I stepped out of the bathroom, she spoke to me.

"Hon," she said with a slight southern drawl, "could you do me a favor?"

"Sure," I replied.

"You see that light up there in the bathroom?" she asked, pointing to a fluorescent light on the wall near the ceiling of the bathroom I had just used.

"Yup, I see it."

"Great," she said. "Do me a favor and clap your hands in front of it." Confused but willing to oblige, I stepped back into the bathroom and clapped my hands near the light.

"It's not working," I called out.

"Try again," came her reply.

I raised my arms and clapped my hands a few more times. Suddenly, I heard a burst of laughter from all three flight attendants. I quickly realized she had just pulled a fast one on me.

Feeling sheepishly silly but appreciative of her clever, smart-ass sense of humor, I burst out laughing too. After a long bout of uncontrollable, full-belly laughter and a few tears, she commented on how good a sport I was. I returned to my seat, grinning from ear to ear.

Five minutes later, she was back on the intercom, making the whole plane laugh again. This time, she ended her message with "And watch out for the young gentleman sitting in seat 25A."

My jaw dropped in shock. That was my seat! Everyone in the front section of the plane immediately turned to look at who she was talking about. I wanted to melt into my chair. I gave everyone a mock look of dismay, rolled my eyes, and slunk down into my seat, wishing I could disappear. Fortunately, this was before 9/11, so no one took her comment seriously.

When we landed in Chicago, I was sad to see the crew and most of the passengers, including the two young women, disembark. We said our goodbyes, and I stayed on the plane, flipping through a magazine to pass the time.

A few minutes later, movement at the front of the plane caught my eye. I looked up to see the fun flight attendant walking toward me.

"Hey hon," she said. "You know the young lady sitting across from you who was celebrating her birthday? She asked me to come back and see if you'd be interested in getting her phone number. She thought you two had a nice connection."

I was flabbergasted and flattered. Before I could respond, she added:

"I told her you might be a little too old for her, but I'd ask anyway. I guessed you were about thirty-four or thirty-five." I paused for a moment, debating whether to tell her how old I really was.

"I'm actually forty-five," I said, trying not to sound embarrassed. Her look of shock was priceless.

"I never would have thought!" she exclaimed. "Good for you. I'll tell her you were flattered." I wished her well and thanked her for making the trip so memorable.

I felt so elated by the experience that I later wrote a letter to the airline's CEO, praising her outstanding service and nominating her for an award—if such a program existed.

Another one of my favorite flying stories is the time I sat next to a woman who was as talkative as I was. In fact, we talked the entire flight. After the plane landed, but before we could exit, we stood waiting, continuing our conversation. Two middle-aged men standing in the row behind us were watching us intently. During a short pause in our conversation, one of them decided to interject.

"Hey," he said, grabbing my attention. "I want you to know I lost twenty dollars because of you."

I gave him a puzzled look, so he elaborated.

"Yeah," he went on, gesturing to the guy next to him, "I bet my friend here twenty bucks that you'd stop talking. But you never did, so now I have to pay up."

My seat companion and I laughed, but I could tell from his tone that he wasn't entirely amused.

My plan, as I boarded my flight from San Francisco to Eugene, was to catch up on some badly overdue sleep. I was in no mood for chitchat, let alone a lengthy conversation.

When I stepped onto the plane, I asked the flight attendant greeting passengers if it was going to be full.

"Not even close," she replied. "You'll probably get a whole row to yourself." That was music to my ears. I couldn't wait to stretch out and nap through the entire flight.

As I slowly made my way down the aisle, scanning the rows ahead of me for an empty one, my gaze briefly landed on a well-dressed, middle-aged woman sitting by herself in the middle seat. As I laid eyes on her, she looked up from her laptop and met my gaze. She smiled warmly and then looked back down as I continued searching for my spot.

I still remember the moment, decades later, as if it's a scene from a movie recorded in my mind. There was nothing romantic or flirtatious about it, but there was definitely something notable. The energy of that moment was subtle, and like parts of a dream we forget after waking up, any significance that moment might have had quickly dissipated into oblivion as I continued searching for a section on the plane to call my own.

The first vacant row happened to be right behind the mystery woman, and that's where I decided to park myself. Once the plane was airborne and the necessary announcements were over, I lifted up the armrests of the seats next to me and lay scrunched up in a fetal position to catch up on some badly overdue sleep.

The next thing I knew, I felt a tap on my hip. It was the flight attendant notifying me that the plane was beginning its descent and that it was time for me to sit up and buckle my seat belt.

I sat up slowly, groggy from the deep sleep I'd fallen into. I sluggishly strapped myself in, rubbed the fatigue from my face, then checked the seat pockets in front of me for any of my belongings. Someone had left a *People* magazine behind, so I pulled it out and flipped through the pages.

While I was catching up on celebrity gossip, I received a telepathic message. It was an unmistakable nudge from within—a personal directive from my inner voice. The request popped into my mind, and in essence, it said, *Keno, I want you to talk to the woman sitting in front of you.*

That was it. There was no *Hey, Keno, how's it going? This is your Higher Self speaking. Are you having a good trip? I've got a great thing set up for you on this flight.*

Instead, it was just a dry, "do-this" type of notification.

What? I thought, momentarily taken aback. It was such a strange and unexpected proposal that I questioned it immediately. But no further explanation came. Welcome to the world of Spirit. I don't know if the lack of detail was an issue with my end or theirs, but in that moment, I was annoyed by the lack of clarity and direction.

Uh, yeah. I don't think so, I replied internally.

I justified my refusal with excuses. Some pretty good ones, I thought. One, I was tired. Two, I was foggy-headed. And three, I had no clue why I was reaching out to her or what I'd even say. My attitude was, if you're not going to help me out here with more details, I'm not going to play the game.

But the inner voice wouldn't let up. Whatever or whoever was prompting me to talk to the woman ignored my excuses and nudged me repeatedly to start a conversation. I leaned over from where I was sitting and peered discreetly through the seats in front of me to see what she was doing. She was holding up loose papers in one hand and writing on others spread out on her tray table, like she was editing a document. I leaned back, content with ignoring the call. But the feeling persisted.

Why aren't you listening to me? I asked, growing more annoyed by the minute. *I'm not going to talk to this woman. I don't have any reason to.*

It was obvious I wasn't the only one doing the ignoring. The voice continued to play the message like a broken record. *Talk to her!*

No, I countered. *Not unless you tell me why.*

But no answer came.

I scooted over to the window seat and stared out at the dense, gray clouds blanketing the landscape below. The view matched my mood—brooding and stubborn. I was determined not to engage.

But the inner prompting was relentless, poking at me like a thorn in my side. Nothing I did or said deterred it. In fact, the longer I ignored it, the stronger the sense of urgency became, and the more annoyed and uncomfortable I felt.

Imagine a child incessantly pestering a parent for something they want, like out in public at a department store, and you'll understand what it was like. At some point, you just have to give in to keep the peace and your sanity intact.

I've had many inner prompts before. That voice, wherever it comes from, has helped me with all sorts of things, from the mundane to the sacred and everything in between. It notifies me when I've missed a dirty towel in the hamper as I'm walking to the laundry room to start a wash. It lets me know if I left a burner on—on the stove. When I had a cat, it told me when my furbaby wanted to come in, or if I was walking to a bus stop, that I needed to run if I wanted to catch the one coming. Sometimes, my inner voice speaks up when I need to pay attention to something around me because it's important for me to do so. (I'm still waiting for it to give me the winning lottery numbers!)

Maybe it was because I was ignoring it so much, but I'd never been so pestered and bothered by my inner voice like that before. The urgings were so persistent that I realized the only way I was going to find peace was to say something to the woman sitting in front of me. I checked the time and saw that we had ten minutes left before touchdown.

Have you ever seen a comedic scene in a movie where the main character practices what to say in front of a mirror before addressing the person they want to talk to, so they don't sound pathetic—but they end up being pathetic, and you laugh? Well, that was me, only I didn't have a mirror, and I couldn't practice out loud for fear someone might think I was crazy.

I slid back over to the middle seat and leaned forward so that my face was in the gap between the seats ahead of me. Trying hard to sound like a normal person with a casual curiosity, I spoke up. "Excuse me."

I waited for her to turn around so she could see my face.

"I know this might sound out of the blue, but I was wondering what it is you do for work?"

I cringed as the words came out of my mouth.

What it is you do for work—Seriously?! quipped my ego. *Could you have sounded any more inept? She's going to think you're some kind of moron.*

Her expression was open and genuine and not at all dismissive like I thought it might be.

"I own a business in town, and I'm a business consultant," she replied, her voice calm and professional. She looked at me for a moment longer, but when I didn't say anything beyond "Oh, that's cool," she turned back around to continue what she was doing.

I leaned back into my seat, at a loss for what else to say, feeling rather stupid.

That was awkward, I thought, regretting that I had let my inner voice rope me into talking to the woman. Then, to my surprise, she turned back around.

"That *was* a little out of the blue," she said, a hint of intrigue on her face. "What is it that *you* do?"

I told her I was a massage therapist at an upscale social club in town. She looked thoughtful and a little surprised.

"Really? That's interesting. My partner and I have been talking about hiring a massage therapist to teach us. My name is Melanie. What's yours?"

"Mine's Keno."

"That's an unusual name," she replied.

I told her the story of how my little sister couldn't pronounce my given name *Kenneth* when she was learning how to talk and how it came out as "Keno" and stuck.

"How cute," she remarked with gentle warmth. "We should exchange numbers. I'm also a member of the club. Maybe we can get together for coffee one day?"

As the plane made its final approach, I felt a mix of relief and curiosity. Exchanging contact information with Melanie brought a strange sense of wonder to the persistent nagging of my inner voice.

Weeks later, over coffee, our conversation flowed effortlessly as Melanie and I each shared stories about our own personal and professional lives. As I listened to her speak that day, and over the months that followed, I realized that my inner voice, which had been so insistent, was not just a random prompting. It was a guiding force to meet someone who would become a close friend and an important ally in my life for years to come.

The inexplicable nudge from within had led to a bond that would enrich both our lives for many years in unexpected ways, proving that it's always a good idea to take heed of what your inner wisdom says. Sometimes, doing what it requests—even when it doesn't make sense—can lead to profound connections, fulfilling friendships, and opportunities you never imagined.

6

Shaman Spirit

The moon glistened against the backdrop of ominous clouds, painting the crisp autumn night with dramatic shapes and tones of smoky indigo and blackened blue. It was another quiet, uneventful evening after work, and as a single, introverted homebody, I relished the opportunity to savor the solitude and cozy up with a good book in the warmth of my humble abode.

A perfect date night for one.

I poured myself a cup of steaming, velvety-rich hot chocolate in the kitchen, its indulgent fragrance wafting through the air as I grabbed my latest read and made my way to the living room. The couch drew me in with familiar ease as I sank into its embrace. With the anticipation of a child at story time, I nestled into the perfect position beneath the soft comfort of my favorite blanket.

With mug in hand, I took in my surroundings with a mindful gaze. The enchanting harmonies of Enya drifted softly in the background as the light from a dozen flickering candles danced across the room, casting a warm glow over my dimly lit living space. A swell of gratitude rose within me as I soaked in the ambiance, relishing the sacredness of this quiet moment and the joy of knowing the rest of the night was mine to do as I wished. A slow, involuntary sigh escaped my lips as my body sank deeper into relaxation.

I cracked open my book, letting the words pull me into their world. I had barely taken in a few sips of hot chocolate when the sharp trill of my landline shattered the silence. The sound ripped through the tranquility like an uninvited guest. I frowned at the intrusion and shot a glance at the wall clock nearby. Just past 9:00 p.m.

Who could be calling me at this hour?

I debated whether to let it go to voicemail, but my curiosity wouldn't allow it. The suspense of not knowing was too much to ignore. Sighing, I set my cup down, threw back my cover, and reluctantly pried myself from the cocoon of my couch to answer the phone sitting in the kitchen.

"Hello, this is Keno," I said.

I recognized the voice on the other end of the line immediately. It was Lila, one of my best friends.

"Hi Keno, it's Lila. Listen, sorry to bother you so late. I have a huge favor to ask you," she said. Something about the tone of her voice caught my attention.

"What's wrong?" I asked. "Is everything okay? You sound like you're in pain."

She let out a small, self-deprecating sigh.

"I did it again. Guess I'm officially the reigning klutz of the year. I was getting up from my chair to check the laundry when I tripped and fell. Landed on my shoulder pretty hard." She groaned. "My neck and shoulder feel awful."

Lila called because I was a massage therapist.

"I hate to ask, and I normally wouldn't, but I'm feeling desperate . . . would you be willing to come by and work on me for a short bit?"

"Of course," I said without hesitation. "I'll be there in fifteen minutes."

As soon as we hung up, I changed into something presentable, carefully blew out my candles, and threw on my coat. Moments later, I stepped out into the night.

Lila was a kind, playful soul wrapped in a slender, petite, thirty-something body. We had been introduced by a mutual friend and became fast friends. Beyond her thoughtful, lighthearted nature, one of the things I admired most about her was her creative genius. She had a well-developed eye for aesthetics and a knack for crafting beautiful pieces using natural materials.

Her home was a reflection of that talent—a cozy sanctuary where altar-like vignettes and artfully placed décor invited admiration. Its soothing ambiance could have easily earned it a feature in an artsy magazine.

I knocked on Lila's door, and from inside, her voice called out. "Come in!"

I stepped into the warm glow of her home and found her lying on her side on the living room floor, shifting uncomfortably. Slipping off my shoes, I made my way to her side, the plush carpet luxuriously soft beneath my feet.

I often felt that my relationship with Lila mimicked the teasing nature of the comic strip relationship between Calvin and Susie in the series Calvin and Hobbes from the 1980s to the 1990s. She even looked a little like Susie with her short, tidy hair. So, as I loomed over her with my hands on my hips in a theatrical flourish, my expression full of mock reproach, I teasingly scolded her. "Oh, jeez, what did you do to yourself now?"

She rolled her eyes and sighed. "I can't believe this happened."

"Not to worry, it happens to the best of us," I said, kneeling down beside her. "Let's take a look at that neck and shoulder of yours."

I placed my hands gently on her neck, moving slowly as I traced the lines of muscle down toward her shoulder blade. As soon as I hit a tender spot, she scrunched up her face and flinched.

"Too much?" I asked.

"No," she replied with a sigh. "I'm just being a weenie. Keep going."

Satisfied that Lila's condition wasn't beyond my care, I instructed her to slowly roll onto her back. I reached for a pillow on the nearby couch and tucked it under her head. I massaged her muscles with gentle precision, moving patiently from one spasm to another, smoothing away each knot I found.

After about twenty minutes and a few deep sighs, Lila let out a breathy, "Wow, that feels so much better!"

I smiled, grateful to have been able to help.

I was about to get up when suddenly, the energy in the room changed. A familiar tingle ran up my spine, my own version of Spiderman's "Spidey Sense." I froze, suddenly hyperaware of my surroundings—every subtle shift, every nuance in the atmosphere, and every sensation in my body. Slowly, I turned away from Lila and looked up from where I was kneeling, toward a spot fifteen feet away.

A powerful spirit had just entered the room.

It's not uncommon for me to become aware of spirits through-out my day. Usually, it's a fleeting glimpse—just a moment of recognition before they're gone.

This was different. Whoever or whatever this was, they wanted me to know they were there. Not only that, but they had an agenda. No alarm bells rang in my head, no instinct to retreat, but some part of me suggested I should stay alert, keep my guard up.

My thoughts drifted back to the first few times I sensed a supernatural presence in my life. Those early experiences had been unnerving—sometimes even downright terrifying—not because they were dangerous, but because they were new and unknown.

It didn't help that I had a runaway imagination, or that, as a kid growing up in the seventies, I spent late nights watching classic black-and-white Creature Feature horror movies from the sixties. But over time, as I grew accustomed to sensing spirits—and once I realized I wasn't about to be dismembered and eaten alive—I learned to relax and open myself to the experiences.

Kneeling there next to Lila, I instinctively held my breath, staying perfectly still, waiting to see if the spirit would make a move. I could feel its presence, but nothing more—no sense of identity or purpose revealed. My eyes weren't much help either—all I could see was a large, transparent wisp of shadow shifting like mist. It had a form, but its edges blurred as if it were veiled, concealing itself from full view.

Lila lay there quietly as I explained what was happening. She was an open-minded, spiritual person, but she had never encountered a spirit before. I could sense her uncertainty, the slight tension in the air.

"Should I be worried?" she asked.

"No," I reassured her. "I don't feel anything malevolent. Whoever this is, they're just . . . watching."

I turned back to the shadowy figure, my awareness sharpening.

Who are you? What is your purpose for being here? I finally asked telepathically.

The moment my mind formed the questions, the energy shifted. The silhouette of mist began to move, floating silently toward me, stopping just a few feet away. Then, suddenly—I was no longer in the room. Or maybe no longer in my body. I couldn't tell.

Whatever was happening wasn't like a waking dream or seeing something in my mind's eye—it was more than that. I was experiencing reality from a place beyond my physical self, beyond the boundaries of human perception. I wasn't exactly seeing. I was knowing. It was as if I had shifted into a state of pure awareness—a consciousness untethered from my body.

The shroud around the spirit evaporated, revealing a tall, middle-aged Native American man standing before me in ceremonial garb. His presence radiated quiet power—a commanding strength that emanated from his being—yet his eyes held a gentle, knowing wisdom. I didn't hear him speak aloud, yet his words echoed within me as if spoken directly to my soul.

I am a healer. A shaman. His voice carried an ancient knowing, something that reached far beyond this moment. Then, he asked me a question. *Do you wish to commune with me?*

I had no idea what he meant or what that would entail, but I knew my answer. With a sense of awe and curiosity, I answered him. *Yes.*

The moment I responded, his aura expanded—shimmering waves of energy unfurling like ripples in water. Then, before I could process what was happening, he moved toward me. Or rather, into me.

His energy enveloped me, fused with me, until there was no separation between his essence and mine. I wasn't afraid. Instead, I was overcome by a sensation beyond words. I had no body. No boundaries. No form. I simply existed—every part of me expanding outward at lightning speed, stretching beyond myself, beyond the room, beyond the planet into the infinite.

A pure, overwhelming sense of peace and love filled every part of my being. It was the kind of love that wasn't tethered to human conditions—it was universal, pure, and all-pervasive.

Everything I had ever feared melted away.

I knew—not through logic, not through thought, but through direct experience—that I was connected to something greater, something limitless. We are not alone. We have never been alone. That knowingness was a delicious elixir, and my soul drank deeply from it.

My exchange with the shaman felt timeless—boundless, infinite. Yet, in our normal reality of time, it had lasted only moments. When the Shaman Spirit was done, I felt myself slowly shrinking back into my physical body. The expansion receded, my awareness narrowing until I could once again feel the weight of my limbs, the ground beneath me, the faint sound of Lila's breathing. I was back.

The Shaman Spirit stepped away, his presence lingering but separate from mine. And yet, something had changed. I could feel it. I knelt there, speechless, as my convoluted mind struggled to grasp what had just transpired. Even as I tried to ground myself, I sensed intuitively that he was preparing to leave. Before he did, he imparted one final message.

I have given you two gifts, he told me. *The ability to channel my voice and the power to be a conduit for my healing energy.*

And then, just like that—he was gone.

No, wait! I cried out silently. *Please, don't leave me like this.* I was baffled, perplexed—beyond words. I tried to make sense of what had just happened, but it was all unraveling too quickly. My mind struggled to find its bearings, grasping for understanding. I longed to be back in that cocoon, to once again feel the splendor and awe of its embrace. And I had so many questions.

I had been touched by something beyond my comprehension. Something incredible, otherworldly. And now, I was expected to do something with it. I sat there, my mind racing, trying to grasp the enormity of it. Who was he? Why had he come to me? What was I supposed to do with the gifts he had given me? The silence offered no answers.

A wave of grief and yearning welled up inside me. The moment of communion had been so profound, so pure, so utterly unlike anything I had ever felt before. And now, it was slipping away, becoming nothing more than a memory. I didn't want it to fade. I didn't want to return to the ordinary world.

Lila had been lying quietly, watching me the entire time. She had no idea what I had just gone through. But she could tell something had happened.

"Keno?" she whispered. "Are you okay? You looked like you were in a trance."

It took a long moment before I could answer. I struggled to put it into words, but how could I? How could I explain something so unfathomable, so beyond language? I tried fumbling through fragments of what had transpired. Lila listened, wide-eyed.

"That's . . . incredible," she murmured. Then, her expression softened. "But you look like you're still somewhere else."

I was. I needed time. Time to process. Time to return.

"I have to go," I said, murmuring an apology for leaving so abruptly.

"Oh, my God, of course! I feel much better, thank you. I'll be okay," she assured me. "Go, do what you need to do."

I groaned as I stood, my body stiff from kneeling so long. Grabbing my things, I stepped out into the chill of the starry night and drove home in a daze.

I wish I could say I immediately and fully embraced my experience—that I boldly stepped into my calling, offering my gifts, touching lives, and changing the world, like some Hollywood fantasy.

But that never happened.

Stepping into that role wasn't so simple. First, I feared that if I told anyone what I'd experienced, they'd think I was crazy and lock me up in a psych ward. I also worried that stepping into the role of a shaman—something many would misunderstand or judge—might scare off my more conservative massage clients.

I had no formal training, no framework to follow—only that one experience at Lila's house. As a young man in my midtwenties, I didn't feel remotely ready to embody a role I barely understood.

And then there was the fact that I was a white guy. Who was I to think I could do the work of a Native American shaman? I had no known indigenous lineage, and the only connection I had to the culture was a deep respect for their reverence toward Mother Earth. The idea of calling myself a shaman—or acting like one—felt presumptuous. It felt inauthentic.

And yet, I couldn't deny it—the spirit of a Native American shaman had come to me, inviting me to share in an alchemical communion.

Me. Why? That question perplexed and haunted me for years, lingering without an answer.

Lying in bed that night, I replayed the encounter over and over, savoring the memory of the profound peace and connection I'd felt. What if this experience was meant to be a catalyst for change— not just in my life, but in the lives of those I would touch? Was I ready to step into this role, despite the uncertainties and the risk of judgment?

I didn't have all the answers. But something within me had shifted, and I couldn't unsee what I had been shown. Like footprints forming on a path I had yet to walk, the journey was already unfolding. All I had to do was take the next step.

At first, I shared my experience hesitantly, offering the Shaman Spirit's gifts only when I sensed that the person lying on my massage table would be open and receptive. I felt like I was working in the dark, guided only by my intuition. Yet every single person I shared this gift with benefited. Still, speaking openly about my experience felt deeply vulnerable.

A few days after I performed the Shaman Spirit work with a new client, I received an unexpected call from her therapist.

"What did you do to my client?!" she exclaimed.

Great, I thought to myself. *Here comes a lawsuit.* I was taken aback by what came out of her mouth next.

"It's like she went through six months of therapy in one session!"

In that moment, I caught a glimpse of the deeper potential behind the work I was doing—something far greater than myself. When I was finally ready to embrace the gifts passed to me by the Shaman Spirit, I began offering shamanic sessions as part of my private practice. Energy work was already familiar terrain, something I had studied for years and gently woven into sessions when it felt aligned.

But chanting? That was an entirely new experience.

I quickly discovered that the moment I opened my mouth to chant, the Shaman Spirit would arrive—his presence unmistakable, his essence weaving through my voice. It was as if he borrowed my vocal cords to use as a tool, his voice blending with mine, melodic tones layered with ancient knowing. All I had to do was step aside, surrender fully to the moment, and allow the sounds to flow through me, trusting in their sacred purpose.

I had always known sound could be healing, and I dabbled in it from time to time. But until I began chanting, I had never experienced its power so directly. These chants bypassed the thinking minds of my clients and reached into their unconscious—opening inner doorways to quiet transformation and deep healing, beyond words or thought.

Sometimes, the Shaman Spirit spoke directly to a client. To their soul. To their inner child. He would sing lullabies, recite prayers, express emotions like grief or empathy, or speak in a language I didn't understand. People often told me the voice coming out of my mouth didn't sound like my own. Many clients also said they could feel his presence in the room whenever I chanted. And I knew they were right—because I felt him too.

The Shaman Spirit was a mystery to me for many years. I had a sense that he once lived in a physical body during the arrival of the white man, so I searched online for clues, hoping to uncover which tribe he had belonged to. But he rarely provided details, and there was no way to verify the information I found.

Over the years, he would share bits and pieces through waking dreams or visions, revealing fragments of his past—like the time his tribe was slaughtered during the white man's arrival. I felt his grief as if it were mine—the anger, the helplessness, the loss—as it cut deep into my heart, racking my chest with sobs so intense they left me shaking.

In my research on shamans, I learned that some have the ability to take powers away from others or share their own—to transfer their gifts. That's when it dawned on me—through that sacred alchemical exchange, the Shaman Spirit had initiated me.

One day, the Shaman Spirit revealed something important to me—something that partially explained why he might have sought me out: He and I had once shared a lifetime together. He had been the spiritual leader of the Native American tribe I belonged to, and we were as close as blood brothers.

Talismans of Healing

One day, as I was performing a shamanic healing session, my hands hovering over my client's body, the Shaman Spirit formed words in my mind. *I want you to start incorporating feather fans and rattles into your practice. They will help you work with the energies.*

I blinked. *Feather fans and rattles?*

I knew they were part of Native American culture, but I had never held either in my hands, nor had I ever seen them up close.

Where am I supposed to find those? I asked.

You'll know, he replied cryptically. And then, like a wisp of smoke, he was gone.

I exhaled, shaking my head. *Well, that's vague.*

That night, I turned his words over in my mind. It made sense—these were the tools he had once used in his own time, his own world. But I had no idea where to find them, let alone how to use them once I did.

At the time, I was living in San Diego, and after giving it some thought, I determined that if any place had feather fans and rattles, it had to be Old Town. The historic neighborhood brimmed with artisan shops, handcrafted goods, and echoes of the past. As fate would have it, I had time the next day to begin my search.

Old Town was once the heart of San Diego, dating back to the early 1800s. Though it lost that title by the 1870s, it remained a lively gathering place during the nine years I lived in the area. With dozens of historic buildings, thirteen art galleries, an array of great restaurants, and over a hundred boutique shops, its main street pulsed with a festive, bustling energy—especially during lunch and dinner hours.

I drove down in the late afternoon, hoping to slip in before the evening crowds clogged the streets. I parked my car and set out on my quest for a feather fan and rattle. A thrill of anticipation stirred in me as I stepped into the first shop.

It turned out that many of the stores carried Native American artifacts, their shelves lined with authentic handcrafted items that spoke of deep traditions. After hours of searching, I found a dozen or so feather fans and rattles but the two or three I liked were well outside my budget.

Disillusionment started to take hold. How did the Shaman Spirit expect me to use feather fans and rattles if there weren't any I could actually get my hands on? I headed back to my car, wallowing in frustration, when another flash of insight whispered in my mind's ear.

Why not make your own?

I stopped dead in my tracks. I had always considered myself a creative person, but aside from cooking, I had never made anything with my hands that I'd be proud to display in my own home—let alone show to others. Ideas came easily to me. I was good at decorating spaces and enjoyed dabbling in graphic design projects like business cards, flyers, and websites.

Make my own? The more I sat with the idea, the more intrigued I became. I was a quick learner, and after seeing enough feather fans, I had a basic sense of what went into making them. It wasn't rocket science, but I still had a lot to figure out. I needed to do some research.

Once I got home, I fired up my trusted desktop computer, pulled up Google, and typed in "Native American feather fans." Instantly, thousands of images flooded the screen. As I scrolled through them, clicking on a few for a closer look, I came across a mention of a place called The Indian Store, located in the town of Escondido, thirty miles north of where I lived.

Curious, I looked up their website—and what I found left me awestruck. The photos revealed a massive shop, a treasure trove stocked with everything a person could ever need for making Native American crafts. My excitement surged. It was too late to make the drive that evening, but I made up my mind: First thing in the morning, as soon as they opened, I would be there.

The moment I entered the store, I was immediately enthralled. I felt like a kid in a candy shop, roaming up and down the aisles, eyes darting from shelf to shelf, marveling at all the neat things. I soaked in every detail, sparking ideas and making inspired plans.

I gathered what I thought I'd need to make a feather fan: a wooden dowel crafted specifically for a handle, small pieces of leather to wrap it with, turkey feathers, and a few decorative touches—ceramic beads, mink fur—anything that might add to its beauty. Since I had never attempted something like this before, I also grabbed an assortment of tools and supplies, unsure exactly what I'd need but determined to be prepared.

When I got home, I eagerly cleared my dining table, spread out newspaper to protect it, and carefully laid everything out. The excitement reminded me of when I was a kid, building plastic models of tanks and airplanes. While my feather fan had far fewer parts than those intricate kits, the feeling was the same. A giddy anticipation took over, and I immediately got to work. Before I knew it, the entire day had slipped away while I tinkered in my creative zone.

When I finished my first feather fan, I held it up with pride, admiring its simple yet sacred beauty. I was mesmerized—not just by its elegance, but by the quiet wonder that I had made it. Some part of me had always longed to be an artist, but until that moment, it had been nothing more than a distant dream. It took me all day to complete, but I didn't care. As I marveled at my creation, it felt like something deep within me was coming alive.

Then, something unexpected happened—something magickal. A surge of creative energy exploded within me, taking hold like an obsession. Suddenly, I wasn't making just one feather fan—with an intoxicating zeal, I felt compelled to make more. Feather fans, rattles, and who knew what else . . . the possibilities felt endless.

The very next day, I drove back to The Indian Store. The first time I had walked through, I carried a shopping basket. This time, I pushed a cart.

Native Americans honor the spirits of the animals they kill by incorporating their body parts into clothing, art, and crafts. With that in mind, I filled my cart with deer bones for handles, soft leather hides in rich hues and textures, turtle shells and gourds for rattles, an entire turkey wing with enough feathers to make plenty of feather fans, a variety of smaller decorative feathers, beads in every color, crow feet, wolf teeth, bison hide, mink fur, and more. By the time I reached the register, my cart overflowed with materials.

My eyes widened as the checker rang up my total—$365.

What started as a simple project to make one feather fan soon became a passion. Several months—and hundreds of dollars—later, I counted over two dozen unique feather fans and rattles scattered throughout my apartment and office space. The Shaman Spirit's suggestion had led me to uncover a talent and a joy I never knew I possessed.

I had always known the spirit world wasn't separate from our own—but this experience deepened that knowing. The tools I created weren't just objects; they were symbols of that connection, tangible reminders that the Shaman Spirit was always with me, guiding and inspiring me. The feather fans and rattles became extensions of not only his energy, but mine as well. At times, they felt almost alive, infused with soul, each carrying its own personality and purpose.

What began with a whisper from Spirit became a creative awakening and, eventually, a sacred practice. These weren't just fans and rattles—they were talismans, each one holding intention, presence, and power. Though I haven't practiced in a while, some of them still sit quietly in my home office—reverent reminders of a time when Spirit called and I followed.

My first feather fan

Some feather fans I created

Turtle shell rattle

An Orchestrated Encounter

The Shaman Spirit wasn't just an entity who appeared during private healing sessions for my clients in the quiet space of my treatment room. On occasion, he would materialize unexpectedly in my personal life, surprising me with requests that carried profound ramifications.

One of my favorite calls to action happened in Los Angeles during the summer of 2012. At the time, I was living in San Diego but making the long drive to Los Angeles several times a week for a ninety-day leadership training program. I would leave early in the day and return late at night, navigating my schedule around LA's infamous traffic. Given how much time I was spending on the road—and the hours of work I was losing in my private practice by leaving early to avoid gridlock—I came up with a practical solution: I would rent a part-time office in LA where I could start a private practice to make up for some of my lost income.

I searched online and found a number of office spaces that looked promising. But after making a few calls, nothing panned out.

During one of my trips to LA, I decided to visit one of my best friends, who had recently moved from San Diego to Venice Beach, just south of Santa Monica. At the time, it seemed like an unremarkable decision. But in hindsight, it was part of an invisible thread weaving itself into the fabric of my destiny. That one simple visit quietly set off a chain of events that would bless my life—and deeply impact someone else's.

Mandy was an attractive, vivacious blonde with a big heart, a sweet smile, and a creative spirit—someone I'd known since my days in Eugene, Oregon, and the same blonde I mention from the story "Night of Divination." We were best buds, and it was always a joy to see her. We were hanging out at her place, catching up on life, when I mentioned that I was looking for an office to rent part-time in the LA area.

"Oh? You should talk to my housemate, Penny," she remarked. "She might be looking for someone to share her office."

Penny was a master herbalist who taught classes in the community. She was home, so I approached her and asked about the space.

"I've already found someone," she said, "but one of my students is married to a chiropractor who has an office in Santa Monica. He might have an extra room for a practitioner to come in on a part-time basis." Her student's name was Francesca, and Penny gave me her contact information.

I immediately typed out a text to Francesca.

Hi Francesca, my name is Keno. Penny Johnson gave me your name and number because I mentioned I was looking for a part-time office space to do massage. She thought your husband might have an extra room to rent. Please call me at your convenience.

It wasn't long before I got a response. We texted back and forth a few times, but ultimately, we came to the conclusion that their office space wouldn't work.

I hadn't planned on reaching out to Francesca again, but the Shaman Spirit had other ideas. He appeared while the buttons on my phone keypad were still warm.

I want you to let Francesca know about me and offer to give her a Shaman Spirit session.

You want me to do what?! I exclaimed.

He knew I had heard him the first time, but he repeated himself anyway, as if humoring me. *I want you to text Francesca. Tell her about me and then offer her a session.*

I immediately felt resistance well up inside me.

What am I supposed to say? I asked. But the Shaman Spirit had already parted, leaving me to figure it out on my own.

I debated what to do. Deep down, I knew there was no question whether I would text her or not. But my shy, introverted self—the part of me that was uncomfortable reaching out to a stranger like this—liked to pretend there was. That part wanted to weasel out of it, but in the end, the Shaman Spirit was going to win. He knew it. I knew it. Still, like a stubborn child not getting his way, I needed to squirm and fuss before finally giving in.

My wiser self tried to offer some reassurance. *If this request came from the Shaman Spirit, it's probably important—and, ultimately, meant to help someone, maybe even you too.*

Wanting to get it over with, I pulled out my phone, rehearsed a few ideas of what I might say, and then transcribed my message, hoping I wouldn't come across as weird.

Hi Francesca, it's Keno again. I know this is an "out of the blue" question, but do you by chance have any interest in Native American healing?

I waited with bated breath.

Her response came just a minute later. *Why yes, I do,* she replied. *Why do you ask?*

A wave of relief washed over me. Knowing now that Francesca had some connection to Native American spirituality—and reassured that the Shaman Spirit wasn't sending me on a wild goose chase—I felt a surge of confidence. I crafted a longer message, giving her the abbreviated version of my Shaman Spirit story, and asked if she'd be interested in a short demo session.

Wow, that does sound interesting, she texted. A moment later, another message followed. *I'm intrigued. I would love to experience your Shaman Spirit work.*

Talking to strangers about my esoteric work without knowing their beliefs always comes with a risk, even if the directive comes from Spirit. There's no guarantee they'll be open to it, and they could even have an adverse reaction. And I'm not immune to the discomfort of being judged.

Still, I was curious. Why had the Shaman Spirit chosen Francesca? Clearly, something bigger was at play. I imagined the session would be meaningful for her—I just didn't realize how profound it would be.

We made plans for me to visit the following week, early in the morning.

Francesca was a tall, slender brunette with a gracious demeanor and an inquisitive intensity about her. She carried herself with the kind of quiet confidence that suggested she was a thinker, a seeker, and ambitious.

Because she had a prior commitment, we had less than an hour, so after a brief conversation, I had her lie down on the portable massage table I brought with me. I took a moment to center myself, grounding my energy, before softly inviting the Shaman Spirit to join us.

I felt intuitively drawn to sit at the head of the table and placed my hands on both sides of Francesca's head. The moment I connected with her aura, an immediate thrum of energy pulsed through my palms. I took a deep breath and invited the Shaman Spirit to use my voice as a vehicle for his healing work.

Chants in a language I didn't understand reverberated from my lips as he spoke to Francesca, weaving wisdom and heartfelt compassion into soulful tones—both high and deep, melodic and resonant.

Francesca was caught off guard. A look of surprise washed over her face as tears rose and spilled down her cheeks. As they often do, the chants bypassed her logical, rational, thinking mind, reaching the deep, primal places of her heart and soul. She wept as I gently held the space, a cocoon of grace and compassion, allowing her to surrender fully to the experience.

I reached for my rattle and feather fan, letting the Shaman Spirit guide my movements. I shook the rattle rhythmically, helping to sustain Francesca's altered state so she could journey where her soul longed to go. With slow, graceful sweeps, I wove the feathers over her body, shifting to quick, flitting motions—like a bird taking flight. Wherever I sensed stagnant or stuck energy, the feathers hovered, calling upon the spirit healers to unblock and clear the affected areas.

As I drew our session to an end, I guided Francesca back to the room from whatever reality she had been experiencing. I had her focus on her breath, the sound of my voice, and the solid feel of the table beneath her.

When she opened her eyes, she looked dazed. Her movements were slow and unsteady as she swung her legs over the edge of the table. Her hands fidgeted in her lap, her gaze fixed on them as if searching for answers. She was still processing, trying to make sense of what had just happened. When she finally spoke, her words came out wobbly, tinged with disbelief and wonder.

I gave her as much time as she needed, knowing from personal experience how disorienting it can be to transition from an altered state—where we experience something profound and deeply emotional—back to the more mundane, less vibrant reality of the physical world.

Stepping behind her, I placed my hands gently on her shoulders. "Breathe," I instructed, guiding her through slow, deep breaths to help her ground. When she seemed more settled, I moved back around the table and took a seat facing her.

"That was amazing, Keno. I—I don't even know where to start. I've never been sensitive to energy work before. It always saddened me because my friends would talk about how wonderful their experiences were, but whenever I went to see a healer, I never felt anything. I eventually gave up going.

"But when you started working with me," she continued, "I was transported into a visceral energetic state so powerful, so palpable that I will never forget it. Parts of my body that I've had issues with in the past pulsated and grew really hot. Different muscles tightened, then released, as if all the tension just melted away.

"I had constant visual images flickering throughout my session, like watching a slideshow on steroids," she said in a quiet voice. "At one point, it felt like my entire body was suddenly flooded with energy, as if a dam had burst. And then, this deep sense of peace came over me—that's when I had this incredible vision."

Tears streamed down Francesca's face as she recounted meeting the Shaman Spirit, as if she had been transported into a past life. Her gaze turned distant, lost in another time, as she described a vivid scene—she was a young woman, riding a horse alongside him. She spoke in detail about the landscape, the rhythm of the ride, and, most of all, the profound sense of safety and love she felt in his presence. He had offered her sage advice, comforting her with his gentle, wise guidance.

I sat there in awe, absorbing every word of her experience. But alongside my wonder, a quiet pang of longing stirred within me. Francesca's journey awakened the sweet nostalgia of my own past-life memories with the Shaman Spirit—recollections that were frustratingly fleeting, never enough to fully satisfy my soul.

A familiar, melancholic sadness swelled deep inside me, a yearning to spend time with him again in a physical body. I longed to feel that deep, soulful connection we once shared—to return to a time of friendship and innocence, before the coming of the white man and all his destruction.

In our last moments together, Francesca thanked me profusely, looking up at me with gratitude shining brightly in her eyes.

"I'm just a conduit," I said. "But I'm honored and blessed to have been a part of this experience with you."

I shared with her the thread of synchronicity that had woven our paths together that culminated in her session, and we both shook our heads in quiet awe, marveling at how a series of seemingly insignificant moments had led to something so profound.

Stepping out of Francesca's office, I was met by the soothing embrace of the Santa Monica sun. Its gentle heat warmed my skin as I drew in a long, satisfying breath, releasing it with a slow, audible exhale. A soft smile graced my lips as I lifted my gaze to the brilliant blue sky above.

I felt on top of the world, uplifted by an exuberant joy and overflowing with gratitude for the gift I had been given—the chance to play a meaningful role in something so sacred. I reveled in the richness of that blessing, basking in its lingering glow for as long as I could before it inevitably faded into the reality of everyday life.

As I made my way to my car, a deep stillness settled over me. The experience was a powerful reminder of the greater intelligence at work behind the scenes of our lives, even in the most seemingly insignificant choices and encounters. Every meeting, every decision, every moment carries the potential to be a thread in an intricate, invisible tapestry.

We may not always know who or what holds the loom, but on days like this, I could feel the presence of the Weaver—the sacred hand orchestrating it all. I wasn't the one the Shaman Spirit had come to serve that day, but I was the bridge, the instrument for someone else's divine experience. And that, I've come to know, is its own profound kind of blessing.

7

My Financial "Wreckoning"

The sunlight streamed through the bedroom window, beckoning me to wake up to a brighter day, as if I were an actor in one of those Folgers coffee commercials from the nineties. On another morning, I might have played the part perfectly—content, carefree, and ready to embrace a wonderful day. But for the past couple of months, my life had felt more like a horror movie, where the monsters are real and bad things happen to good people. That morning, I woke up in the clutches of a beast, and no ray of sunshine—or even Folgers coffee—was going to save me.

Before I tell you about the monster in my bedroom, though, you'll need to understand how my life got into the mess it was in.

On the surface, my life looked pretty good. I had a busy massage therapy and shamanic healing practice, a cute girlfriend, a nice car, and a cat I adored. The roof over my head wasn't half bad either. But beneath it all was a fault line no one could see—a crumbling financial foundation waiting to collapse.

I handled money like a chimpanzee with a banana—devour it quickly, toss the peel, and expect there'll be another one. If that sounds like you, that monkey business will have you hanging by the ropes like it did for me.

At fifty years old, I was drowning in $16,000 of debt, making only minimum payments, with no savings, no investments, and behind on paying my taxes.

An injury the previous year had sidelined me from being able to work for months, leaving me with a growing stack of medical bills I couldn't pay. You'd think that would've been enough to motivate me to get my finances in order. But it wasn't.

If you asked me what my monthly expenses were, I would have given you a blank stare. I knew how much money was coming in, but apart from that, my money management skills were nonexistent. My finances were a ticking time bomb.

One balmy day in September, the bomb's countdown mechanism was triggered when my twelve-year-old cat started showing troubling symptoms that something was wrong with her health. A vet visit, followed by a flurry of tests and a second opinion, left me with two choices: Euthanize my furbaby or cough up $2,500 for an investigative procedure, $2,500 I didn't have. The cracks in the foundation of my life began to grow and spread.

As if things couldn't get worse, my once-thriving private practice eerily nose-dived. It was as though all my clients called one another to say "Let's not see Keno for a while."

The experience was like the engines of a plane suddenly quitting midflight. In less than fourteen days, I went from seeing twenty-five clients a week to a meager seven. And it stayed that way for over a month. (Cue the sound of a plane crash-landing and bursting into flames.)

There's an old adage in new age ideology: If the Universe sends you an important message and you ignore it, the intensity of the message increases in the hope that you'll eventually listen.

A gentle nudge can turn into a brutal shove—or worse—if you don't pay attention. That's exactly what happened to me. I kept ignoring the messages (and opportunities) to get my finances in order, which brings me back to that Folgers coffee morning when the sun was streaming into my bedroom.

I was still drifting in that dreamy, half-conscious state where the world feels soft and distant. The sun poured in, warm and golden, and for a fleeting moment, I allowed myself to bask in its delight.

But a moment later, reality came crashing down like a sledgehammer. I remembered the mess my life was in.

Then came the detonation. I felt a sharp, nasty pain shooting through my jaw as if a ghoul in the night had taken a pair of pliers to my teeth and yanked on them while I slept. The shock of it snapped me fully awake.

"What now?!" I groaned, pushing myself upright and back into the headboard. I instinctively reached for my jaw, fingers pressing and probing, trying to pinpoint the source of the pain. A tidal wave of self-pity welled up within me, threatening to overwhelm and pull me under. *How much more can I take?* I wondered.

I couldn't believe what was happening. It felt so unfair. My life was crumbling around me, and now this? The pain in my jaw was a slap in the face—another blow in a series of hits that left me reeling. Desperation clawed at me, but I latched onto one lifeline: Molly, my girlfriend, lying peacefully beside me, was a dental assistant.

"Molly, Molly," I whispered urgently. "Molly, wake up!"

Groggy but concerned, she sat up, brushing the hair from her face. After I explained what was happening, she didn't miss a beat. Within minutes, Molly was on the phone arranging an appointment with her boss. There was at least one piece of good news: I could be seen later that morning.

Grateful but still anxious, I got myself ready. By the time I was dressed and driving the thirty minutes to the dentist's office, my thoughts were spinning. I wasn't expecting good news, but I wasn't prepared for the setback I was about to face.

After a quick exam, the dentist delivered his verdict.

"Son," he said, "I'm afraid this tooth needs an immediate root canal. You've also got three other teeth that are decaying and need crowns as soon as possible."

It was worse than I imagined. My stomach sank as I thought about the cost.

Getting the root canal done was a no-brainer; I couldn't have lived with the pain another hour. Thanks to Molly, I qualified for the family discount, which softened the shock. I still had to come up with $1,000. As much as I hated to add to my debt, I had no choice but to pay for it with a credit card.

The crowns were another story. While they were necessary, they weren't urgent. I would have to get them done another time.

An hour later, I stumbled out of the office and into the parking lot. My mouth wasn't the only thing that was numb. I suddenly felt a strong urge to cry, but I was so scared, the tears wouldn't come.

I looked up and stared at the sky. It was breathtaking—an endless expanse of brilliant azure, dotted with soft, dreamy puffs of white clouds that seemed to float without a care in the world. I wished I could trade places with them—untethered and free, far above the mess my life had become. I tried to hold onto that feeling, but reality was cruel, and there was no escaping mine.

As I approached my car, a slow dread seeped into my mind, thick and toxic, spreading like poison. Each step felt heavier as if the weight of my situation wrapped around me like a python, tightening its grip with every passing second.

I had been living from month to month, and now I was teetering on the edge of financial ruin. This crisis had pushed me to the brink. Where would the money come from? How would I pay my bills? The questions churned in my mind, each one sharper and more suffocating than the last.

By the next day, that dread had twisted itself into full-blown terror. It clung to me like a parasite, draining my faith and resolve, eroding my self-worth until I felt hollow and ashamed, devoid of hope. I stumbled through the following week like a zombie, my body moving through the motions while my mind spiraled in an endless loop of doom, playing out scenes of a bleak future. Every step felt like I was wading through quicksand, dragging me deeper into despair. I began to toy with thoughts of ending my life.

My nights were just as bad. I tossed and turned, seeking peace in the comfort of my pillow, but solace was nowhere to be found. When I grew weary of that fruitless search, I'd roll onto my back and stare into the abyss of my dread, haunted by visions of living on the street, destitute and alone.

Those fears of homelessness weren't mere figments of my imagination. They were rooted in harsh reality. Years before, when I was struggling to establish my massage practice, I went through a period of living out of my car. It was one of the darkest times of my life and an experience I never want to relive.

I'm not a religious man, but I've always been spiritual. And like many do when their backs are up against the wall, I prayed. Looking back at that time, I feel pity at how desperate my prayers sounded—more like frantic begging than solemn words of faith. But at the time, I clung to them like a security blanket.

As the days of my financial nightmare dragged on, I kept asking myself, *Why is this happening to me?* At first, I blamed everything but myself—life, bad luck, the Universe. But as I took a deeper look and was more honest with myself, it became harder to ignore the truth: I had created this predicament. My question then became *How did I get here?*

Over the years, I had received messages to get better with money more times than I cared to admit. A friend told me about a book he was reading on managing personal finances, my brother mentioned a podcast he had heard by a financial guru, and I'd even seen ads in magazines touting the benefits of money management. Each time, I brushed them off, convincing myself it wasn't for me or that I'd deal with it later.

There were times when I tried to learn how to manage my money better, but they were half-hearted at best. My old habits always crept back in, sabotaging whatever small progress I made.

When I finally owned my part in creating my reality—when I realized that I was responsible for the results I was getting, and that it all could have been avoided had I taken the time to learn—things started turning around. I realized my relationship with money wasn't healthy. I knew my life with money had to change, but I just didn't have a clue where to start. No one had ever taught me how to manage money.

Until that moment, I had never been motivated enough to do anything about it. Nothing like a crisis to get you going!

During the second week of my ordeal, I drove to my neighborhood library to return a few overdue books. Hoping for a distraction from the gritty reality of my life, I decided to search for something to read. I wasn't much of a reader, but desperate times called for desperate measures. All the ice cream I was eating could only help me cope for so long before I'd have to buy new clothes.

As I wandered toward the back of the library where the books were kept, a tall, freestanding bookshelf on my right caught my attention. It looked out of place, as if someone had moved it there and then forgotten about it. The shelves were mostly bare, but one item stood out like bait on a hook, silently luring me to take notice. Normally, I would have stopped to satisfy my curiosity, but I was on a mission to find more books to take home. As I continued past the bookshelf, I told myself the materials were probably still being processed and not available for me to borrow.

I was about six feet past the bookcase when a sudden, unshakable feeling tugged at me to reconsider, as if something essential hinged on my turning around. The feeling was so strong that it stopped me in my tracks. It felt like the item called out to me in a voice only I could hear. "Pssst, Keno! Come over here. I've got something important to show you."

Intuition has a unique signature, a kind of calling card—and in that moment, I thought I recognized it. I stood there for a moment, deciding what to do. I felt so compelled to take a closer look that

I turned around and walked back to the rack. I picked up the item that had caught my eye. It was an audiobook on CDs about personal finances: *The 7 Money Rules for Life: How to Take Control of Your Financial Future* by Mary Hunt. I turned the packaging over to read the description on the backside. *This looks interesting,* I thought.

As I reflect back on that moment, I realize I had no clue how significant that audiobook would become. It's strange, really. Struggling with serious money issues, you'd think I'd be searching for answers in books or online. But I wasn't. Part of that came from my naivete, but most of it stemmed from fear and resistance.

Facing my money problems meant confronting the fallout of my choices—and that was something I hadn't been willing to do. Denial, avoidance, and rationalization are incredibly powerful coping strategies that often keep us stuck. They were for me. Looking back, I'm just so grateful I had enough sense to listen to my intuition. The audiobook was available to check out, so I took it home and immediately placed the first CD in my computer.

The narrator's voice was warm and encouraging, explaining how to master the fundamentals of finances in a simple, easy-to-understand way, with clear, step-by-step instructions. I sat there, completely captivated, as Mary Hunt demystified the essentials of building a healthy relationship with money. Her words felt like hope—like being handed a glass of water after wandering through the desert for far too long. Every passage I heard made it feel as if she was speaking directly to me, addressing my financial struggles with remarkable clarity.

Within a short time, a profound epiphany struck me. A current of electricity coursed through my body. "Oh my God," I whispered. In that moment, I realized I was the recipient of divine intervention. My prayers for help had been answered. The seemingly mundane act of going to the library had been Spirit's way of guiding me to the right place at the right time, delivering the information I needed to transform my relationship with money.

From that day forward, my life took a dramatic 180-degree turn. I read books and took courses from various financial counselors, implementing the strategies that resonated with me.

I used to think *budget* was a four-letter word in disguise, but now I embraced the practice wholeheartedly. What I once saw as a hindrance to enjoying my money, I now saw as a tool—a road map to financial prosperity and security. I began to meticulously track my expenses, with eye-opening results that led me to shift my spending priorities to reflect my newfound, healthier financial mindset.

I was surprised at how much my outlook on life immediately changed just by making the decision to take control of my finances. My depression vanished instantly.

Within a few months, I started seeing real progress. My debt slowly started to shrink, and I even managed to set aside a small emergency fund. I felt a renewed sense of control and purpose. My practice began to flourish again, and the peace of mind I achieved was absolutely priceless. Even though I had a ways to go, I was no longer living in fear about my finances.

My wake-up call shook the very foundation of my life like an earthquake, but it became the catalyst for a profound transformation in both my relationship with money and the overall quality of my life.

Decades ago, a teacher of mine shared a profound quote: "Pain is inevitable; suffering is optional." It's applicable to many areas in our lives, finances included.

When it comes to facing your issues with money, yes, there will most likely be pain in addressing them—but the alternative is to suffer until you do. The longer you wait, the worse the suffering becomes. An ad in a magazine for a dental office I once read put it perfectly with this slogan: "Ignore your teeth long enough, and they will go away." The same applies to money.

Another of my favorite quotes is this: "It's not how much money you earn that determines whether you'll become wealthy. It's what you do with it once it comes in."

Looking back, I realize that my wake-up call wasn't just about fixing my finances. It was about reclaiming my life. Money was a source of fear and shame for so long, but now it's become a tool I use to enjoy life and to build a better future.

Did the transformation happen overnight? Not at all. Were there moments I wanted to quit? Absolutely. Were the challenges and sacrifices I made worth it? Most definitely!

If you're reading this and can relate to my experience, know this: It's never too late to change. The first step might feel like the hardest, but it's also the most liberating. Start small, stay consistent, and trust the process.

Healing your relationship with money isn't really about money. After all, money is just paper—symbols we've collectively agreed to believe in. It has no power except the meaning we give it. And yet, for so many of us, that meaning becomes tangled with fear, shame, self-worth, and survival.

True healing begins when we stop avoiding numbers and start untangling the stories behind them. It's about reclaiming your power from something you grew to fear out of ignorance. It's finding the courage to say "Enough is enough. I want a better life."

When I pressed play on that audiobook, I knew I needed help—but I had no idea just how deep or how far the lessons would take me.

Like a single drop in still water, that one act rippled out, unleashing a surge of energy that became swollen waves, dramatically altering old beliefs, carving new edges, and reshaping the shoreline of my identity forever.

Today, my bank account no longer rules me. It reflects me—my peace, my growth, my self-love. I'm not even talking about the amount of money, either—I'm talking about the systems I've put in place to make sure every known expense is covered and every unexpected surprise is planned for. Whenever I look at it, I feel proud and empowered because my wiser adult self—not my child-like impulses—is in control of my finances.

And that shift, I've learned, is priceless.

If you've been thinking it's time to master your finances, I can help you. Check out my website at kenompowers.com and schedule a complimentary 15-minute consultation.

8

Parking Angel GPS

If you know anything about the Gaslamp District in downtown San Diego, you know that finding street parking between 5:00 p.m. and 8:00 p.m. is like trying to thread a frayed, limp piece of yarn through a small sewing needle. You might start off feeling optimistic, but by the end, you're late, frazzled, and ready to throw in the towel.

I speak from experience, having lived in San Diego for nine years, from 2008 to 2017. For a stretch of time, I made a weekly pilgrimage to the Gaslamp during rush hour to attend a meditation group. By the time I finally walked through the door, it often felt like I needed the entire session just to recover from the ordeal of getting there.

On a good day, the drive from my house took a reasonable twenty minutes, a bit longer during rush hour. With the parking challenge, I had to tack on an extra twenty to thirty minutes because of the likelihood that I would have to drive in circles looking for a spot. I also had to factor in the time it took to walk from my parking spot to the building where the group met, which was usually a distance.

The odds of snagging a parking spot close to your destination in a timely manner during those peak hours are so slim that the

Vatican is considering certifying it as a miracle when it happens. Okay, I'm joking, but they should because it sure feels like a miracle.

My meditation group was one of the highlights of my week, not just for the benefits of mindfulness and reflection, but also for the chance to connect with other like-minded folks. But the parking fiasco began to steal my joy. It got so bad that I asked myself whether the class was worth the hassle. I hated the thought of giving it up, and for a couple of weeks, I wrestled with what to do.

Over the years, I've learned some powerful lessons about what's possible when we focus our minds on what we truly want—from walking on fire to winning races as a competitive runner to manifesting experiences and achievements that once felt out of reach. Those experiences taught me that right thoughts, paired with right action, can influence reality in remarkable ways.

In those two weeks, I devised a plan to solve my parking dilemma. I drew inspiration from one of my own past experiences, a story you can read in this book, titled "The Power of Intention."

For my parking predicament, I decided to set a similar intention—but with a twist. This time, I planned to call on a parking angel for help.

If you're not familiar with the concept of a parking angel, let me explain. As a new age friend once told me years ago, there are spirits, or angels, who are available to help us with anything we want, from something as significant as manifesting our soulmate to something as mundane as finding misplaced keys, or in my case, a parking space in downtown San Diego during the busiest time of day.

"All it takes is faith—and the courage to believe it might work," she said.

At first, I scoffed at the idea. Why would an angel waste their time helping someone find a parking space? It seemed absurd. But I respected my friend enough to set my skepticism aside, and I gave it a shot not long after.

To give myself the best chance of finding a parking spot near my meditation group, I decided to utilize a visualization technique along with my appeal to the parking angels. It was the same process I used as a successful competitive runner, back before visualization was mainstream or even widely understood. To this day, I credit those visualizations with helping me win races.

Before every competition, I'd close my eyes and visualize myself surging ahead of all the other runners to the finish line while electrifying melodies from Van Halen and AC/DC blasted from my boombox. I immersed myself so deeply in the visions that I would break out into a sweat as if I had truly run the race.

My preparation for finding a parking space wasn't nearly as extreme, nor did I crank up Van Halen or AC/DC to psyche myself up. Instead, hours before each class, I'd sit in a quiet space, close my eyes, and visualize every step of the journey—from getting into my car and driving down the highway to pulling into one of the coveted spaces right in front of the building. I imagined feeling the satisfaction of finding a spot with ease and the calm that followed.

The first few weeks proved unsuccessful. Not once did I find a decent parking spot. I felt discouraged, and with every passing week, my frustration grew. My inner critic sneered, dismissing my efforts as nonsense and a waste of time. I began to wonder if it was right. Quitting started to feel like a viable option.

If you knew me, though, you'd know I don't like quitting. The very idea of it unsettled me. *What if success was just around the corner and only needed a little bit more time or effort*, I wondered? *How would I feel about myself if I did quit?* I only had to think of the handful of times in my past when I had given up to know that quitting now would haunt me for the rest of my life. This debate gnawed at me as I wrestled with my commitment to manifesting parking spaces and the growing frustration of my apparent inability to do so.

Ask my wife, and she'll tell you I can be pretty stubborn. Stubbornness, like most traits, has its upside and downside. The upside—and one of the most valuable lessons I've learned in life—is that perseverance pays off. And perseverance, I've come to realize, is just stubbornness in a nicer suit. With that in mind, I decided to keep trying.

Another couple of weeks passed with the same disappointing results. And then, something remarkable started happening. Each time I went to class, I would find a parking space either directly in front of the building or just a short walk away. This continued for several weeks as I kept up my practice of visualization. I was amazed—and of course, delighted—by what felt like a streak of serendipity. It was as though a spot with my name on it was always there, quietly waiting.

Then one day, as I prepared to leave for class, something unusually mysterious happened. I had gone through my usual ritual earlier that day, visualizing my parking spot as vividly as ever. But just as I wrapped my hand around the front doorknob, a soft voice whispered in my mind like a telepathic communiqué. *Don't leave just yet. Wait till I tell you to go.*

I froze, hand on knob, questioning whether the thought was just my imagination. *What? Who is this?* But the voice didn't respond. I hesitated as I stood by the door, keys in hand, caught in a curious mix of wonder and skepticism. The recent spree of finding perfect parking spaces already felt unusual, to the point where I wondered whether my success was entirely my own doing or the result of an unseen force lending a hand. My wonderment begged me to ask if this message was the latest twist to some otherworldly plan. The questions swirled in my mind as I lingered, unsure of what to do.

The part of me prone to superstition had been questioning when my luck of finding a great space was going to run out. It offered a stark warning as if any changes to our routine were bad. *Go ahead, follow that voice, and watch our luck dry up. You'll end up with a lousy spot—or worse, no spot at all—and wind up late for class.*

I was tempted to heed my mind's advice. Doubt has a way of

sounding convincing, especially when fear is riding shotgun. But the wiser, calmer part of me assured me that the opposing voice was the same one that had guided me countless times before, often leading to outcomes far better than I could have imagined.

To this day, I don't know for sure where my intuition comes from exactly, whether it's my Higher Self, my future self, or some other being in the spirit realm. What I do know, as I knew back then, is that when it shows up, it's always a good idea to heed its message. Ignoring it had never ended well for me, and there were more times than I care to admit when I didn't listen.

As I reflected on the memories of my regrets, I chose to trust the silent nudge. Even after I made what I thought was the right decision, my doubt still lingered. It felt both heavy and dismissive. I let out a sigh, not entirely sure if it was relief or resignation. Then I turned away from the door and headed back to my desk.

My plan was to pass the time surfing the internet on my desktop computer. I tried to focus on what I was looking at, but all I could do as I sat there was try to calm the mounting anxiousness, *try* being the operative word.

The rational, linear-thinking part of me that couldn't understand or believe in spiritual guidance or the concept of the Higher Self kept insisting I grab my keys and drive to class immediately, before it was too late. My agitation grew, but I held steadfast in my decision to wait.

I was surprised and intrigued when another message arrived.

"*Okay,*" it said telepathically, "*time to go.*"

I didn't know what was happening, but I couldn't deny how good the wave of relief felt at finally being able to act. I grabbed my things and headed to my car. Five minutes later, I was cruising down the four-lane highway toward downtown San Diego.

I was two lanes right of the fast lane, content and unhurried. The speed limit was 55 mph, but to keep up with traffic, I had to maintain a speed of 65 mph. Was I concerned about getting a ticket? The thought crossed my mind, but I figured I was okay since the cars in the two left lanes were passing me like I was standing still.

Less than a mile down the thoroughfare, the voice chimed in like a back-seat driver.

Speed up a little.

Wait, you want me to speed up and risk getting a ticket? I asked, incredulous. Again, there was no response. No explanation, no courtesy, not even a shred of consideration to help me make sense of the request or what was going on, something like: *Hey, Keno, your parking angel here. We're running a little behind schedule, so pick up the pace. Five miles an hour faster will do, thanks!* That would have been great.

But no, nothing like that. Just a curt and indifferent, *Speed up a little.*

I didn't think driving faster was a good idea. I imagined getting pulled over by a black-and-white with flashing lights and telling the officer of the law that I was speeding because Spirit told me to. The next scene I pictured was me being handcuffed and taken to a place where the staff wore crisp, white coats.

Despite my doubts, I turned on my signal and moved into the lane to my left, accelerating to draft the car in front of me doing 70 mph.

After ten minutes of steady, uneventful driving, Spirit made another announcement, just like the audible notifications of a GPS.

Now I want you to slow down, it said.

Something prompted me to look ahead into the lane on my right, as the voice continued, *See that guy driving the gray car up ahead? Pull in behind him and drive at his speed.*

Okay, this is weird, even for me, I thought. But I was also fascinated by what was going on and intrigued to see where this rabbit hole was leading me, so I turned on my signal and pulled into place.

As I approached the heart of San Diego, a low, nearby roar suddenly cut through the air. It was a commercial airline on its final approach to the airport, situated to my right.

One of the city's unique features is that the airport sits right next to downtown, overlooking the bay. Planes fly in so low that you can practically reach up and touch them. There's even a bar downtown in the flight path of many planes with an open ceiling where patrons can marvel at the underbellies of incoming planes as they prepare to land.

The noise grew exponentially sharper, more urgent, drawing my gaze skyward. The massive jet screeched overhead, close enough to make my heart race. Instinctively, I gripped the steering wheel tighter, bracing against the sudden rush of sound and adrenaline. I glanced over to follow its flight path, catching a quick glimpse of the shimmering waters of the San Diego Bay like a fleeting postcard scene.

Then, as I looked back to the freeway ahead, the downtown skyline loomed into view as if it were appearing for the first time. Against the majestic blue sky, the buildings gleamed bright, their sharp lines standing in stark contrast to the organic curve of the bay. I couldn't help but take a breath and let it out slowly as I marveled at the sight, feeling grateful to be living in such a beautiful place.

As I neared my exit, my GPS angel uttered more instructions. *Okay, pass this guy in front of you and speed up.*

How fast should I go? I asked.

I don't know why I kept thinking I was going to get a reply. I must have been a terrible back-seat driver in a past life, I mused, because it felt like this was payback for my karmic debt. But I was a good sport and played along. I did what I was told. I put the pedal to the metal and relived my younger self's joy for speed, if only for a brief moment.

Once I exited, I coasted down the long and lazy Front Street off-ramp until it dumped me near Little Italy, about twenty blocks from where my class was located. Stoplights illuminated most of the intersections along the way. Some were green, some were red, and two or three were yellow. I tried my best to stay calm and relaxed as I waited for the red ones to change, but I wasn't able to stop cursing at every yellow light I braked for.

I had mapped out the fastest route in my head, but Spirit had other intentions.

Turn left here, it said as I came up to an intersection a few blocks away from class. I was planning to go straight and was confused about why I was turning at this intersection.

Are you sure you want me to go this way? I asked, questioning Spirit's route savvy. I didn't have time to wait for an answer that was never going to come, so I just shrugged my shoulders and made the turn.

Maybe we're taking the scenic route? I wondered with a pinch of sarcasm.

Patience, Grasshopper, came its reply, a reference to one of my favorite TV shows as a kid from the early seventies, the popular *Kung Fu* starring David Carradine.

Okay, truth be told, the voice didn't actually say that, but I thought it would have been really cool if it had.

You can always tell when it's early evening in downtown San Diego by the number of cars circling around like vultures, looking for a good spot to land. The sight of them stirred my fear. We were all competing for the same spot, and I fretted that I was going to miss out on a good space. I was told to ignore them and not to worry.

The wide downtown streets were lined with angled parked cars, their noses touching the sidewalks. Crowds of people milled about the usual downtown mix of restaurants, bars, and towering buildings that made up apartment complexes, banks, and insurance offices. I motored ahead slowly down two blocks until I reached another stop sign where I was given instructions to make a right.

I turned, keeping an eye out for any open spaces, and navigated toward the next stop sign at a busy intersection. Pedestrians crossed from every direction in scattered groups while cars jockeyed impatiently, eager to dart through any opening. I held my breath, waiting for the right moment to move, trying to time my acceleration without hitting anyone while eyeing the other cars suspiciously to see if they were going to be diplomatic and follow the rules or not. These moments tend to bring out the worst in people.

I inched forward, spotting a narrow gap, and carefully squeezed through, honking at another driver who dared tried to cut in. Relieved that I made it through without incident, I continued on.

What next, I asked?

Make another right at the next intersection, came my answer.

I flicked on my blinker as I approached the stop sign. I was less than two blocks from my class. I looked in every direction. The coast was clear. As I rolled into the turn, a parked car to my left suddenly flashed its white backup lights as if waving to get my attention. A moment later, in perfectly timed fashion, it pulled out from its spot, putting me in position for first dibs.

"No way!" I exclaimed. I was stunned. I slowly pulled my car into the parking spot, turned off the engine, and sat quietly in the stillness, mesmerized by the magick of what had just transpired. The voice, the instructions, the traffic, the stoplights, the timing— everything aligned perfectly, like it was orchestrated. It was as if someone or something took control of my reality and pulled some strings to grant me this small yet significant success. Stepping out into the cool evening air, I felt a profound sense of connection to something greater than myself. The frustration and skepticism of my ego that had plagued me vanished, replaced by an unwavering belief in the power of intention and faith. I felt incredibly grateful. This experience had not only solved my parking dilemma, but it also reaffirmed my trust in the mysterious and powerful ways of the universe.

I shook my head slowly at the realization that I could have easily missed this experience if I had not listened to my inner voice. It's a common theme with intuition, that narrow escape from logic and skepticism that, if heeded, would lead to a much different outcome.

Only in hindsight, looking back to the moment with 20/20 vision, was I able to be keenly aware just how razor-thin the line was between following the subtle suggestions and prompts of my intuition versus the louder, more familiar, no-nonsense reasoning of my rational, analytical mind.

Every time I choose to follow that voice—to hear it and then do what it suggests—I strengthen my ability to recognize it. And because I listened, I was rewarded with this magickal mystical moment of manifestation. I felt like I had won the lottery. Not the monetary lottery you win by buying a ticket, but a sacred, spiritual lottery made up, not of chance, but of mindful choices, trust, and faith.

Gratitude wasn't a big enough word to express the appreciation I felt as I slowly made my way to class.

9

More Than a Name

alk into any Las Vegas casino, and you'll see my name, Keno, lit up in lights everywhere. It's a popular game of chance, but my name? That wasn't chance at all. That was destiny, tied to something far more meaningful than a roll of the dice. If you enjoy hearing the stories behind people's names, you'll love this one.

Keno, the game, is a lottery-style numbers game. I'm not much of a gambler, but on a business trip to Vegas, I tried my luck on a penny slot machine and won forty dollars. That's four thousand pennies that came flying out of the machine! You can bet I kicked myself for not playing the dollar slots instead. I moved on to the blackjack table and promptly lost it all.

When people comment on my name and jokingly ask if my parents gave me that name because they were gamblers, the trickster in me likes to tell them this: "My mom was overdue with me when she and my dad took a trip to Las Vegas. My mom played the game Keno and hit it big. She got so excited that she went into labor. And just like that—boom!—I was born. So, naturally, my parents named me after the game."

I tell it so convincingly that people gasp in awe. I wish it were true because it's a cool story, but it's not. If it were, I'm sure I would have gotten some royalties out of it—or at the very least, a contract as their poster child for marketing.

But the real story? It's actually pretty cool too. My given name at birth wasn't Keno—it was Kenneth. When my sister learned to talk, around the time I was eight, she couldn't pronounce Kenneth. It came out as Keno—and it stuck. I've been Keno ever since.

When I tell that story, people often share their own endearing accounts of how nicknames in their families came to be. I never tire of hearing them. As I reflect on those anecdotes, I realize that words—especially nicknames—aren't just letters strung together. They have soul. They are an expression of a rich, meaningful history that embodies belonging, love, and identity.

I've experienced how much a name can influence the way people see you. But what fascinates me just as much is how people sometimes rewrite a name in their own minds—even when I introduce myself clearly.

When I lived Down Under in the early 1980s, a curious thing happened. Aussies often defaulted to calling me Ken, even after I introduced myself as Keno. It happened so often that I eventually stopped correcting people. And so, for three years as a teenager, I was Ken to most and Keno only to my close friends and family.

It still happens here in the States occasionally as well. But in an interesting twist of timing, the very day after I wrote this, someone I had just met on LinkedIn called me Ken in several different messages—even after I initially corrected them.

The story of my first name is a heartwarming one—a gift I cherish from my sister. But that's not the focus of this narrative. This is about my last name: Powers.

Divine guidance comes in many forms. Over the years, I've learned that when you're open to it and pay attention, Spirit will guide you—sometimes in ways you'd never expect or ever imagine, even with something as simple as a new name. To understand why changing mine mattered so much, I'll first tell you about my fathers and their names.

Growing up, I had two fathers: my biological father, Bert Gore, and the man who raised me, William "Bill" Weingarten. Their names carried their own stories, but I needed a name that reflected my own journey.

If you've ever seen the movie *Midnight in Paris*, starring Owen Wilson, you understand well how it captures the magic the city once held for artists and dreamers back in the day. My biological father, an American artist from Texas, didn't need a time-traveling taxi to step into that world—he moved to Paris to live the Bohemian dream during the golden era of the 1950s art scene. At the time, the city attracted creatives from all corners of the world, and he fully immersed himself in that vibrant energy.

My mom, born and raised in Minnesota, knew at a young age that she belonged somewhere more exotic. She was a sophisticated yet down-to-earth soul with an adventurous spirit, captivated by Paris's allure—its history, culture, fashion, and culinary arts.

After graduating from college in 1951, she turned her dream into reality, moving to Paris with her best friend and securing a job at the US Embassy. She turned out to be a die-hard Francophile, living for more than twenty-five years at different times in her life in a city her heart called home.

Bert Gore was the quintessential charmer—tall, dark, and effortlessly magnetic. So it was no surprise when my mom was instantly drawn to him at a lively Parisian gathering. Their romance blossomed in the heart of Paris, with moonlit strolls along the Seine, afternoons in lush gardens, and quiet moments in cozy cafés. The city's charm wrapped around them, deepening their connection, and in 1955, they were married.

Seven years into their marriage, my brother was born, followed two years later by me. As we grew up, my mom realized that Bert wasn't cut out for family life. His true love was art, and selling his work often took him away for months at a time. He saw the responsibilities of raising a family as a hindrance to his ambitions. This strained their marriage, leaving my mom feeling neglected, unsupported, and bitter. After years of emotional distance, she asked for a divorce.

With my biological father out of the picture, another man stepped in to fill the void—Bill Weingarten. But he didn't just step in, he became the man who truly embodied what it means to be a dad. He was the one who would raise me, love me, and support me in so many ways.

Many years later, when I was in my fifties, I became my parents' caretaker, looking after them during the last three years of their lives. During that time, I came across a wooden placard that read,

ANY MAN CAN BE A FATHER, BUT IT TAKES SOMEONE SPECIAL TO BE A DAD

The moment I saw it, I knew it was the perfect description of who Bill was to me. I bought it for him as a gift—because no one deserved those words more than he did.

After college, Bill joined the army and served thirteen months in Korea as an intelligence officer. But he quickly realized military life wasn't for him, so he set his sights on law and the Foreign Service, both of which suited his intellectual and ambitious nature.

Eventually, he had to make a choice: Harvard Law or the Foreign Service. In the end, practicality won out. The immediate paycheck of diplomacy was more appealing than taking on a mountain of student debt from law school.

After his first three years at the State Department in Washington, DC, he received his first overseas assignment—a highly coveted post in Paris. He packed his bags and set off to begin his life as a diplomat.

Legend has it that when my dad first walked into the office where my mom worked, he was smitten and kept finding reasons to return—whether for an official matter or just to catch her smile. Bill was sharp, ambitious, and kind. He won my mom's heart with his Long Island charm, his steady nature, and a genuineness that contrasted with the artistic, carefree world she had known.

In 1968, my dad proactively signed up for a two-year post as a civilian adviser in Vietnam, knowing it would reflect well on his record and advance his career. They were going to draft him for the war anyway, so he took control of his fate and chose a path that aligned with his ambitions. Determined to stay close, my mom relocated our family to Manila in the Philippines.

One of the most endearing things about my dad, besides his playful, warmhearted nature, was his love for storytelling. He never tired of recounting the adventures of his past, and I never tired of hearing them.

Some of his favorite stories were about the time my mom flew from the Philippines to Vietnam in 1968, right in the middle of the war, to marry him. Pulling off a wedding in a foreign country's war zone was anything but easy, yet somehow, they made it happen. I know because, as a kid, I used to look at their boring wedding photos and wonder what all the fuss was about.

But what they did was actually unheard of—the perseverance, the bravery, and the great lengths they went through to make it happen. Just getting to the altar was a feat in itself. My mom had to secure special permissions to enter Vietnam while my dad, as a United States government adviser, had to get official approval to marry. Wartime travel was unpredictable, and finding a safe place for the ceremony was another challenge, with movement restricted in a country at war.

Even basic wedding essentials—like a dress, rings, or a venue— weren't guaranteed. And with no modern communication, they planned everything across multiple countries through slow telegrams and expensive phone calls, knowing that at any moment, the war could upend their plans.

Of all the stories my dad told about my mom's trip to Vietnam, one of my favorites was about the night mortar shells rained down on the compound where she was taking shelter—the same place Bill's platoon ate and slept. The explosions jolted everyone awake, and they scrambled out of bed, rushing to the bunker. My mom, the only woman there, looked around at the men gripping their rifles—only to realize they were all huddled together in their underwear.

After two years of dodging bullets and ambushes, my dad eagerly returned to Washington, DC, with our family in tow. He had been offered a three-year post at the US embassy in Belgrade, Yugoslavia, and so he spent the next year immersed in a language program studying Serbo-Croatian in preparation.

We arrived in Belgrade in the summer of 1971, a time when Yugoslavia was still under the rule of Marshal Tito. It was a country caught between East and West—Communist but independent from the Soviet Union, open to the world yet tightly controlled. For a child, it was an intriguing place to grow up.

After Belgrade, we returned to DC for a three-year domestic assignment. By the time I was ten, Bill had cemented a place in my life and in my heart. It felt only natural that he would make it official by legally adopting me and my brother.

In that moment, I was no longer a Gore but a Weingarten, taking the name of the man who had committed his life—not just to my mom, but to our family.

After my mom's divorce from my biological dad, I never saw or heard from him again. It was as if he had never existed. My mother never spoke of him, and there was nothing in our home to remind me that he had once been part of our lives.

When I was twenty one years old, I felt curious enough to search for his whereabouts, only to find out that he had died six months prior. Not knowing what to do with my feelings, I put a lid on them and moved on.

Months later, I met his spirit in a guided meditation and realized that he had meant far more to me than I had let myself believe. That encounter set in motion a series of synchronicity that led me to his widow—a magickal, heartwarming three-week long journey where I got to learn more about him.

That experience tapped into a well of grief. I struggled with the mystery of who he was and what that meant for me. I wanted to know him, not just for the sake of knowing him but because I believed understanding him would help me understand myself. Coming to terms with that longing wasn't easy. It took years to untangle what his disappearance truly meant in my life. But that's a whole other story—for another book.

Bill was the one who raised me, who was there through my formative years, and who became the man I would always think of as my dad. I came to appreciate just how fortunate I was to have him in my life.

I loved Bill and was grateful for everything he did for our family, but I never felt at home with his last name. It suited my parents well—fitting for two people who loved wine, since Weingarten is a German name that literally means "garden of wine."

But for me, it was cumbersome. People constantly mispronounced and misspelled it, and I grew tired of correcting them. No matter how long I carried it, it never felt like it truly belonged to me.

I longed for a name that was short, easy to pronounce, and memorable—but more than that, I wanted a name that represented the kind of man I aspired to be. An affirmation to help me embrace my power and share it with the world.

When I made the decision to change my name, I spent time reflecting on what it should be. Then, during a meditation, the name Powers came to me. It resonated in a way Weingarten never had. It carried strength, simplicity, and a spiritual energy that felt undeniably right. Still, changing my name was a big decision, and

I wanted to be sure. So I took my time, letting it settle, making certain it was the one.

One of my biggest concerns was how my parents, especially my dad, would feel about me changing my last name. I knew the request would be sensitive for him. No matter how much love we shared, there was a part of him that still felt the weight of not being my biological father. The last thing I wanted to do was hurt his feelings. Ideally, I would have talked to them in person, but since we lived on opposite coasts, I decided to call and ask for their blessing.

There was never a perfect time to bring it up, so after months of procrastination, I finally made the call. My dad's knee-jerk reaction was to get upset. But once I explained my reasoning, he understood. He let go of his initial resistance and was able to relax, realizing it wasn't a personal rejection. By the end of the conversation, he reluctantly—but graciously—gave me his blessing, as did my mom.

I often ask Spirit for guidance in important matters, and changing my name was no exception. Not all signs from Spirit are obvious, but in my case, Spirit didn't disappoint. The ones I received were impossible to miss.

The first sign arrived when I was sitting at my desk, casually surfing the web on my desktop computer. Out of nowhere, a random video thumbnail popped onto my screen. It was the strangest thing—this had never happened to me before, and it hasn't happened since. I probably should have ignored it, given the risk of phishing, but something compelled me to click on it.

The video was a thirty-second clip from some low-budget B movie that had clearly seen better days. A woman sat in a medical examination room, facing the closed door as if waiting for someone to enter. A moment later, a man walked in wearing a white coat with a stethoscope around his neck and holding a chart in his hand.

Flipping through the papers on his clipboard, he took a moment to scan them. Then, the patient looked up at him and said, "So, Dr. Powers, what's my prognosis?"

I sat there, dumbfounded, caught between disbelief and wonder —my mind reeling from the odds of this happening.

The second sign came just two days after my encounter with the video clip. I was attending a business networking meeting with a new group that was meeting for only the second time. More than twenty people had attended the first meeting, so I expected a similar turnout. But when I arrived, much to my surprise, there was only one other person at the long table where we had gathered before.

Becky had been at the first meeting and was just as surprised as I was by the lack of turnout. We weren't early, but we waited another ten minutes to see if anyone else would show up.

When no one else did, we ordered our drinks and began the meeting. With just the two of us, we kept things informal. At one point, Becky mentioned that a friend of hers was moving to Australia and that she was tentatively planning a visit there once her friend got settled.

When the conversation shifted to what I was up to, I naturally brought up that I was contemplating changing my last name to Powers and had asked the Universe for a sign to confirm my decision. I told her about the random video clip and how I had taken it as a sign but admitted I was still hesitant to go through with it.

Becky's face lit up with excitement.

"What's with that big grin?" I asked.

"That friend I've been talking about—the one moving to Australia—her last name is Powers!"

I stared at her, stunned. "You're kidding!"

"Nope," she said, still grinning. "Isn't that crazy?"

I leaned back in my chair, letting it sink in. The random video clip was one thing, but now this? I had asked the Universe for a sign, and it seemed determined to make sure I didn't miss it.

"That's wild," I finally said, shaking my head. "What are the odds?"

We wrapped up our meeting, and as I sat in the parking lot in the quiet of my car, I took a moment to thank Spirit, not just for affirming my name choice, but for the breathtaking synchronicity used in its confirmation.

One reason I like the name Powers is because of a certain well-known movie character, Austin Powers. Maybe you've heard of him?

I get a kick out of referencing him when people ask for my last name while taking down my information—whether I'm signing up for a service or placing an order. Instead of spelling it out, I'll say, "That's Powers, as in Austin Powers." Sometimes, I even joke that we're cousins. You'd be surprised how many people actually believe me when I tell them that.

My favorite incident involving my last name happened at a Williams Sonoma store one Christmas season. I was shopping for my wife when I came across a display of mugs, each engraved with a large, beautiful golden letter of the alphabet. I decided to get one with the letter *P* since her first name starts with a *P* and she loves drinking tea. The fact that my new last name also started with a *P* was a bonus—I could use the cup too, kind of like when my dad would buy a book for my mom and end up reading it first.

I looked at every cup on display and couldn't find one with a *P*, so I walked up to the counter to ask the clerk for help.

"Can I order a mug and get it before Christmas?" I asked.

"Of course, love. I can help you with that," came the reply from a thirtysomething woman with a distinct British accent. "Let me get your information, and we'll get it ordered."

When she asked for my last name, I immediately saw an opportunity. "My last name is Powers—like Austin Powers," I said with a big grin. Then, for good measure, I threw in a rusty, not-so-great impression of Austin's famous, "Yeah, baaaaaby."

She suddenly stopped writing and raised an eyebrow as she

looked up at me. Then, in a perfectly deadpan tone, she said, "That's the worst Austin Powers impression I've ever heard."

Her delivery made me laugh so hard that everyone in the store stopped what they were doing to look our way. If you've ever heard my laugh, you'd understand—it's loud, distinct, and impossible to ignore.

Fun aside, Powers is more than just a name. It's a call to action and a reflection of the person I strive to be—bold, courageous, and authentic. It wasn't about rejecting the past but about fully stepping into my potential.

In January 2020, I legally changed my name from Kenneth Bertram Weingarten to Keno Powers. I didn't keep my middle name or choose a new one because I didn't see a need for one.

My wife is from India, where middle names and initials aren't as common as they are in most Western countries. When they are used, they're typically derived from the father's name, family name, or the village where a person was born.

Superstition and numerology play a significant role in Indian culture, especially when it comes to names. Many individuals and families modify their names—adding initials, inserting extra letters, or making slight variations—to align with numerological beliefs or to attract good fortune.

My wife is one of them. She wasn't given a middle name at birth, but later in life, after consulting a seer, she was told to add the middle initial *S*—taken from her father's first name. She swears that doing so changed her life dramatically.

My wife follows a number of other superstitions, but those are stories for another time.

One day, she sat me down to discuss something important. "I have an idea," she exclaimed.

That's never a good sign in my household. She caught the mock look of fear on my face as we sat across from each other in the living room.

"Just hear me out," she insisted. "I think you should add a middle initial to your name."

At the time, I had an LLC established under my name: Keno Powers LLC. My wife, once again, retold her story about adding the middle initial to her own name—this time with even more dramatic flair, emphasizing how it had transformed her life. Then she looked at me with expectant eyes, waiting for me to agree to her idea.

I groaned inside. Changing my name meant dealing with the hassle and cost of terminating my existing business registration and applying for a new one. On top of that, I'd have to notify the IRS to ensure they wouldn't get confused by two nearly identical business names.

After a few rounds of back-and-forth, I finally agreed to add a middle initial. My wife knew how much my mom meant to me and suggested using M for her legal name, Mary.

My mom never cared for her first name. From an early age, she chose to go by her middle name, Traci.

I tested out both by writing my name with each initial and saying it out loud. But it wasn't until I wrote down the M and heard myself say it that I realized how it transformed my name. That's when it hit me—M Powers could be read as empowers.

Keno M. Powers.

How cool is that?!

Although I haven't made my middle initial legal (changing your name is a lengthy, involved process), I've considered it. It's one of those *I wish I'd had this conversation with my wife before I initially changed my name* moments.

Life has a way of weaving threads together in unexpected ways, doesn't it?

To some, changing my name might seem trivial. But to me, Powers is an affirmation that I am a powerful man. It's a reminder of my ability to redefine myself, to claim a life that empowers me to live boldly, pursue my dreams, and fulfill my destiny.

More than that, it's a reminder that we all hold the power to shape our own stories—if we have the courage to live in a way that is true and authentic. Sometimes, it starts with something as simple as adding a single letter to your name.

CHAPTER 2

Encounters from the Other Side

10

Australian Rescue 2.0

I lived in six different countries before the age of twenty, when I moved to Oregon for college. Moving every few years was part of my dad's job. New countries, new schools, new friends—rinse and repeat. While I would never trade the richness of experiencing different cultures for the benefits of living in one place, uprooting myself from one continent and establishing a new life in another was never easy.

The move we made in the summer of 1981 was especially difficult. I was a sophomore in high school, finally finding my groove after four years in one place, when my dad came home one night and informed us that we would be relocating from our home in Brussels, Belgium, to the small city of Canberra, Australia, located thousands of miles away on the other side of the planet.

I was fifteen and furious.

There were a host of reasons why moving Down Under was significantly challenging. Besides leaving our familiar way of life and the people in it, we made the heartbreaking decision not to take our dog and two cats with us. The Australian government required a yearlong quarantine for all animals coming into the country, and since we didn't feel it was morally right to put our pets through that kind of ordeal, we found new homes for them. This was especially agonizing for me because I was very attached to my cat.

To add to the stress, once we arrived in Canberra, we spent months in temporary housing without our personal belongings before finding a home to call our own. Because Australia is in the southern hemisphere, their seasons are opposite ours—summer in June in the United States is winter down there. Their school year also follows a different schedule: Instead of starting in September and ending in June like ours, it begins in January and ends in December. Moving there in June, like we did, meant that I walked into the middle of a tenth-grade year. And because Australians have a separate school for eleventh and twelfth graders, I had to adjust to a new school for my last two years.

Going through life without pets was like living without an arm or a leg for our family. While we could get by without them, animals added immeasurable joy to our lives. As soon as we were situated in our new home, we drove to the local Humane Society in search of a new addition to our family.

A chorus of yowls and barks filled the air as we entered the building where the dogs were housed. The task of finding a dog was given to the youngest of our family—my little sister. After some lip biting, back-and-forth pacing, and reassurance from the rest of us, she made her choice. Bega was the one to make our family whole.

Named after a small town our family had visited near the Australian coast, Bega was a slender two-year-old mix of Lab and pointer with a shiny black coat. We quickly discovered she also had a large dose of retriever because—next to eating—chasing a ball was her favorite thing to do.

Given that I was a competitive runner, it fell upon me to be the one to take her out when she was bounding with hyper energy (which was nearly every day). Bega and I quickly established a routine. We would drive to a nearby park, where I'd let her loose so she could chase after her ball without the restrictions of a leash.

I would pull over and park at the edge of a large field, framed by quiet streets on two sides and a fenced playground on the third. The fourth side, a fair distance opposite me, descended out of sight and down an embankment behind a grove of gnarled, moss-filled oak trees.

Bega never attended dog obedience training, but she came back often enough when called that I felt it was safe to let her off the leash in large, open spaces.

At least, that's what I told myself. The truth was, as I think back to the times when she was running free, I often worried that I was taking too big a risk. I conveniently and quietly pushed my concerns into the back of my mind, rationalizing my decision by telling myself the area we were playing in was too large and far enough away from traffic for me to need to be overly cautious. It was a choice I would come to regret deeply.

One morning, before the summer heat arrived, Bega and I were in the field, running our usual circles around each other, playing tag, and chasing after her tennis ball. With ball in hand, I cocked my arm back, watching Bega's steely eyes lock on in anticipation of another hot pursuit. I let out a dramatic groan as I hurled the ball with all my might up and away toward the clouds in the wide-open sky. Bega wasted no time in answering my challenge. She tore across the grass in a fierce sprint, carving out a straight line under the arc of my throw.

I watched with glee and wonderment as her body hurtled through space, twisting and turning with fine-tuned adjustments to grab the ball after the first bounce. How she was able to track its trajectory from so far up was both a mystery and a marvel to me. Once that slimy, green joy was gripped between her teeth, she would bound back, her tail whipping wildly behind her, eyes gleaming, so we could do it all over again.

After one catch, Bega took a few loping strides toward me as she always did. But then suddenly, her demeanor changed. A jolt of instinct seemed to take over. She froze; her body stiffened with alertness. Without a second thought, she dropped the ball and, with the eagerness of a hound on a fox's trail, zigzagged in wild abandon from one part of the field to another, periodically dipping her nose close to the ground, dashing here and there, searching the field for whatever had hijacked her attention.

Alarmed, I called out for Bega to come back to me. To my chagrin, she ignored my commands. My concern exploded into panic as her trajectory changed. I stood in horror as she weaved in a frenzy across the field, away from me, picking up speed toward the woodland, hundreds of yards away. I screamed at the top of my lungs, but nothing persuaded her to stop.

I shook myself out of my mortified stupor and exploded into motion, fueled by the adrenaline of fear. My legs fired like pistons, and my feet pounded the hardened ground, each step charged with raw power like a lightning strike. Every nerve screamed with urgency, my lungs pumping furiously, my heart jackhammering in my chest as I tracked her path with laser focus.

Before I was halfway across the field, Bega's body vanished over the crest of the hillside, beyond the sparse cluster of trees. My mind yelled a multitude of expletives, cursing my decision to let her run without a leash and lashing out at the heavens for allowing this to happen. In the same desperate breath, I offered up promises to God in exchange for her safety.

Like a drill sergeant yelling threats at a group of cadets, my fear pushed my body to run faster. Hoarse cries filled my ears as my lungs desperately clawed at the air, sucking in oxygen with breathless fervor. But my body had nothing more to muster. Afraid I'd run out of steam before reaching her, I reluctantly slowed my pace, gauging the distance I had left as I scanned the area ahead of me, hoping Bega would reappear any second.

Suddenly, the prolonged blare of a car's horn shattered the stillness. Tires screeched, followed by the thud of a soft body struck by something hard and big. I raced past the tree line and descended a short but sharp slope that spilled onto a four-lane highway, with a wide grassy strip separating the two directions.

Bega had run onto the road and was hit by an oncoming car. I arrived at the scene to find her lying still in front of a stopped vehicle in the lane closest to the park. The car's horrified driver, a middle-aged woman, had gotten out and was rushing toward Bega's body when she saw me darting onto the scene.

"Are you the owner of this dog?" the woman screamed, a look of shock written on her face. When I acknowledged that I was, she began to apologize profusely.

"I'm so, so sorry," she cried. "The dog just appeared and ran in front of my car."

"I know," I yelled as I ran up to Bega. "It's okay. We were in the park up there," I said, pointing to the trees above. "She ran off following a scent. It's not your fault," I assured her.

We both reached Bega at the same time. She was alive and trembling, but it was clear she was badly hurt. A pool of saliva grew wide around her head as moans of pain emanated from her.

"Please, let me take you to the animal hospital. It's not far," the woman cried.

I agreed and knelt beside Bega, offering what little comfort I could with my voice and soft strokes. I scooped her into my arms as carefully as I could while the woman opened the passenger side door. I gently maneuvered into the seat, placing Bega on my lap. Her breathing was quick and shallow, with frequent whines rising from her heaving chest. I consoled her as best I could until we reached the hospital.

We didn't have far to go, but in the end, it didn't matter. Bega had sustained too many internal injuries to survive.

I called my parents from the hospital to give them the bad news. I waited an excruciatingly long twenty minutes for them to arrive.

Following the advice of the vet, we made the heart-wrenching decision to have her euthanized.

There are two types of dog owners when it comes to the loss of a pet: those who replace a loved one sooner rather than later, and those who wait a long time, unsure if they're ever going to get another. My sister was the former while I was the latter. No one blamed me for Bega's death, but that didn't stop me from feeling racked with guilt.

Less than a month later, my sister asked my parents if we could get another dog. I was averse to the idea, but after some family deliberation, my parents agreed to let my sister pick out another rescue.

I reluctantly drove my sister back to the same facility where we got Bega. I swallowed my grief as scores of canines—from young to old—peered at us with desperate eyes. Some were boisterous, tails fluttering, while others sat in the back of their cages, looking destitute. My mind wanted to run out of there screaming, but my heart wished I could take them all home.

A scrappy, funny-looking puppy with a dull, black, short-haired coat peered at us through the bars of her cage. Her soft eyes tracked our every move as we approached. Her oversized, moth-bitten ears framed a sweet, pear-shaped face. Her small tail gave a tentative wag when we noticed her. But when we stopped to say hello, it thumped into overdrive, eliciting smiles from both of us. While her quirky body made us laugh, it was her soulful eyes and gentle, loving nature that sealed the deal.

I didn't think I was ready for another dog. My heart was still raw from losing Bega, and part of me felt disloyal even stepping into that shelter again. But sometimes the animals we love leave us—not to break our hearts, but to make space for the next soul we're meant to love.

As we were filling out the necessary forms to adopt her, the staff at the RSPCA gave us the somber news that our little dog was due to be euthanized that week because she had been at the shelter for quite some time.

Tathra, named after a tiny coastal town near Bega as a kind of tribute to our lost love, was a mismatched mix of Spaniel, black Lab, and Pointer. It was as if her maker had hastily thrown body parts together in a distracted fashion. She had the paws of a much bigger Lab but the body size and shorter legs of a cocker spaniel. Whether it came from neglect and undernourishment or God's design, we didn't care. She became our second Australian rescue—a mini 2.0 version of Bega—who quickly won our hearts as we nursed her back to health.

In the three years I spent in Tathra's life before I ventured off to college, we developed a close relationship. It was hard to say good-bye to her, but I felt consoled knowing she was in good hands with my parents and younger sister.

Over the next decade, she joined my parents in their globe-trot-ting lifestyle, moving from Canberra, Australia, to Ottawa, Canada, then on to Washington, DC, and finally settling in Paris, France, where she spent the remaining years of her life.

In the summer of 1994, my parents discovered that Tathra had a tumor growing in her sinuses. The vet told them it was inoperable and that she would need to be euthanized once it became too large. Unbeknownst to me, that day would come shortly before Christmas.

That same summer, I was going through my own crisis. I sustained debilitating injuries from a serious car accident and spent the next six months recovering—not only from my physical injuries but also from major depression.

I had two menial jobs that barely kept me afloat, and to top it off, that November, I became homeless, living out of my cramped Ford Escort hatchback. None of my friends or my family had any idea what I was going through because I was too proud to ask for help and too embarrassed to let them know the straits I was in. I did everything I could to hide the truth from everyone.

Later that month, things dramatically changed for the better (you can read about it in the story "The White Light"). I landed a position that catapulted my career, and at the same time, I received a fateful call from one of my best friends, Isabelle—a call that would alter the course of my life.

Our friendship dated back almost a decade and had seen the highs and lows we each went through. Isabelle was calling to thank me for the birthday card I had mailed her and to check in on how I was doing. It had been a while since we last spoke.

Being an astute, sensitive soul, she read between the lines of my card and knew something was wrong. Despite my ego's attempt to dodge her questions, the one thing I didn't want to do was lie to her. So I surrendered my pride and told her the truth: I was homeless. Without hesitation, she invited me to stay with her and her husband until I got back on my feet.

As I sit at my desk writing this story, I think back to that phone call and appreciate, with a deep sense of gratitude, how Isabelle's offer and friendship saved my life. Sadly, Isabelle passed away fifteen years later from stage four breast cancer; otherwise, I would call her right now to thank her one more time.

While we made some great memories during that winter, having me in their house as I struggled to pick up the pieces of my life wasn't always easy for them. I fought hard with my inner demons, marked by tears, depressed moods, bouts of anger, and many hours curled up in a fetal position.

One night, a couple of weeks before Christmas, I asked my friends if I could make a long-distance call to my parents in Paris, France. This was before cell phones were commonplace, so I had to use their landline. I hadn't talked to my parents in a long while, and I suddenly felt compelled to reach out.

It was during that conversation that I found out Tathra had been euthanized earlier that day. I hung up the phone in a daze and walked into the dining room, where my friends were sitting down for dinner. As I sat to join them, Isabelle asked me how my call went. I told them the news about my childhood dog in a matter-of-fact tone and then proceeded to eat dinner as if nothing significant had happened. Isabelle looked at her husband with concern but said nothing, and the conversation moved on to other topics.

Late that night, I decided to take a walk around the neighborhood to calm my nerves. I had spent the last few weeks living with my friends, and as gracious and polite as their invitation to stay with them until I got back on my feet was, I grew concerned that I was overstaying my welcome and imposing on our friendship.

On my way back, less than a block away, a car pulled up and parked on the street in front of a home just thirty feet from where I stood. I watched as all four doors of the vehicle opened simultaneously. Five lively young adults and a small black dog without a leash piled out of the car and strode toward the house. The dog caught sight of me and came bounding over like a puppy, wagging its tail and expressing its infectious joy and affection.

I was immediately struck by how much this dog looked and acted like Tathra. It was uncanny—the same scrawny tail whipping back and forth like hummingbird wings. It was jumping up and down with its oversized paws and had a sweet, loving demeanor. We played for a few moments as the owner stood by beaming at our interaction.

As if following the lines of an invisible script, the dog suddenly ran back to its master and scampered into the house. I bid them good night and walked the last two hundred feet to Isabelle's house. I pulled the front door key out of my pocket and placed it in the lock. As I turned the key, a wave of emotion overcame me, and I burst into tears.

Isabelle and her husband, Mark, had gone to bed, so I pushed back my grief and quickly but quietly tiptoed through the house to the guest bedroom to grab my CD player. Then I made my way down to their basement so I could feel free to cry as loud as I needed to.

I switched on the light at the top of the stairs, then clambered down the rickety wooden steps into their unfinished basement. The space was dark and dingy, a graveyard for boxes and miscellaneous discarded household items strewn across a dusty cement floor. The only light source was a lone bulb hanging from the ceiling by a scraggly wire. The light cast a sickly bluish-white glow over a single piece of furniture—a well-worn couch sitting in front of an old tube TV set that had seen better days. There was nothing comforting about it, but it was what I had, and I was going to make do with it. I programmed my boombox to play my "sob" song on repeat. The CD was *Watermark* by Enya, and my go-to song for catharsis was "On Your Shore" for its haunting melodies and soulful lyrics.

I sat on the couch and opened the shutters of my heart. The grief blew in like a hurricane. I sobbed uncontrollably, shaking to the core of my soul as the sadness of Tathra's passing overwhelmed me. Memories of Tathra played in my mind like video clips, fueling the unapologetic drip from my nostrils and the continuous stream of tears running down my face, making a mess of my shirt.

As I cried, I became aware of something else—something insidious that had been lurking in the shadows of my subconscious. It was guilt with a capital *G*. My tears were no longer just for grief. They became cries for forgiveness—for not being there for Tathra at the end of her life.

I had moved to the other side of the country when I was nineteen to go to college and had lived the rest of my life absent from hers, except for Christmas visits. Tathra spent her final years in Paris, France, and because of the distance, cost of travel, and my constant excuses for why I couldn't go, I never made the trip there while she was still alive.

As I wept, my calls for redemption were met with a profound and unexpected response. From out of the darkness, a silent swirl of energy appeared, gliding toward me with deliberate grace. Its radiance intertwined with my aura, filling my heart with a sweet and tender love.

I knew instantly what—or rather, who—it was. Tathra. Her spirit had answered my plea, bathing me in pure love and impressing upon my soul a message that rang with absolute clarity.

There's nothing to forgive. Let go of your guilt.

I didn't think I could cry any harder, but I did. Held in the warmth of her affection, the guilt and sorrow I had carried melted into a flood of fresh tears. Like a river, they carried my burden away until I was left with nothing but the serene hush of grace. When her purpose had been fulfilled, and without any fanfare, Tathra's spirit turned quietly and drifted back into the ether.

In all my visitations by Spirit, I've never had a say in how much time I could spend with them. This encounter was no exception. As much as I wanted to continue basking in Tathra's beautiful energy, I had to let her go.

Gratitude, pure like glacial waters, welled in my heart and overflowed into the heavens after her, thankful for the priceless miracle I was given. As my tears dried, I felt cleansed—like the freshness that comes after the passing of a storm.

I sat on the couch for a while, processing the events of the night: the phone call to my parents, the news about Tathra's passing, my nonchalant reaction, and the "chance" encounter with her doppelgänger that became the catalyst for my healing catharsis. And then, of course, there was the climactic visitation by Tathra's spirit.

As I reviewed the details of the evening, I was mesmerized by how one action seemed tied to another and by the precise timing of the run-in with the puppy. Everything played out like it was predestined. I felt like the lead actor in a movie someone—or something—else was directing. Was it my Higher Self's doing, Tathra's doing, someone else's doing, or was it a group effort? It was tantalizing to think about.

I became aware of how late it was and decided I had better head to bed. As I slowly unfolded my body, soft groans escaped my lips, my muscles stiff from my having stayed curled up, crying in the same position for so long.

I lifted my weary bones off the couch and shuffled over to the stairway until my hand grasped the rail. I stopped and looked back at the sad, empty couch, then scanned the dark, dreary room one last time, searching for any signs of Tathra. But there weren't any.

I let out a deep sigh with the involuntary rise and fall of my chest. As unsightly as the basement was, and no matter how late it was, I didn't want to leave. I yearned to hang onto the magick of my interaction for as long and as deeply as I could, but it was already fading fast.

These kinds of experiences with the world of Spirit were beyond amazing, but my mind couldn't help but lament that they never lasted long enough and didn't happen as often as I wished. And while such gifts were extraordinary, they came with a price. Moments of mystical magick left behind a residue of yearning—a tender ache, a longing that ordinary life could never fully satisfy.

But I didn't let myself dwell on the downside. Instead, I focused on the beauty of the gift and let gratitude anchor my heart, humbled by the rare blessing of witnessing such spiritual splendor and having the awareness to truly receive it.

I turned and slowly climbed the stairs. I was still sad, but there was a calm in my heart and a lightness to my step. Tathra's spirit was gone, but the love she left behind walked with me—soft and glowing—into the night.

11

Spa Day Visitation

Sadie and Margie were lifelong friends in their late forties, planning to spend a perfect Sunday together—a day of pampering with massages, facials, and brunch, followed by a peaceful stroll along the sun-drenched shores of La Jolla, California. Sadie was visiting from out of state, and they wanted to make the most of their time together.

Back then, I was a massage therapist at the spa they had chosen for their day of relaxation. On that particular Sunday, I was the only therapist available. To keep things flowing smoothly, the women took turns—while one enjoyed a massage, the other relaxed with a facial. Margie chose to go first for her massage while Sadie opted to begin with a facial.

Margie was a tall, quiet woman with a no-nonsense, let's-get-down-to-business demeanor. As is often the case with certain clients, our conversation was limited to the customary formalities: reviewing her intake form and discussing which areas she wanted me to focus on.

Margie was feeling stressed and requested a relaxing massage. I obliged, gently kneading her muscles as the room settled into silence.

Not long after I started, a sudden change in the room's energy made my pulse quicken. I felt a swirl of energy in the upper right-hand corner behind me, where the walls met the ceiling. Glancing over my shoulder, I thought I caught a movement from the corner of my eye. Unwilling to disturb Margie's reverie, I quickly turned back and refocused on the massage.

Then, a vivid projection flashed across my mind's eye—as if a holographic movie screen had been activated in my brain.

Up near the ceiling, a large circular blur spiraled in motion, expanding rapidly and creating an opening in the fabric of reality—like a hidden door revealing itself. A split second later, a spirit passed through and hovered by the portal, looking down at me.

She was a middle-aged woman, and without speaking, she informed me telepathically that she knew both Margie and Sadie. Though her presence was palpable, her features remained indistinct—a shadowy impression rather than a clear image.

I continued the massage, waiting with bated breath for our visitor to speak. But she didn't.

After a long silence, I projected a thought toward her: *Can I help you with something?*

Her response came as a planted thought in my mind—she wasn't here to deliver a message, nor did she need anything from me. She simply wanted to make her presence known.

A quiet sigh of relief echoed in my mind. From my brief interaction with Margie, I doubted she would be open to the fact that I had just communicated with the spirit of a dead person—even if the spirit claimed to know her.

As I refocused on the massage, the spirit's presence faded, like background music dissolving into a quiet hum. Soon, it seemed that she was gone.

Time passed without incident as I finished Margie's massage. We exchanged pleasantries, and I took a few minutes to reset the room for her friend, Sadie.

Sadie was a short, talkative woman with an effervescent, heart-warming presence. Our conversation flowed effortlessly, an engaging volley of back-and-forth banter that continued even after her massage began.

"I used to be a massage therapist myself," she said, settling onto the table as I prepared to begin.

"Oh really?" I replied. "That's neat! What inspired you to pursue massage, and why did you stop?"

We carried on a relaxed conversation, drifting through different aspects of her life as I worked to ease the tension from her muscles.

It's common for people to talk during the first part of their massage and then eventually drift into a quieter, more contemplative state. You can always tell when they reach that point—the conversation naturally fades into a lull.

As soon as that happened with Sadie, the energy in the room suddenly intensified as if someone had turned up a dimmed floor lamp to full brightness.

The mystery spirit was back.

This time, she made her intentions clear. She wanted me to let Sadie know she was there—and that she had a message for her.

I wasn't comfortable with the idea of interrupting Sadie's blissful state to tell her a dead person's spirit was hovering above us in the room. I rarely talk to strangers, let alone someone on my table in a professional setting, about the fact that I sometimes communicate with the dead. This moment with Sadie was no exception.

Instinctual fear reared its head, and a familiar monologue rattled through my mind: *Do you really want to embarrass yourself in front of this woman and risk looking like a fool? What if she doesn't believe in this kind of thing and gets upset with you? She might even get up off the table and leave. And what's the owner of the spa going to say when she complains?*

I cringed at the thought.

But then, I heard another voice—a voice with the same calming intonations that a loving, thoughtful father might use to console a scared child. *You have nothing to fear,* it said.

I recognized it instantly—the voice that had occasionally showed up during pivotal moments in my life.

She's not going to complain, it continued. *You know she's open to this based on your conversation with her. Trust your intuition.*

My apprehension softened, gently shooed away by the voice's tone and reasoning. But, like a child just learning how to swim, I wasn't quite ready to dive into the deep end and tell Sadie outright that a spirit was in the room. Instead, I chose to wade into the shallow end first.

I softly intruded into her dreamy state with a whisper. "Sadie, can I ask you a personal question that might seem a little out of the blue?"

"Sure," she replied sleepily.

"Did a woman you know—a friend or someone you were close to—pass away in the not-so-distant past?"

Sadie thought for a moment.

"Well, let me see," she pondered. "I can think of a couple of guys I know, but I can't think of a woman I know who died. Why do you ask?"

I was caught off guard. The spirit in the room had been insistent that she knew Sadie.

While I'm not always completely confident in my ability to interpret messages from Spirit, in this instance, I felt certain—I knew I was getting it right.

I decided to fill Sadie in on what was happening. She wasn't fazed in the slightest by my disclosure but struggled to come up with a woman she knew who had passed. I reached out again, hoping for more from the spirit, but to no avail. It became clear she had left the room.

Sadie shrugged and sighed.

"Guess it'll just have to stay a mystery," she said. She was clearly clueless as to who I could be talking about.

After our session came to an end, Sadie thanked me for the great massage and wished me well before heading back to the changing room to meet up with Margie.

I closed the door to the treatment room so I could have some privacy for the tantrum I was about to unleash. I shook my head in disbelief, frustration knotting up in my chest . . . more frustration than I care to admit. My jaw clenched as I waved a fist at the corner of the room where the spirit had entered.

"Why did you embarrass me like that?" I blurted as if someone were actually there.

Caught off guard by my sudden outburst, I reminded myself that I was in a spa and needed to keep my voice down. Lowering my tone, I rasped, "Why didn't you give me more information?"

I felt humiliated and let down. I had been so sure I was getting the information right. Bewildered, I kept questioning what had happened and why. But no matter how much I ranted, my questions were met with silence.

I took a few deep breaths, exhaled slowly, and tried to calm the storm inside me. Why was I so upset? I paused, examining my thoughts and feelings. Then it struck me. My pride had taken a hit. A memory of an important lesson one of my psychic teachers had drilled into me years ago surfaced.

"Make sure to keep your ego in check when you read for people," she would say. "Ego is only interested in looking good and being right. It will create attachments to outcomes and taint your ability to be objective. Your ego can't see beyond the next corner, but Spirit can view the entire horizon and beyond."

I recognized that my ego was only trying to protect me from feeling judged. I carry a deep-seated fear of being abandoned. Some part of me believes that if I make enough mistakes, people will leave me. Perfection was my ego's antidote to make sure that never happened. My frustration was a byproduct of that fear.

I comforted the fearful part of me with whispers of self-forgiveness. "It's all right," I softly said. "It's okay that you're not perfect. You tried your best. That's all you can do."

I continued to inhale deeply, mentally working to release the knots of my frustration with each exhale as I tidied up the treatment room for my next client. I grabbed a pile of sheets from the hamper and headed toward the laundry room.

Just as I was stepping out of the room, I saw Sadie walking down the hallway toward me—her eyes red and puffy, streams of tears falling down her face.

"I can't believe what just happened!" Sadie exclaimed as she walked up to me. She struggled to meet my eyes as if she were embarrassed.

I motioned for her to come back into the room, and I set my linens back in the hamper.

Sadie took a breath, then explained that she did have a close female friend who had died recently, named Evelyn. She had completely blocked the memory of her death.

"When I met up with Margie in the changing room, I told her what happened during my massage," she continued. "Margie gave me the strangest look. She had to remind me that our friend Evelyn died. How could I have forgotten that?"

Sadie's grief poured out of her as she stepped up and wrapped me in a hug.

"Thank you so much for your amazing gift," she said, her voice choked with emotion as she held me tight for an extended hug. Her body softened against mine as her sobs eased.

We stepped apart, and I placed my hands gently on her arms, gazing into her eyes. I swallowed hard, fighting back a flood of my own tears.

"You're so welcome," I said. "It's an incredible honor and a blessing to be a voice for loved ones who have passed on."

Sadie nodded, wiping her eyes. "Well, I'm grateful you said something," she replied tearfully. "This whole experience has made me realize I have some work to do around my friend's death."

We stood in silence for a moment, letting the weight of her confession settle between us. Then Sadie let out a deep sigh. We hugged goodbye, and I lingered in the doorway, watching her walk down the hallway to the front desk.

I grabbed the dirty linens from the hamper, closed up the room, and headed down a different hallway to the laundry room—with an armful of sheets and a heart full of gratitude.

On my way, a realization struck me—I had forgotten to give Sadie Evelyn's message.

I dropped off the sheets and hurried up to the front receptionist area, relieved to find them both still there. Margie was at the counter paying for their treatments while Sadie stood beside her, tears still streaming down her face.

I walked up to Sadie and gently pulled her aside.

"Evelyn wanted me to give you a message," I said softly. "She says you're carrying around a lot of guilt, and you don't need to. She wants you to let it go."

Sadie nodded as if she understood, fresh tears welcoming the news.

We embraced for another heartfelt hug, immersed in the blessings of the moment, until I tenderly let her go and wished her well.

Sadie rejoined Margie, who was waiting by the entrance. They waved one last time as I watched them walk out into the brightness of a fresh new day. In that moment, I imagined that Evelyn was also peacefully walking into a brightness of her own.

An immense sense of gratitude settled on me, resting on my face and in my heart as I slowly turned and headed back to the treatment room.

As I went about the rest of my day, I reflected on my experience with Margie, Sadie, and Evelyn. I was reminded of the importance in trusting myself and trusting the process when it comes to receiving intuitive information. I saw clearly how my ego had stirred up my frustration and how crucial it is to let go of the need to be in control, to be right, and to understand why things happen the way they do in the moment.

What astonished me upon reflection was that Sadie's experience wouldn't have been nearly as powerful or profound had she figured out who Evelyn was when she first appeared during her massage. And because of that, neither was it my role to tell her or to explain Evelyn's intention nor to give her the message until the moment I did.

The fact that Sadie had completely blocked her friend's death from her conscious mind wasn't just tied to a significant lesson around guilt—the realization itself that she had blocked out the memory became a doorway to her healing on a much deeper level.

Receiving information and delivering messages are a continual dance for me—a push and pull, soft and hard, yes and no, trust and doubt. Learning how much to say, when to say it, and how best to deliver the message are skills I'm still mastering.

Just like a dancer improves with practice, refining their movements with every performance, so does a psychic. My experience with Sadie and Spirit was both a boon and a blessing to my confidence, but it also served as a reminder to stay humble.

I'm not a religious person, but I'm comfortable using the word *God*, and I do think the age-old adage applies here: "Let go and let God." Or as a dear friend of mine says when asking for something she wants, "For this or something better, and for the highest good for all."

12

K-9

editative music drifted in the background of my massage treatment room, its soothing tones setting the mood for my practice. As I sat at my desk, catching up on paperwork before my next client arrived, an intuitive nudge to check the clock confirmed I only had a few minutes left before the appointment.

I scanned the large room from end to end, making sure everything was in its proper place. Satisfied that the space was set for the session, I turned my attention back to my paperwork.

My private practice was located in a two-story commercial building across from Mission Valley in San Diego and featured a spacious eighteen-by-thirty-foot treatment room and a separate, cozy waiting area. Ambiance and aesthetics have always been important to me, so both rooms were furnished and decorated to reflect that. Rich bronze-colored barrel chairs, elegant accent tables, and striking art-piece armoires adorned the space. Plush area rugs, lush green plants, and towering real-wood bookshelves added a touch of warmth while carefully chosen wall décor tied everything together, creating an inviting retreat.

When I heard the familiar sound of my waiting room door opening and closing, I tidied up my desk. Picking up my leather-bound clipboard, I slipped a new-client intake form under the clasp and headed out to greet my first-time client, Mike.

Stepping into the waiting room, I found myself facing a gruff-looking man in his midsixties with a solid build and a distinct macho presence—the kind I'd associate with someone from a military background. It came as no surprise when I later learned that he was a sheriff with a long history on the force.

Mike's powerful physique and athletic stature were hard to ignore as he stood up to greet me, extending a well-worn hand in a firm handshake. I met his grip with equal strength, then gestured toward his seat and handed him the intake questionnaire. I explained that we'd go over it together in my treatment room once he was finished.

As we sat across from each other to review his answers, Mike's discomfort was palpable. He shifted in his seat repeatedly, avoiding eye contact as much as possible. It was clear he felt uneasy. I mused that it might have been due to my office's strong new age vibe with its overtones of spirituality and shamanism.

I was reminded of the time a new client walked into my treatment room to get ready for her massage, only to dart out less than a minute later, exclaiming she wasn't comfortable getting a massage from me. She practically ran out of my office without stopping to give me an explanation. Bewildered, I wondered what had alarmed her so much. Maybe it was the little Buddha statue sitting on my massage table as part of its decorative display. It wouldn't be the first time that little Buddha had sparked a strong reaction.

Just weeks before, a woman from a previous generation came for a massage scheduled by her daughter. As I followed her into my treatment room to go over her intake form, she took two steps in and then stopped dead in her tracks as if she'd seen a ghost. With a dramatic flair that made me raise an eyebrow, she pointed to the Buddha statue on my table and exclaimed that she couldn't walk into the room until *that thing* was removed from sight. Yikes!

Of course, I immediately removed the Buddha and stashed it in the armoire. Given her outburst, I was afraid it was going to be a session from hell. Fortunately, things went better than expected. Not only did we strike up a pleasant rapport, but her daughter later reached out to tell me her mom had loved the massage. Phew!

Shaking off the memory, I refocused on Mike and the task at hand. One question on my intake form asked, *Have you ever had a massage before?* Mike checked the box indicating that he hadn't. Considering his wife had scheduled the appointment for him and the way he was acting, I put two and two together.

I often see this scenario: One partner signs up their significant other for a massage because the massage recipient either doesn't know how to relax, doesn't take care of themselves, or both. It was clear that getting a massage wasn't Mike's idea. I imagined he was here to placate his wife. I empathized with his discomfort, and, like I always do with nervous or uncomfortable clients, I addressed the elephant in the room.

"I see that you've never had a massage," I stated. "Let me guess. You're here because your wife made you come, even though you don't feel comfortable getting a massage."

Mike looked at me, surprised and a little off guard that his uneasiness was so obvious. He forced a brief smile, acknowledging that my observation was true. His reaction gave me the impression that he didn't like being vulnerable or transparent. I supposed that those weren't ideal traits in his line of work.

"Don't worry," I said in a lighthearted tone. "It happens all the time."

People who have never had a massage, and especially those who wouldn't get one of their own volition, typically feel uncomfortable because they don't know what to expect or they feel uneasy with the idea of a stranger touching their body.

I explained to Mike in detail what was going to happen: We would finish going over the intake form, then I would leave the room, and he could undress to his comfort level and lie stomach-side down under the sheet with his face in the cradle. After I finished my explanation, I asked if he had any questions. He was noticeably more relaxed as he stated he didn't.

"Okay, great," I said. I stepped out of the room so he could get undressed and onto the table.

When Mike let me know that he was ready, I reentered the room, dimmed the lights, and walked over to the massage table beside his upper body. I gently placed my hands on his back and held them there for a long moment. This was my usual starting point—a way to connect both physically and energetically to whoever was on my table.

That act also served another purpose: It gave my clients a moment to absorb my touch—to register it and get used to it. That simple act sent a signal to a nervous client's brain, letting them know they could begin to relax and unwind.

I could immediately tell Mike needed a lot of bodywork by the sheer amount of tension in his muscles. I assumed it was from the emotional and mental strain of his job, as well as its physical demands. Mike wasn't the talkative type, so I carried on in silence, checking in with him a couple of times in a soft, reassuring voice to ensure he was comfortable and that I was using the right amount of pressure.

As I worked, my mind settled into a deep meditative rhythm. I had learned to quickly enter this altered state from years of experiencing the runner's high during my long runs and from the practice of focusing my attention intently during the thousands of massages I had done.

There was something about the stillness of those moments—the quiet, the deep concentration—that seemed to act as a beacon for unexpected visitors from the Other Side.

Before I realized I could initiate contact at will with souls who had passed on, spirits from the Other Side would occasionally show up in my treatment room during a session when their loved one lay on my table. This time would be no different.

Spirit communicates with psychics and mediums through the five senses. These include clairvoyance (seeing visual images), clair-cognizance (receiving telepathic knowledge), and clairsentience (feeling emotions or sensations). Less common are clairalience (smelling scents associated with the deceased) and clairaudience (hearing sounds or voices).

Like most psychics and mediums, I receive information in multiple ways at once. My naturally developed modalities are claircognizance and clairsentience. On rare occasions, I will hear or smell something attributed to the deceased.

I don't usually see spirits clearly or in much detail when I interact with them. More often, I catch a fleeting glimpse of their form in the corner of my eye when they first appear. This tends to happen when I'm at home and lost in thought or focused on a task—like washing the dishes. A spirit will pass by me, and I'll see a movement in my peripheral vision. If I shift my attention to them, I sometimes receive impressions of who they are, or if they decide to engage me, they project images onto the screen of my inner sight.

Such was the case when I was massaging Mike.

As I worked on his right shoulder, I caught the movement of a shadow in the corner of my eye—to my left, near the foot of the table. My intuition told me it was the spirit of a dog.

To my rational, analytical mind, the idea of a dog's spirit showing up in my treatment room seemed a bit outlandish. It suggested that my overactive imagination was playing tricks on me, conjuring shapes out of the darkness. When I turned to look, it appeared my rational mind was right—there was nothing there.

I was about to dismiss my intuition altogether when the shadowy presence reappeared, this time in sharper focus, exactly where I had first glimpsed it. An image of a face formed telepathically in my mind—the countenance of a beautiful, middle-aged German shepherd. Normally, I wouldn't associate German shepherds with sweetness, but that's exactly the kind of energy she radiated. Her presence warmed my heart as if I were interacting with the innocence of a child.

All the animals in my life have been considered family. That was how I was raised, and I carried that philosophy into adulthood. Even now, as a married man, my wife and I refer to our adorable Havapoo as our furbaby. When he's up to mischief—which is at least ten times a day—my wife will often point it out with an amused admonishment: "Look what *your* son is doing," as if his antics are somehow a reflection of me.

I've had several profound experiences communicating with living animals and insects, but never had I communicated with the spirit of a dog from the Other Side like this. Without breaking the flow of Mike's massage, I sent her a telepathic *hello*.

Hello, she replied.

Are you here for Mike? I asked silently.

In response, a flood of memories filled my awareness—glimpses of her life with Mike. Thoughts and images fluttered across the screen of my mind, each one imbued with a deep, unwavering love. I was surprised when she gave me the impression that she saw herself as "Daddy's little girl"—a sentiment I had only ever associated with human fathers and daughters.

I didn't receive her name in our exchange, but for the sake of this story, I'll call her Sheila. In the dimly lit cocoon of my office, I became a silent witness, blessed to experience Sheila's soul-stirring tribute to the man she loved. It was a beautiful homage—but it was also tragic. This radiant soul let me know that Mike had been part of a K-9 unit and that she had been his partner.

I tried to remain poised as she conveyed to me the events of that night—the night she lost her life in the line of duty. While on patrol with Mike, they were called to a crime in progress. When they arrived at the scene, the perpetrator made a run for it. Mike threw open the door of his vehicle and gave Sheila the command to apprehend.

She leaped into action without hesitation, sprinting after the man at full speed. Mike took off running too, but he was much slower than she was and struggled to keep up.

As Sheila closed in, the assailant spun around, raised a gun, and fired several shots, killing her instantly. Her body crashed hard to the ground, tumbling into a lifeless heap—a violent finale to her life.

I swallowed thickly, pushing back tears while the vision played out in my mind like a holographic video. As a massage therapist, it was important to maintain my professionalism. The last thing I wanted was to start crying with a new client on my table.

Just when I thought it couldn't get worse, Sheila revealed that Mike carried a heavy burden, believing her death was somehow his fault. She wanted me to tell him it wasn't—that he didn't need to carry that weight any longer.

My heart both melted and sank.

I found myself in a difficult position. The tricky thing about visits from the dead is that not everyone is ready—or willing—to believe their loved ones' spirits live on and still watch over them. Just because a spirit reaches out doesn't always mean you should act on it. I had learned that lesson the hard way years before while giving a regular client a massage.

James was a successful artist who came in regularly for massage. He didn't strike me as spiritual or new age, so I kept my woo side to myself. James was a private man of few words—an introvert with an air of muted intensity. We never spoke at length and had only the occasional brief conversation.

Halfway through this particular session, I instructed James to roll onto his back and close his eyes. Once he was settled, I scooted my stool to the head of the massage table, facing James, cupped his head with both hands, and began channeling healing energy to promote deeper relaxation.

As I sat there quietly, holding his head in my hands, enjoying the tranquility of the moment, I suddenly felt compelled to ask him if there was anyone who had inspired his work. Normally, I wouldn't interrupt a client's repose. It wasn't even a question I was particularly curious about. But the urge was undeniable—almost as if an unseen force was nudging me to speak. So, I asked him.

James slowly opened his eyes. He was so relaxed that it took him a moment to reorient himself. I could see by the look on his face that he was mentally searching for an answer. With my hands still cradling his head, he methodically began listing several names, adding a few words about their influence.

When he was done, I felt an energetic shift in the room.

It only took me a second to realize what was happening. A soul from the Other Side had just entered the room. I knew immediately who it was: James's father.

James hadn't mentioned his dad as one of the people who influenced his work. But when he finished talking, his father's voice chimed in telepathically, letting me know that he had, in fact, played a significant role in shaping James's career.

I was puzzled. Why hadn't James included him? Before I could overthink it, I found myself speaking.

"What about your dad?" I asked.

James hesitated for a moment, then confirmed that his father had indeed encouraged and inspired his career. As those words left his mouth, I felt a sudden surge of energy. His father's soul moved toward me and entered my body.

A delicious wave of pure, unadulterated love radiated from my chest, flowing down my arms and out through my hands, which were still cradling James's head. It was an experience straight out of the 1990 movie *Ghost*—the moment when Whoopi Goldberg's character allows Patrick Swayze's spirit to inhabit her body so he can share one last embrace with his wife.

For me, it was nothing short of ecstatic. But James? He didn't seem to notice. He just lay there in silence, completely unaware of what was happening.

I ached to tell him. Maybe, if he knew, he could feel what I was feeling—the incredible depth of love, pure and unconditional.

I debated silently but ultimately decided against it. James didn't strike me as someone who would be open to this kind of experience. The last thing I wanted was to upset a paying client and have it come back to bite me if he complained to upper management.

As if on cue, his father's spirit drifted from my body and evaporated into thin air. At the end of our session, I bade James farewell as if nothing extraordinary had just happened.

That night, I couldn't stop thinking about the interaction with James's dad. The experience left me wonderstruck—in awe at what had transpired and deeply moved by his father's adoration.

Despite my reluctance, and against my better judgment, I decided to write James a handwritten letter.

Days passed. Then weeks. James never responded. And when he quietly disappeared from my schedule, I had my answer.

Months later, I ran into James and mustered the courage to ask about the letter. I acknowledged that he hadn't come in for a massage in a while and carefully asked if it had anything to do with what I had written. Avoiding my gaze, he hesitated before admitting that the experience I described didn't align with his religious beliefs.

A sudden rush of heat radiated across my face, his words landing like an accusation. I fumbled for an explanation, mentioning how I had wrestled with whether to write the letter at all, then apologized for making him uncomfortable.

I walked away telling myself I hadn't done anything wrong—but my sweat-soaked underarms and clammy palms told another story. Despite the shame and awkwardness, I was grateful for the closure.

But I also made a silent vow: Next time Spirit speaks, I'll listen—but I won't necessarily share it.

Back in the room with Mike, I contemplated what to do about Sheila. She had moved to stand by my legs, looking up at Mike on the table as if she still had a body. It was an endearing moment—not just because I could see, in my mind's eye, the love radiating from her face, but because I could feel it. A deep, unwavering devotion. A desire to ease his pain.

I wanted to say something, but I was torn. Just like with James, I sensed Mike wouldn't be open to the idea that the spirit of his K-9 was in the room—let alone that she was communicating with me. I was caught between honoring her request and respecting not only his boundaries but mine as well. In the end, I knew I had to say something.

I hate to admit it, but part of me wanted confirmation—to know that what was happening wasn't just my imagination, that Sheila was real. That she had, in fact, been his partner. I chose my words carefully. In a gentle tone, so as not to jar Mike's relaxed state, I initiated a conversation.

"Hey, Mike, I was curious about something."

He took a moment to emerge from his silence. "What's that?"

"Are you part of a K-9 unit?"

"Yes, I am," he replied.

A spark of excitement shot through me. I waited for him to say more, but he didn't. The fact that he didn't struck me as odd—and with it came the first flicker of doubt. Had I made the right decision in bringing this up? My excitement began to fade, but I figured I had already started the conversation, and there was no turning back now.

"Were you partnered with a German shepherd who died in action?"

"Yes, I was." His tone was even, almost unreadable—no trace of emotion, no hint of what he was thinking.

Those were the only words he spoke. I was left puzzled as to why Mike didn't engage with me any further. Here was a beautiful, healing opportunity around the loss of the dog he had loved profoundly, one I felt deep in my gut. If it were me, I would have been curious and full of questions: How did you know? Are you psychic? What's going on? But for whatever reason, Mike wasn't willing to say much of anything.

Sometimes, spirits insist I pass on a message, no matter my reluctance. In Sheila's case, she simply wanted to express her love and for Mike not to carry so much unwarranted guilt. While I wasn't getting the sense that it was urgent for me to tell Mike she was in the room, I did feel that Sheila wanted me to say more. I continued to tread carefully.

"I imagine you had a close relationship with your dog. That must have been hard. I'm sorry for your loss."

"Yes, it was." His response was stoic as ever.

Sheila stayed by my side, radiating a quiet, unwavering love as she looked at her human companion with sorrowful eyes. Her expression made me gently continue.

"I imagine she felt the same way," I offered tenderly, "and that she was lucky to have you."

True to his nature, Mike didn't utter a single word. I let the silence settle, sensing the conversation, and Sheila's mission, had reached its end. She slipped away into the ether without a trace, and Mike remained quiet for the rest of his session.

When it came time to leave the room so he could get dressed, I encouraged Mike to schedule another massage, given how much his body needed it. He agreed, and we got him in the books for the following week.

After Mike left, I sat at my desk, jotting down notes about his session for future reference. My thoughts drifted back to Sheila's visitation—how it unfolded, the warmth of her presence, and the quiet devotion she carried for Mike. I kept shaking my head in quiet amazement at the profound nature and beauty of that experience. A warm glow radiated from my heart, filling me with a deep sense of peace. It was an incredible privilege and an honor to be a messenger for Sheila's spirit.

Despite feeling blessed, I couldn't help but second-guess myself. Had I made the right choices in how I handled things? Should I have been more direct? Should I have told Mike, plain and simple, that his dog's spirit was in the room? His lack of engagement left me feeling sad and disappointed. Her visitation was an opportunity for profound healing, and I feared it had passed him by.

I didn't like the thought that I might have had a hand in that by not being more open and honest. To appease my guilt, I reminded myself that not everyone is open to the idea of life after death, or that some people can communicate with spirits from the Other Side, whether human or animal. Nor was it for me to know the greater plans the Universe had for Mike. Maybe our paths crossing—and the interaction we did have—was the plan, and I just couldn't see it. I told myself I would consider telling Mike about Sheila's visit during his next appointment.

But I never got the chance. Mike canceled his next massage a few days later, and I never heard from him again.

13

Beyond the Veil of Death

On February 29, 2020, as COVID-19 was just beginning to wreak havoc on the world, my dad passed away. On March 8, I delivered his eulogy at a celebration of life service held at the retirement center where he and my mom lived. The very next day, everything went into lockdown.

My mom was heartbroken. Her health declined rapidly, and by the following day, it looked like she was going to pass as well. But true to her Irish nature, her life force rallied, bringing her back from the brink of death. It was just another testament to her strong constitution, which had helped her survive cancer and other medical ailments throughout her life.

Mary "Traci" Weingarten was a down-to-earth woman with a natural beauty, her appeal enhanced by her charm, keen eye for aesthetics, and refined sensibility. She carried herself with an undeniable grace—classy yet never pretentious. Her allure and elegance were cultivated by a lifetime of worldly travel, born from an adventurous spirit and an openness to the marvels of different cultures.

It was a cruel reality that she would suffer from the ravages of dementia in the last years of her life. The disease brought short-term memory loss, violent shifts in personality between sweetness and unrestrained fury, an inability to reason, cognitive decline, and the endless repetition of the same questions again and again. It was a devastating blow to her dignity and a heartbreaking decline that challenged everyone around her. During the last three years of her life, as I cared for both parents, there were times I had to step away from our interactions, retreating to the bedroom to scream my exasperation into a pillow.

Yet before the disease took hold, she was the rock of our family—the emotional glue that held us together. I would often go to her for comfort and guidance as I faced the challenges of growing up, benefiting from her love, care, and emotional intelligence.

She was also an exceptional cook, and her love of food brought the family together for many meals. If someone who had previously dined at our home was lucky enough to receive another invite, they canceled any conflicting plans to be there. Her love of food also inspired my brother to become a chef and sparked my own joy of cooking.

Although she was a devout Episcopalian, I never thought of her as a spiritual person. Her beliefs about the spirit world seemed limited by the constraints of religious dogma. When I once dabbled with tarot cards as a teenager, she told me it was the work of the devil. In that moment, I decided not to share anything about my psychic abilities or experiences with her or my dad, who was equally unaware and dismissive of such things.

For some reason that doesn't make sense to me, I mistakenly assumed those limiting beliefs would carry through to the Other Side once she passed, equating her lack of spirituality with a sign of underdevelopment. So, I was quite surprised by the sheer will and force with which her spirit showed up in my life after she took her last breath, as you'll read about in this book.

With my dad gone, my mom relied on me more than ever. So, when the retirement center went into lockdown, barring all visitors, family, and caretakers, it was especially hard on both of us. One of the staff members was kind enough to bring a laptop into my mom's room every day so we could see each other via video calls, but those makeshift visits were a dissatisfying alternative to being there in person.

Within weeks of starting our internet chats, my mom's condition deteriorated significantly. By the second week of May, she could no longer carry on meaningful conversations, and it was clear she was nearing the end of her life. The specter of not being there with her in person during her final days haunted me.

I believed my mom was going to a better place. But losing my mom, who defined so much of my life, was already tough. There was no way I was going to let anyone stop me from being there for her last few days. Much to the chagrin of the nursing ward's director, I made it clear that I was weighing the option of moving my mom into my home so we could be together.

To this day, I count my blessings that it was a drastic, unwieldy choice I didn't have to make. When it was clear death was imminent, I was allowed to visit her in person. I spent the next three days by her side. She couldn't speak clearly or beyond a whisper, but as I peered into her eyes with my face close to hers, I could tell she understood the words I most wanted her to hear, "I love you, Mom."

Her eyes focused as best they could before she mouthed, "I love you too."

I tenderly kissed her forehead as she closed her eyes, a quiet peace settling over her.

I believe spirits on the Other Side try to help us by whispering encouragement and advice in our ears in the hopes we can hear them. On the day before my mom died, as I sat for hours at her bedside, I received one of those prompts. It was a quiet, almost imperceptible thought: the idea to play her favorite song.

Why didn't I think of that before? I wondered. I thought back to a documentary I had watched years ago, titled *Alive Inside: A Story of Music and Memory*. This film, directed by Michael Rossato-Bennett, explores the profound impact of music on individuals with dementia. It chronicles how personalized music can reawaken memories and emotions in patients, improving their quality of life and reconnecting them with their loved ones. The documentary features numerous personal stories and expert insights, demonstrating music's ability to combat memory loss and lead to remarkable improvements in patients' engagement and emotional well-being.

Though my mom was nearing death, I still imagined she would appreciate hearing music she was fond of. The song that came to mind was a popular tune from the early '70s called "Morning Has Broken" by Cat Stevens. I hadn't heard it in decades, but after a quick search on YouTube, I was able to play it for her on my iPad. We listened to it several times, along with one of my favorite songs: the very soulful version of "Somewhere Over the Rainbow/What a Wonderful World" by Israel Kamakawiwo'ole.

Unbeknownst to me, the night of Wednesday, May 20, 2020, would be the last time I saw my mom alive. As the silver light of the moon lingered in the night sky, I decided it was time to go home and bid her goodnight. I kissed her forehead, whispered how much I loved her, and left her to the care of the nurses' aides.

My home was just minutes by car from the retirement community, and within an hour, I had showered, eaten dinner, and was ready to relax for the rest of the night. It had been an emotionally tiring two days, so I was looking forward to the simple pleasure of vegging out in front of the TV.

I sank back into the comfort of my plush couch, propped my feet onto the coffee table, and reached for the remote. As I was scrolling through thumbnails of shows on Netflix, something strange happened. The internet quit abruptly, as if an invisible hand had pulled the plug.

That's odd, I thought. It had never done that before. I sat still and looked out the window, waiting and watching for any signs of lightning that might have caused an outage. My head cocked to one side, straining to hear any rumbles of thunder. There was nothing to indicate a storm was passing through. While I felt irritated by the unwelcome interruption, I couldn't shake the feeling that something eerie and otherworldly had just occurred. I reached for my phone and called my internet provider.

"I'm sorry, sir, but there are no reports of an outage in your area," came the reply to my inquiry. "Did you try resetting your router?" I ran downstairs to where the router was located and unplugged it, counting out loud for ten long seconds. Then I ran back upstairs to see if it was working. It wasn't. I ran back down to the router and unplugged it again, leaving it unplugged for several minutes. Nothing. I stood in front of my TV, my inner victim cursing at the disruption of my much-needed escape. When that didn't work, I gave up.

Resigned to the fact that there was nothing I could do to fix the internet, I called my wife for our nightly check-in. She was still my girlfriend at the time, and because she lived on the outskirts of Baltimore, a two-hour drive away, we typically saw each other only on the weekends. Our conversation was cut short by the beep of an incoming call.

"Hang on a sec, babe," I said. "There's another call coming in." I looked at the screen of my phone and saw that it was the skilled nursing ward.

"It's the retirement community," I told her. "I'll call you back."

A call from them was not unusual, even at this hour of the night, but given my mom's state, my mind raced, wondering if this was "the call." Before I had time to dwell on it, I answered.

With a quiet, empathetic voice, the night nurse informed me that my mom had passed away. My heart swelled as she recounted what transpired after I left: how the aides had come in to bathe her and tuck her in for the night, and how she herself had returned a short time later to find my mom resting peacefully.

Mixed emotions flooded my mind as I tried to register the

finality of the moment. I knew anecdotal evidence suggested that a significant number of people wait until they are alone to die—often after family members step out briefly for a break or rest—but I had hoped that my mother would breathe her final breath with me there.

The night nurse continued her account as I struggled to focus.

"On my next rounds, I peered into your mom's room and sensed a change. That's when I checked for a pulse and realized she was no longer with us."

I was amazed and fascinated by how nurses could perceive things like that. When my dad neared his death, he entered a near-comatose state. It had been a tough week, and I was due for a much-needed break. Because his vitals were okay, I left him in the care of the floor nurse while I drove the ninety miles to visit my wife. Not long after I arrived, the nurse called and informed me that if I wanted to say goodbye to my dad, I should head back immediately. If it weren't for her, I would have missed that opportunity. He died later that night.

"Mr. Powers, would you like me to call the funeral home for you?" Her question brought me back into the moment.

"Yes, please," came my solemn reply.

"Would you like the funeral home to wait until you arrive before taking her?"

"Yes, I'd like to come down to see her before they take her away," I replied. "I'll be there in about fifteen minutes."

I hung up the phone, dazed by the news. I felt both sad and relieved: sad my mom was gone but relieved she didn't have to suffer living a life that was a mere shadow of her younger, more vibrant years.

As I prepared to leave, it hit me. The strange feeling I had when the internet went out—it wasn't caused by an act of nature. I realized it had been my mom, marking the moment of her passing. The idea seemed a bit wild, even for me, but it was a feeling I couldn't shake. I would later come to learn that my mom did indeed have the power to influence electricity from the Other Side.

In fact, as I sat at my desk editing this very part of the story from my manuscript in the cloud, my internet momentarily cut out—not once, but twice. Coincidence? Not one bit. Loved ones from the Other Side often communicate with us in remarkable ways to let us know they're watching over us. You just have to be aware that they do and recognize that the signs are often deeply personal and subtle—and sometimes not so subtle, as you're about to find out.

As my parents' health deteriorated, my wife and I began to discuss what our next steps were going to be when both my parents died, once I was free to do whatever I wanted. Her job was a remote position, and I was going to be unemployed, so we weren't anchored to any one location. Neither of us wanted to stay in Maryland. I yearned to be back in San Diego, California, and my wife had her sights on Tampa, Florida, for the warm weather and no state income tax. I had no interest in moving to Florida, but after researching real estate in California and comparing the prices to those in Florida, followed by numerous discussions between the two of us, I reluctantly agreed to fly to Florida with her to see if we liked the area enough to move there.

Because of COVID, there was no ceremony to plan for my mom, so days after she passed away, we flew into Tampa. It took less than seventy-two hours for both of us to realize we didn't like it. We were about to cut our trip short when mutual friends suggested we drive down to Sarasota to check it out. We did. While I had my reservations about living in Florida, we both immediately felt that Sarasota was a viable option.

Lakewood Ranch, a planned community close to Sarasota, consists of over two dozen developments with their own style and amenities, each with model homes for prospective buyers to walk through. As we sat in the waiting area of one such community for a guided tour, I passed the time watching other couples milling about and discussing their plans while soft music piped into the room from speakers built into the ceiling.

Suddenly, I heard the start of a familiar tune. I froze, not believing what I was hearing. My heart swelled while I pondered the improbable statistics of what was happening. Playing from the speakers above was the song "Morning Has Broken" by Cat Stevens—my mom's favorite song and the one I had played by her bedside that day just before her death.

As if that wasn't enough, my mom made sure I understood that she was watching over me with another profound sign.

After our trip, we flew back to Maryland from Florida so I could take care of my parents' estate affairs as their executor. The first night I was back in Chestertown, I was home alone and decided to relax for the evening by watching a movie. I scrolled through a number of pages of thumbnails on Netflix until I found an interesting movie I had never seen or heard of before. It was an independent movie from 2017 with the intriguing title *The Healer*.

The Healer is a drama about a gambling, womanizing, bankrupt young man who discovers he has the ability to heal others, a gift he initially resists. As he grapples with this newfound power, he embarks on a journey of self-discovery and acceptance. I decided to watch it, and with less than thirty minutes left in the movie, I was brought to tears as a song started playing during a montage. It was Israel Kamakawiwo'ole's rendition of "Somewhere Over the Rainbow/What a Wonderful World," the same song I played for my mom on her deathbed.

While my mom took center stage with her dramatic displays, she wasn't the only one giving me signs.

Just the other night, as I was preparing dinner, I stopped to think deeply about my parents. Waves of gratitude flowed from my heart as I marveled at the lives my mom and dad lived and how much they did for me while they were alive—especially my dad, whom I silently paid tribute to for his unwavering dedication to our family.

The next morning as I was moving my printer's power cord around a filing cabinet, my elbow inadvertently cocked up and back, hitting the wall next to me. It was an odd movement that seemed unlikely to ever happen naturally. I also felt my elbow bump into something on the wall. When I turned to look, I realized it was a framed photo of my dad and me, taken decades earlier during one of my annual Christmas visits. How my elbow reached that high, I don't know. The frame hung crooked, like a wry smile from my dad.

I love you, Dad, I mouthed as I straightened the photo.

Moments like these always leave a soft ache behind—a mix of wonder and longing that tends to linger. That ache was especially present the night my mom passed as I drove to the retirement center's main entrance, flooded with memories of the past and thoughts of the future without her.

I checked myself into the building, briefly spoke to the attending nurse, and headed for the room that was home to my parents and a second home to me for the last year and a half as their full-time caregiver. As I stepped into their one-room space, I took a moment to soak it in with a slow, sweeping glance.

On the left side lay what was designated as the living area. Two drab, vinyl, oversized recliners sat next to each other, facing a flat-screen TV perched atop a family relic: a secretary's desk made of teak that once organized my mom's daily homemaking life. A small, inexpensive computer desk sat crammed into the corner behind the recliners, where I used to spend my time monitoring the lives of my parents. On the right side, just a reach away, the space was neatly lined with two hospital beds lying next to each other, each with its own nightstand. A tall, skinny bookshelf in one corner displayed a clutter of their personal belongings.

Despite only having one double window, the twelve-foot ceilings created the impression that the room was much larger than it actually was. Covering nearly every available inch of wall space was some of the artwork collected over my parents' lifetime. It was a marvel to behold—and the talk of the ward when they moved in. Staff and residents alike would stop by to appreciate the richness their framed prints exuded.

I walked over to my mom's bedside and forced myself to look at her frail, lifeless body. Without her soul, it was just a decrepit shell—far removed from the once-beautiful mother she had been. I couldn't bear to look at her corpse for very long. I scanned the area, my focus lingering over her personal belongings. Artifacts that once held purpose and helped define her life now cluttered the space with a quiet emptiness of their own. As I stood there in the silence of the room, I was struck with a visceral, soul-deep epiphany.

I had a sudden awareness of how utterly lifeless and barren the room felt. What struck me was that the room's vitality had come not from the decorations and personal belongings, as I once had led myself to believe, but from the life energy that had emanated from my parents. I knew my mom was going to a wondrous place, but at that moment, my heart fell and drowned in a deep well of sadness.

I walked to the center of the room and stood with my eyes closed. I had devoted the past three years of my life to taking care of my parents. Memories of that time flooded my mind like a life review. As I thought of them, I silently sent a prayer full of blessings to wherever my parents were.

As soon as I was done, I felt a presence enter the room. My back faced the door, but I could tell it wasn't coming from there. I opened my eyes. Out of the corner of my left eye, I caught a glimpse of movement in the upper corner of the room, near where the walls met the ceiling. In that moment, my awareness shifted into a heightened state. In this altered consciousness, I was able to process my experience in nanoseconds. It was as if time stretched and expanded like a rubber band, creating an extended timeline within just one normal second—giving me the illusion that everything was happening simultaneously.

I recognized what was happening. It was what I call a warble in the fabric of reality: a swirl of energy I had experienced before when visited by a spirit who had crossed over in death. The movement of energy was a buildup that transformed into what appeared to be a portal—a threshold between their world and ours.

I turned my body to face the corner, recognizing who was there even before I looked up. It was my mom and dad. I couldn't see them, but I had no doubt. It's often said that loved ones meet us when we pass. My dad and mom had been married for over fifty years, and now, less than two months after he died, he was back to guide her through her transition.

They stood next to each other, facing me, as they hovered above me in the air, about fifteen feet away. I placed my right hand over my heart in a solemn, heartfelt salute to them for all the things they did for me throughout my life. An incredible wave of warmth and calm passed through my body in return as they showered me with acknowledgment and gratitude for the sacrifices I had made for them and the level of care I had given them. Tears of joy and sadness streamed down my face as we held an energetic embrace.

After a moment, and with gentle finality, my parents indicated it was time for them to go. I reluctantly bid them farewell, wishing I could hold onto the beauty of the moment forever. No words—not even those of a master poet—could truly capture the experience. I continued to stand in the middle of the room after their departure, absorbing the remnants of love and calm, cradling my experience like a newborn wrapped in warm cloth.

My parents were icons who defined so much of my life. And now they were both gone. I used to dread the coming of their death before I became their caregiver, even fearing that I might go into a depression once they were deceased. But as I stood there, I knew I was going to be okay. The three years I spent taking care of them helped me prepare for this day. Yes, I was going to miss my parents. But the intensity of losing them was softened, their passing made more bearable, by their priceless gift of love from beyond the veil of death.

14

Turn on the TV

"Babe? Babe!" My wife's disembodied voice traveled down the single flight of stairs, past the front door, and through the short hallway to my office. The pocket door was closed to signal I didn't want to be disturbed, but her summons ignored it, disrupting the eloquence of my quiet solitude. When my wife wants something, boundaries don't exist, and there's no stopping her. Her voice continued to ring from upstairs.

"I think your mom is up here," she declared matter-of-factly. "You should go talk to her."

A groan of annoyance echoed in my mind.

Really? Now?

I raised my voice so she could hear me.

"If my mom wants to talk to me, she can come down here and talk to me," I shot back, my tone carrying a not-so-subtle hint that I didn't appreciate the interruption.

I heard the familiar cadence of her feet descending the long, straight flight of wooden stairs. A moment later, the whooshing whisper of the pocket door wheels gliding along their tracks filled my ears. The door disappeared into the wall, revealing my beautiful, stubborn wife—reminding me of the TV show *The Price Is*

Right, when the large doors slide open to reveal the prize sitting behind them.

Her tone raised a small red flag in my brain.

"Your mom is upstairs."

She stood in the threshold, waiting for a response. I pretended to ignore her, my fingers tapping at the keyboard as I kept my eyes glued to the monitor, my expression set in a stern, don't-bother-me look.

My wife knew better than to disturb me, but she couldn't help herself. It was in her nature to be nosy and bossy. It didn't matter what I was doing.

"I think you should go and talk to her," she announced again.

I am psychic, but I didn't need to be to know I was in a losing battle. Was it pointless to argue? Yes. But I did it anyway.

"Babe, I'm busy. Why can't she come down here and talk to me?"

My wife ambled next to my desk in a calculated move. I turned my head to look up at her. Big mistake. She locked her piercing doe eyes on mine. My wife is not only stunningly beautiful, she's also petite with a "high cuteness factor."

That's actually a scientific term I learned from a fascinating BBC Earth documentary about how baby animals across species have certain features that make them more attractive to their parents, ensuring the parents will stick around to take care of them. It's called *The Code for Cuteness.* Check it out.

But I digress. With a sweet, persuasive inflection, she continued her deliberation. "I think you should go upstairs and talk to her. Come on, just go. I think it's important."

I let out a pronounced sigh.

My wife's lips curled into that endearing little smile of hers. She knew exactly what that exhale meant. Pleased with her victory, she pivoted back toward the door and wandered off to do her own thing, either unaware or completely unbothered by the fact that she'd just interrupted my personal, creative space.

I wrapped up what I was doing at my desk, pushed back my chair, and made my way upstairs.

My mom had passed away six months ago, when we lived in Maryland, yet she found ways to make her presence known in our new home in Florida. Flickering lights, the sudden blare of a smoke detector for just a second or two, telepathic hellos, and fleeting glimpses of her energy occurred from time to time.

My wife has occasional flashes of intuition, but as I headed up the stairs, I didn't put much stock in her proclamation. As an intuitive, I pick up on Spirit's presence now and then, but most of the time, the subtle visitations don't have much of an impact on my life.

My mom's passing was still fresh in my mind, but I felt at peace about her transition to the Other Side. She had lived a great life, full of experiences most people will never have. Spending the last three years of her life taking care of her had helped me gently and gradually prepare for her death. So as I reached the landing at the top of the stairs, it was with a mild sense of curiosity, without any expectations of grandeur.

I slowly opened the door to our second-story suite, a space that included a decent-sized family room, a bedroom, and a full bathroom. As I stepped over the threshold into the main room, a dense, almost palpable silence greeted me. It hung thick in the air, wrapping around me like a tomb. The wood floor creaked once beneath my weight, the sound swallowed by the stillness, only making the silence feel heavier.

My nostrils flared as I caught the stale warmth of the air, baked by the afternoon sun through windows that had been shut for too long. A faint scent of leather drifted from the new recliner facing our TV, mingling briefly with the residual smell of untouched space. Light streamed through a wall of windows to my left, its intensity softened by the swaying branches of a palm tree and the delicate ripple of sheer curtains. Golden beams of light stretched across the room, casting a quiet glow on the beautifully decorated wall across from the windows.

As I acclimated to the space, I realized my wife was right. My mom was here. I could sense her presence. Out of the corner of my eye, I thought I saw a concentration of translucent energy hovering near the doorway. Just as I was about to send her a telepathic hello, she vanished, gone in an instant, like a light switch being flipped.

In the split second before she disappeared, however, she left me with a message. It wasn't spoken. It was an imprint on my mind. A directive that simply said, *Turn on the TV.*

Turn on the TV? It was an odd request, but the pull to obey it was undeniable. The remote lay on a decorative storage chest that acted as our makeshift coffee table in the middle of the room. I walked over, picked up the remote, and took a couple of steps back before sinking comfortably onto the couch.

The screen soon came to life. It was a smart TV, so a multitude of app thumbnails filled the display. Not knowing what I was looking for, I browsed my options. My default go-to was Netflix, but this time, I felt an inexplicable pull toward Amazon Prime.

Numerous rows of thumbnails materialized, showcasing a variety of shows. I let my eyes drift across the top row—nothing stood out. I clicked the arrow to shuffle the row to the left, revealing the next set of thumbnails. Again, I scanned from left to right. One, two, three—stop.

My gaze landed on a thumbnail.

What is that? I wondered. It was for a show I'd never seen or heard of before—*Seatbelt Psychic.*

That looks interesting, I mused and clicked on the thumbnail to read the synopsis.

Seatbelt Psychic is a reality TV show featuring psychic medium Thomas John, who poses as a rideshare driver and delivers messages from deceased loved ones to unsuspecting passengers while chauffeuring them to their destinations. It was a feel-good show—warm, heartfelt, and best of all, it featured a guy who talks to dead people. My kind of program!

I started watching, and within moments, I knew I was going to enjoy it. I paused the episode and called down the stairs for my wife to come up.

"You're not going to believe what just happened," I said as she entered the room. I recounted the experience with my mom and her message and motioned for my wife to join me. She shares my interest in all things woo, and soon enough, we were snuggled together, happily hooked on the series. With popcorn in hand, we binged the entire season in one night.

After several episodes and a bowl of popcorn under our belts, my wife turned to me, completely unaware that what she was about to say would change everything. She spoke the words that would become Spirit's dramatic call to action—the very reason we were meant to watch this show together.

It was a coup de grâce, the perfect cherry on top of Spirit's well-orchestrated plan.

"You have a gift," she said, referring to the moments she'd witnessed my psychic abilities and mediumistic tendencies since we'd been together. "You should do something with it. You're so good with people, and I know you like helping others."

Her words struck a deep chord in me, like the haunting melody of a cello—stirring something ancient, something primal in my soul. An old, weathered door that had been shut for years creaked open, inviting me to step inside.

I sat there in silence, on the verge of tears, absorbing the weight of what she'd just said. We paused the replay to take an intermission break. My wife went downstairs to make more popcorn while I sat on the couch, deep in thought.

Little did I know, my mom's message was only part of a bigger plan—one that would change the trajectory of my life. And Spirit wasn't going to make me wait long to find out what they were up to. My mind drifted to a night in January 2009—a moment of epiphany that had a profound effect on my life. It was the night I discovered I could read people's energy at will, that I could look into a person's heart and mind and know things about them—intimate, meaningful details.

As faint sounds of popcorn popping reached my ears, I reminisced about that time, thinking back to the months that followed my discovery—the camaraderie of like-minded folks in Meetup groups and the profound, magickal moments I'd experienced during practice sessions with peers and volunteers who came to get free readings so we could practice.

I fondly remembered how those times hummed with excitement—the wonderment of this uncharted spiritual horizon and the possibilities that came with developing my newfound abilities. I was eager, ambitious, and fully committed to nurturing my potential, with plans to offer psychic readings as a career.

But that was not the path fate had in store for me.

As part of my efforts to build confidence and refine my craft, I sought mentorship from a psychic who, instead of guiding me, became a detriment to my growth. Maybe she was jealous of me, or maybe she had issues with men—but whatever the reason, she made a point of belittling me, masking cruelty with misaligned, underhanded behavior.

The damage was profound. She decimated my confidence like an infestation devouring the succulent buds of a tree, stripping away its potential, until I was convinced that I had lost my ability to connect with and interpret the subtle world of Spirit. Disheartened and disillusioned, I turned entirely away from developing my gift.

Throughout the years that followed, I would occasionally revisit my interest in developing my psychic abilities, but never for long—never seriously enough to make anything of it. Of course, I continued to have extraordinary experiences with the spirit world, and I did use my intuition in my private practice as a shaman, but I never took classes or actively practiced giving readings with the intent of pursuing a career as a psychic.

Until that night watching *Seatbelt Psychic*, I never envisioned myself as a medium—or even someone who could develop that skill. I had colleagues who were mediums, but in my mind, they were a different breed. Yes, I had experienced visitations and communication with souls from the Other Side throughout my life, but I had always seen those encounters as anomalies, as something beyond my control. They were amazing events that happened to me—not something I initiated of my own volition.

Deep into the night, as we watched Thomas John touch the lives of his commuters, the resonance of my wife's declaration continued to reverberate in my psyche. Portents of my destiny, yet unknown to me, swirled in the air, hinting at things to come.

Over the next few days, that poetic strum of my soul's chord serenaded my heart—a melody that reverberated deeply, unearthing long-buried memories of how I had once touched people's lives with my intuition. Each note carried the weight of a desire I had buried more than a decade earlier—a calling that refused to be silenced, echoing deep in my heart.

An ocean of thoughts about that night surged through me, energizing me like a surfer catching the perfect wave. This wasn't just an idea; it wasn't just nostalgia—it was an awakening, a summons, a force that demanded my attention. The question was no longer if I should return to my path, but how could I not?

I was moved by the magick of what had transpired that night, no doubt about it. However, an equally powerful force pushed back, preventing me from effortlessly embracing the calling. The reasons threatened to quell the wave of euphoria I was riding.

First, it was my belief (and fear) that most people in our society hold negative associations with psychics, mediums, and the mere mention of supernatural phenomena. Up until that night, even I hadn't been comfortable with the label—let alone stepping into the public eye as one.

It was going to take some serious inner work to get past my reservations about publicly claiming and advertising that I was a psychic—let alone someone who could talk to the dead.

I also wasn't sure I wanted to take on the emotional weight that comes with reading for people. I recalled a conversation I had a few years ago with a friend who was also intuitive. She had chosen not to pursue a professional career using her ESP because, as she put it, "I don't want to deal with the performance anxiety or the responsibility that comes with doing readings for people. It's too much pressure. It's too stressful!"

Those were the very same sentiments I was struggling to come to terms with, and some of the reasons why I never chose to become a professional psychic. I was also keenly aware of my propensity for perfectionism. That affliction, combined with my aversion to being wrong or looking incompetent, was a trait that would hamper anyone's ability to read and correctly interpret the subtleties of energy. I worried about it a lot.

Another hurdle I faced was my more immediate focus in life. I was building the foundation for a new career as a mindful money coach, author, life coach, and motivational speaker. I wasn't sure I wanted to dilute my energies any more than they already were by adding an additional pursuit to my plate. Yet, despite all the resistance my rational mind threw at me, I began researching psychic and mediumship development opportunities online.

Because of COVID's grip on the world, in-person classes and studies weren't an option. I had serious doubts about the efficacy of taking classes via the cold, impersonal setting of an online video chat room, but I didn't let that stop me from looking. I scoured the internet, hopping from one website to another, following the rabbit hole wherever it led until something piqued my interest. Within a week, I had a list of several suitable prospects for teachers.

I found myself at a crossroads, asking many questions. *Do I really want to take this journey? Am I committed enough to follow through? Do I even have what it takes to be a professional? Can I develop my abilities remotely, through a screen? Do I even want to learn that way? Is it worth the time and money to pursue this as a career? And how will this affect my ability to pursue my other passions?*

What my reluctance ultimately couldn't argue with was the undeniable sense that Spirit had orchestrated the evening's events—from my wife's innocent request to talk to my mom to my mom's cryptic message to turn on the TV, to us watching *Seatbelt Psychic*, to my wife's seemingly innocent statement that reawakened my desire to share my intuitive abilities for the betterment of others.

In January 2021, I committed myself fully to psychic and mediumship development, taking numerous classes every month from different teachers, like a full-time student. This went on for a year and a half.

But in the end, I had to accept a difficult reality—the anxiety leading up to each reading weighed on me. My ego's attachment to perfectionism stripped the joy from the experience. Instead of feeling in flow with Spirit, I was locked in a battle with my own self-doubt. I was fine once the reading started, but the stress beforehand was something I couldn't overcome.

So I made a choice to step back. Maybe I'd return one day, maybe I wouldn't. But one thing is certain: The story isn't over.

15

One Tough Cookie

When souls who have transitioned to the Other Side appear for their loved ones here on Earth, they display the same personality they had when they were alive. It's how we've known them, and it's how we can recognize them when they show up.

Have you ever known someone—maybe a grandparent—who had a strong personality, and the worst thing you could do was cross their good side? Lordy, lordy, if you ever did . . . then there was no hope for the skin of your hide.

I met one such grandmother from the Other Side in the parking lot of Whole Foods.

As I was exiting the store with bags in hand, I noticed a middle-aged African American woman walking in front of me, heading out into the parking lot in the opposite direction from where I was parked. I glanced at her in an absent-minded way for just a moment, long enough to observe what she looked like, before I headed to where my car was parked.

I placed my bags in the back of my hatchback, got in, turned on the ignition, checked my surroundings, and then backed out of my space. As I slowly headed toward the exit, I suddenly became aware of the presence of a spirit in the back seat of my car, sitting in the middle, between the two front seats. She was a slim, petite elderly lady, I'm guessing in her seventies. She grabbed the backs of the two front seats, leaned forward slightly, and made a request.

"I would like you to speak to my granddaughter," she said in a pleasant but assertive tone. She indicated to me that the woman she was referring to was the woman I'd noticed walking in front of me as I exited Whole Foods.

People who have met me may be surprised to hear that I'm an introvert. What that means is I like solitude. While extroverts are very comfortable interacting with groups of people and feel recharged from being social in crowds, I prefer one-on-one interactions, and I rejuvenate while alone in a quiet space. I believe there's a spectrum. It's not either-or. I consider myself to be an introvert with extrovert tendencies—that's how I like to put it. Maybe it's because I moved every two to four years growing up that I had to learn to be extroverted in order to meet and make new friends. I used to be shy, but now, once I get over my initial shyness, I'm very comfortable walking up to strangers. I enjoy striking up conversations with people I come across in my day-to-day, talking up a storm.

This woman's request was a different matter. She wasn't just asking me to start a conversation with a stranger—she was asking me to approach someone I didn't know to tell them that I talk to dead people. I've watched those TV shows in which mediums walk up to people in public, divulging that they have a message from their deceased loved one. They're touching moments. But I can't help wondering how many people are approached who aren't open to hearing what the medium has to say. The programs never show you *those* interactions.

I had been studying mediumship for several months by the time I found myself conversing with this elderly woman. It's one thing to practice communicating with spirits from the Other Side with like-minded people in a controlled, supportive environment. It's another to approach a complete stranger in public, especially in this day and age when people find it more acceptable to be rude and mean.

I was very uncomfortable with the idea and told her so, telepathically speaking. *I'm sorry*, I said. *Besides, as you can see, I'm just about to head out now. I don't really want to take the time.*

Oh, was that the wrong thing to say. I got an earful like you wouldn't believe. I think if she could have twisted my ear, she would have. She made it clear that I had better do what she asked or there would be trouble.

Okay, okay, I acquiesced. *I'll see if I can find her*. I got the distinct impression this elderly woman was not someone you wanted to mess with when she was alive.

I turned the car around and headed for the far side of the large parking lot while the grandmother looked over my shoulder to make sure I was doing her bidding.

I drove slowly up and down the rows, darting glances left and right, craning my neck in search of the woman I'd spotted walking through the front doors, hoping we weren't too late.

As my car crawled forward down the third row, I spotted her just as she was about to step into her SUV.

I stopped my car behind her vehicle, rolled down my window, and tried my best to sound normal and calm. I held onto the steering wheel with sweaty palms as if I were bracing for impact. With a raised voice, I called out to get her attention.

"Excuse me, ma'am, excuse me."

The woman stopped and turned to look at me.

"I'm studying mediumship, and as I was pulling out of the parking lot, your grandmother appeared in my car and asked me to talk to you."

I cringed as the words came out of my mouth. My inner critic rolled its eyes like I was a complete failure. I could see in the way the woman was looking at me that what I had just blurted out was a lot to process.

"Do you believe in that kind of stuff?" I asked, filling the silence out of nervousness, realizing too late that I should have started with that kind of question. I was trying not to let my inner commentary about how poorly I was doing interfere with my conversation, but I felt like a deer caught in the headlights of an oncoming car.

"I'm a believer," she finally replied.

Feeling some relief, I commented, "That grandmother of yours—she was a tough cookie, wasn't she?! I didn't really have a choice about coming over here. She wouldn't let me leave the parking lot without first coming to speak to you."

The woman chuckled, recognizing the truth of what I was saying. She was clearly taken off guard, and I could tell she was still trying to find solid ground.

"That sounds like my grandmother," she replied.

I spent the next couple of minutes giving her a physical description of her grandmother and mentioned that she loved purses when she was alive. Despite her small stature, she was a firecracker—not to be messed with—the matriarch of the family.

As I was talking, love radiated from my celestial passenger. It became clear that this was her favorite grandchild. When I told her that her grandmother loved her, tears fell from her granddaughter's face.

When I delivered that last message, my riding companion vanished as quickly as she had appeared. I said my goodbyes and headed back home.

As relieved as I was that I'd gotten it right and that the grand-daughter was receptive to hearing from her grandmother, I still wished I had been calmer and more confident in the delivery. Being a medium between the living and the spirit world is not just a sacred honor—it's an act of service as personal and intimate as it gets. And while I wished I'd carried it out with more grace, I took comfort in knowing I delivered a grandmother's message of love—one that reached straight into her granddaughter's heart.

CHAPTER 3

Epiphanies
That Empower

16

The Tortoise Way
to Winning

Cool temperatures and the sunny skies of an early spring morning created ideal conditions for running a road race. But as my feet pounded the pavement, I was in no frame of mind to appreciate the weather. My once relaxed, powerful stride had lost its finesse, and the rough sound of my labored breathing betrayed just how quickly fatigue was setting in.

I wiped the sweat from my brow and out of my eyes with a tired arm and looked down the long stretch of road ahead of me. I searched its gentle curve with my gaze as it wound through a swath of undeveloped land between neighborhoods dotted with sparse groves of pine and open grassy fields. As I surveyed the area, my eyes zeroed in on my target: a lone figure running two thousand feet ahead of me.

I stole a glance behind me. The pack of runners I had started with was nowhere to be seen. I wasn't worried about them catching up to me. What I cared about now was the runner ahead of me: the guy in first place.

The sun hadn't yet dried the wet sheen on the asphalt, left behind by the rain the night before. I was annoyed by the droplets that splashed onto my calves, kicked up by the heels of my shoes. I knew I was in trouble when my mind started griping about a minor irritation like that. It meant I was tired, frustrated, and losing focus.

Eugene, Oregon, is known as the running capital of the nation, largely due to the legendary coaches at the University of Oregon and the impressive performances of their runners over the years, and for being the birthplace of a running shoe company, the world-famous Nike. As a result, a plethora of road races took place in the spring and summer months. The one I was in was a 10K that wound its way through the outskirts of town. Hundreds of men and women, spanning all levels of fitness, had lined up at the start—with a core group of serious runners at the front. I was one of them. And I was in it to win.

I loved racing, both on the track and on the road, but these events weren't fun for me so much as they were a challenge. They were hard—sometimes grueling—because I chose to test myself beyond what I believed my limits were, pushing through the pain and discomfort of both mind and body as I raced others of the same ilk.

That morning, the two thousand feet between me and the first-place runner might as well have been two thousand miles. I glanced at my watch to check the time, gauged my progress, and plotted my strategy. A sharp twinge in my shoulder made me grimace as I moved my arm. My legs weren't the only parts suffering from the strain.

I had a mile and a half to go—about seven minutes to catch up to the runner ahead. But closing the gap was only half the battle. If I caught up to him, odds were he'd fight to hold his position. A duel would unfold, each of us pushing harder, vying for the coveted title of winner. We could end up in an all-out sprint. There was also the chance he'd spot me gaining and accelerate before I even reached him. I had to be mentally prepared for any and all of it.

I took an inventory of my condition: my attitude, energy levels, and the location and nature of my aches and pains throughout my body. I also took a moment to observe the runner in front of me. I couldn't tell what his state of mind was, but I could watch his movements to see if I could glean anything about his physical condition. Was his stride fluid and confident, or did he move like he was tired? Was he looking back to check on his competition, and if so, how often? From what I could tell, he was in better shape than I was.

I took all that information and came up with an evaluation of what I thought I was capable of—namely, whether I could catch the runner in front of me and what it would take to do so. I grimaced at the results of my analysis.

Winning the race was going to involve pain. Not a brief moment of pain like the prick of a finger—this would require sustained, voluntary suffering. I was going to have to endure both mental anguish and intense physical discomfort. I didn't believe I had it in me to win in my current state.

As I sit here at my desk writing about my experience, a memory floats into my mind. It was the late 1980s when I looked at a comic strip of Snoopy from the *Peanuts* gang called "Snoopy the Fitness Fanatic." In it, Snoopy is out for a run, and each frame depicts a different snapshot of him running, highlighted by commentary from different parts of his body. I chuckled as his feet, lungs, back, nose, and even his lips had something to complain about. Each part quipped that life was comparatively more difficult for them than for the other body parts.

A similar process was happening with my body during the race, but nothing about it was humorous. I was about to have a Snoopy-style pep talk. I gathered everyone and laid out my plans.

If we want to win this race, we have to work harder and run faster, I told them. Different parts of my body balked at the idea. Some put up a fuss.

Lungs: *What?! You want us to work even harder? We've been huffing and puffing for miles already. It's not fair. We're doing all the heavy lifting, and the legs get all the credit!*

Butt: *Hey, no need to be so cheeky! My job's just as important—we're bringing up the rear.*

Legs: *Ha, lungs! You're full of hot air! We're working just as hard as you are.*

Kidding aside, unlike the comic strip version, my body's complaints were genuine and painful. My mind became the drill sergeant, and every body part became a cadet, ordered to dig deep and find the strength to win. I cracked the whip with my determination and pushed myself to run faster.

The ache of physical exhaustion permeated every fiber of my body as I surged ahead. I gained a few yards but paid dearly for them. Every part of me screamed louder in protest. I could sense a mutiny brewing.

Come on! I want to win! Don't you? Think how good that'll feel. The only way to get there is to suck it up and run faster, I argued. I forced my legs to pick up the pace, but it was immediately clear the effort was futile. I felt like I was dragging a donkey by a rope—one that had no interest in budging.

"No pain, no gain" was a popular slogan in those days, and as a competitive runner, I understood that pain was inevitable during training if I wanted to become faster, stronger, and better. The same was also true in racing if I wanted to win.

As I chugged along, I thought back to a motivational talk one of my high school running coaches gave me before the start of a race during a track meet. He raised one of his hands just above his head, palm down, and the other just under his chin—framing his head between them. His sermon was brief as he looked me in the eye.

"Ninety percent of winning happens from here to here," he stated, moving his hands slightly to emphasize his point. *Mindset. Mind over matter. Where there's a will, there's a way.* But those are only concepts until you're face-to-face with a significant challenge. I tried to draw inspiration from the memory.

But I also believed there was a place for common sense when it came to pain. Sometimes pain is a warning—urging us to stop, slow down, or change course. Sometimes it's hard to know the difference. I knew perseverance paid off, and that morning, I was determined to win. If I had to fight through some pain, so be it.

My inner drill sergeant blew his whistle and barked orders. I quickened my pace, only this time, every part of me revolted at the command, instigating a mutiny. I was suddenly overcome with intense fatigue and an overwhelming desire to quit. My body had had enough. I was on the verge of giving up and walking the rest of the way. The ferocity of my body's reaction surprised me. I had never quit a race before. It was clear that I was running on thin ice.

How are you going to live with yourself if you quit? I asked myself. My body had drawn a line in the sand. There was nothing left to give. I was so close to quitting when I heard a whisper of a suggestion in my head.

Relax, try slowing down, it suggested. *Don't be so hard on yourself.*

Slow down? Slow down?! retorted my inner drill sergeant. *That's preposterous! The only way we're going to win is to keep pushing hard. Slow down? That's the silliest idea I've ever heard! Don't listen to that voice, Keno. And stop being a baby. Try harder,* it clamored.

Logically, it made sense. Slowing down was counterintuitive to winning. It was like saying 2 + 2 = 5. It was just plain wrong.

But the voice was softly persistent. It had an air of enlightenment that made me take note and a tone that enticed me to trust it.

You don't have to push so hard, it said, with an implication that good things would come from listening to it.

As I reflected on my experience while writing this story, I was reminded of the classic fable, "The Tortoise and the Hare," and felt compelled to revisit it through a bit of research.

It's a well-known fable credited to a man named Aesop, a Greek slave and storyteller thought to have lived between 620 and 560 BC. Each of Aesop's stories espoused morals designed to teach and encourage desirable virtues to his audience.

In this story, a tortoise is made fun of by a hare for being slow. The tortoise replies that she can reach the destination sooner than the hare thinks.

"I'll run you a race and prove it," the tortoise says.

The hare takes on the bet, laughing at the tortoise for being so foolish. Moments after the gun goes off, the hare races out of sight.

When the cocky hare nears the finish line, he decides to further humiliate the tortoise for thinking she could beat him in a race. In his clever arrogance, he formulates a plan. He decides to take a nap, thinking he'll wake once the tortoise catches up. Then he'll cross the finish line in front of her, rubbing his victory in her face. He finds a suitable place by the road and soon thereafter falls asleep.

In the meantime, the tortoise slowly but steadily makes progress and eventually passes the hare, who is still sound asleep. When the hare wakes up, he realizes he's overslept. He dashes after the tortoise, but by that time it's too late. The tortoise crosses the finish line before the hare can reach her.

The morals of Aesop's fables were often revealed at the end of the story, written as a separate line, almost like a punch line to a joke. The moral of this story was written as "The race is not always won by the swift." There are variations in how this line is interpreted, but after careful consideration, I took it to mean that the race is sometimes won by the strategist. As I pondered what that meant, I began to see striking parallels between my experience and the fable. I'll reveal them shortly, but first, let's get back to the story.

I don't know how Aesop came to his understanding of this moral, but I experienced it firsthand when I had an epiphany during that pivotal point in my race—a watershed moment that held the power to determine whether or not I would win.

Back on the pavement, I was trying to figure out the best plan of action and weighing my options. I had tried the "no pain, no gain" way, and it hadn't worked. As a result, I was dangerously close to quitting. I examined my need to win and came to a compromise. I decided I would rather finish the race in second place than quit.

I loosened my grip on the reins and relaxed to a more comfortable pace. The drill sergeant threw his arms up in dismay.

When I set aside my rigid plan of attack and heeded that voice, something unexpected and remarkable happened. I suddenly felt a flood of energy. In an instant, all my physical and mental fatigue vanished. In its place, I felt an incredible lightness of spirit. It was a moment of sheer exhilaration that defied expression.

Rather than feeling fatigued, achy, and ready to give up, I felt relaxed and infused with seemingly limitless energy.

What the hell is going on?! My mind tried to make sense of what I was experiencing, but it was so far beyond its realm of understanding. As I reveled in the pure joy of my transformation, I refocused on the race. That's when I had my epiphany.

Since that spring day in the 1980s, I know from the many experiences I've had that we, as human beings, have the capability to tap into incredible, breathtaking power that defies the laws of reality as we understand them—feats that appear miraculous, surreal, and impossible.

I realized it was my mind's attempt to bulldoze my body into running faster that acted as a barrier between me and these extraordinary resources.

My attitude created tension in my body, which prevented me from accessing my life energy. By focusing on how far I had to go to catch up to the runner ahead and on how tired I was, my perspective fostered feelings of overwhelm and unrelenting pressure to perform. My body parts were throwing a tantrum in response. Those parts of me didn't feel heard; they didn't feel their needs were being met, so they resisted and rebelled.

When I trusted the wisdom of that voice and slowed down to a comfortable pace, I unknowingly acknowledged those parts of me.

The act of surrender—and responding with compassion—changed everything.

With my newfound rush of energy, I kicked things into another gear. I thundered ahead like a champion horse coming out of the last bend into the final straightaway, given free rein to unleash the joy of my passion and power. I ran effortlessly, as though I had wings on my feet.

Closing in swiftly, I surged past the lead runner, catching him completely off guard. He briefly tried to challenge me, but once he saw the ease and determination in my stride, he knew he couldn't match me and surrendered the race. I went on to win with a comfortable margin.

The moral of the story is that if I had continued to let my ego force the effort, I would have been asleep to my power—just like the hare napping on the side of the road. The hare lost because he let his ego dictate his attitude and actions, overriding his wiser self. But when I embraced the words of my inner voice and surrendered, I opened the door to something far greater than muscle or will. I didn't win the race by pushing—I won by yielding, by trusting, by allowing a deeper wisdom to move through me. That shift awakened a quiet, divine strength that had been within me all along.

Sometimes, winning isn't about effort or trying harder—it's about softening, listening, and saying no to our ego so we can trust in something greater to guide us toward right action.

17

I Love That Song

The year was 1987. Cassette tapes and CDs were the way of the world, while smartphones, the internet, and streaming services were just ideas in someone's imagination. It was a time when people listened to the radio far more than they do now.

I was a young man at the time, scraping together a living while I pursued a calling to become a licensed massage therapist. My day job was as a produce clerk at a mom-and-pop health food store in the relatively small town of Eugene, Oregon, while I took classes in the massage program at the local community college.

I arrived home early one evening, after a tiring day at work, and decided to take the rest of the night off from my studies. With my belly full, my body clean, and my pajamas on, I was ready to kick back for the evening.

The heat of the midsummer sun waned as I collapsed onto my living room couch. Savory traces of charcoal-grilled meat wafted through the open window of my apartment, catching a ride on the current of air blowing from my window fan. I stared at the ceiling as I absentmindedly listened to a mix of hits playing softly from my favorite radio station. My thoughts wandered aimlessly, like a daydream adrift, lost to the outside world.

I let out a deep sigh as I stretched out on my back, my head resting on a pillow. My couch was the most important piece of furniture I had. It was a Zen sanctuary—a place to unwind, reflect, or simply nap.

I could feel the tension of the day slowly dissipating as the cushions yielded to my weight with just the right amount of give, cradling my weary body. I embraced this much-needed chance to relax and clear the mental clutter of frustrations and worries that came from the toils of my work and studies.

Suddenly, I was brought back to my living room by the opening notes of a familiar melody. It was one of my favorite songs from years past. I was surprised that even though it was a song I loved, I had completely forgotten it. I wondered how many other songs were tucked away in some forgotten corner of my mind.

I let go of my ruminations and focused on the music. A smile spread across my face, and I rocked my feet rhythmically as a flood of memories from more innocent days filled my mind. My heart swelled as I sank into the warmth of it all.

After a couple of minutes, it dawned on me that the song was soon going to end. Melancholy crept into my reverie, tainting my joy with its unwanted presence. A yearning for the song to last longer rose up to the heavens like a prayer. But I knew it was in vain. The closer the end got, the more disheartened I felt.

In those days, there were no streaming services, so if you wanted to hear a song more than once, you had to go out and buy the record or call up the DJ on the radio and plead for them to play it again. (I tried that once—it didn't work.)

The unavoidable end of the song finally came, but my sadness and disappointment continued into the lull between songs, poised to linger indefinitely.

What happened next surprised me and sparked an epiphany.

The next track cued up. It was another ballad I hadn't heard in ages. The kicker? I loved it even more than the first one. And like the first song, it stirred long-forgotten memories that I savored.

Once the song ended, I sat with the experience, turning it over in my mind. I was struck by the contrast between what I was anticipating after the first song ended and what actually happened. I assumed I was going to continue feeling disappointed because, well, I didn't think it was possible that the next song could be better. Why had I assumed that? The experience was an eye-opener that inspired me to examine the inner workings of my thought process.

I was both intrigued and troubled by my assumption that the future wasn't going to be as good as the present. I was surprised too when I realized that I wasn't even aware that's what I was doing. How often—and in what other corners of my life—did I make that kind of assertion? I discovered that my attitude about the future was, in general, more negative than positive—far more than I cared to admit. (There's probably enough material there for another book or two.)

When the immediate future turned out better than I'd imagined, I was surprised not just by how quickly my mood lifted, but by how fleeting my feelings were. Despite my strong sentiments of disappointment and longing, they shifted on a dime once the second song started.

As a humorous aside, while writing this, I came across an intriguing video clip on YouTube that exemplified just how impermanent our emotional state—and by extension, our reality—can be.

The video shows a girl, between two and three years old, standing on the front passenger seat of a parked car, wailing away as if her world were ending. After a short time, music starts playing. The moment she hears it, her crying instantly stops, and she's seen bobbing up and down contentedly to the music. Her shift from one state to another was so quick that the experience was surreal. I was spellbound as I replayed the video numerous times.

As I reflected on my own experience, I remembered a conceptual framework for understanding life transitions I had read about in a book by William Bridges, titled *Transitions: Making Sense of Life's*

Changes. His model breaks the process into three stages: the Ending (death), the Neutral Zone or the Gap (the uncertain, in-between period where the old is over but the new isn't fully formed), and the New Beginning (the birth of a new identity, value, or circumstance).

Transitions are a constant in life. It's a death-to-birth cycle. Sometimes transitions are major, like losing a job or the end of a long-term relationship, and can take months or years. Sometimes they're minor, taking only seconds or minutes, like going from one song to another.

What I found helpful about this model was learning that transitions have universal truths—that people from every walk of life go through similar thoughts, feelings, and experiences. Understanding that we're not alone can be comforting—it reminds us that there's a good reason why we feel the way we feel, whether it's frustrated, lost, confused, or something else.

Just as understanding the stages of grief can help when we've lost a loved one, recognizing we're in a transition helps us surrender to the process rather than fight the current. The transition blueprint serves as a simple yet powerful road map for navigating change, reminding us that there's a method to the madness.

Major transitions—especially when we don't know what the new beginning will look like or when the gap will end—can feel especially rough.

It's a very common tendency for people to pine for the way things used to be. In my work with clients and in myself, I've witnessed a tendency to reminisce and glorify the past—to long for it simply because it's familiar and comfortable, even if it wasn't the best of circumstances. The longer we linger in limbo, the stronger the temptation to romanticize the past.

Feelings of grief, sadness, confusion, and even anger are normal, natural emotional states to experience in the space between an ending and a new beginning. So are self-doubt, fear, and the feeling that the Universe or God might not have your back. From the healing work I did with clients, I found that many people who felt stuck in long, drawn-out transitions began to wonder if they were destined to live in the gap without ever finding a new beginning—or their way back to meaning, purpose, and happiness.

My epiphany was sparked by a relatively mundane experience—the end of one song and the beginning of another. But it was profound nonetheless, and the lesson I took from it applies to any transition in life, no matter the circumstances. Whenever I shared my story and the resulting epiphany about the gap with my clients, they found comfort in it, drawing strength and peace from the insight it offered.

The gap isn't a barren landscape—it's sacred ground. It's where the old dissolves and the soul reshapes itself in silence, like a caterpillar surrendering to the darkness of its chrysalis. In the stillness, something new is already forming.

Next time you're in the gap, remind yourself: Feeling unsettled and anxious is part of the process, and what's coming around the corner could very well be much better than what you had or currently expect. Remember this: Faith is a melody heard in the heart, not something seen with the eyes. Trust the process. Believe there's a plan and be willing to act when the need arises. The mechanisms of destiny are working, even if you can't see them.

18

When Fear Has a Name

Fear often feels like the bane of my existence. When I was twenty-six years old, I worked part-time at a local health food store as a produce clerk while trying to get my massage career off the ground. After several years of pushing vegetables and fruit around, I was more than ready to move on to something else.

One late evening, as the moon cast a bright glow from high in the autumn night sky, I closed up the store with my coworkers and hopped on my bike for the short ride home.

My body felt heavy after another long, draining day at a job I now despised. I pedaled slowly, trying to muster some positivity. My mind had been consumed all day by how much I loathed my job and how frustrated I was that my private practice wasn't taking off as quickly as I'd hoped. No wonder I felt exhausted.

The steady rhythm of pedaling away from work and the cool wind in my face were a welcome relief, helping me unwind and reclaim some sense of joy. It also helped to know I was heading toward the comfort of my home.

The final stretch of the commute was my favorite. My house sat on the lower slope of a butte, and the road leading up to it resembled a weathered country road with tar-patched cracks, faded paint lines, and ragged edges. Light was sparse as the road meandered upward with twists and turns, leading travelers away from the town's bustle. It was a stark contrast to the more civilized streets below with their smooth surfaces, clean lines, streetlamps, and sidewalks.

Wild brush, tall oak, and towering firs lined the road, their branches stretching toward the sky, welcoming visitors with a rich canopy. Every time I entered it on my bike in the dark of night, my imagination conjured a fantasy that I was passing through a magical threshold into the mysteries of the Earth's shadows, where the fullness of the moon could not penetrate.

The crisp scent of pine filled the cool air as I slowly ventured through. I breathed deeply, savoring the freshness with each measured inhale and exhale. Scattered homes dotted my path—some glowing faintly with light while most others sat in darkness—leaving me to navigate long stretches of starless, pitch-black night with the faint glow of my bike light. The early autumn air whispered through the trees, carrying with it a quiet stillness, broken only by the occasional rustle of leaves or the soft crunch of gravel beneath my tires. As I rode, the shadows seemed to deepen, enveloping me in a sense of calm tinged with the wild mystery of the night.

When I neared the quarter-mile mark to my home, I dismounted my bike, opting for the slower, meditative pace of walking. The road was narrow, with sharp bends that made it difficult for cars to see me, so I kept the bike between myself and the street. With no sidewalks, I stayed alert to the uneven terrain on the roadside, prepared to scramble for safety if any vehicles came barreling around a curve.

Half a block from my house, I passed a dark, unlit home set about twenty feet from the road. A nearby streetlamp cast an eerie light that abruptly stopped at the edge of the property, leaving the house and yard cloaked in a dense, impenetrable shadow. There was a clear, distinct line where light met dark, creating the illusion of a veil between two worlds. I peered intently into the blackness while passing, straining to make out more details, but all I could see was the roof's silhouette and the edges of an expansive paved driveway that ran up to the winding road. The darkness was so thick it seemed to pulse with life, coaxing my imagination to conjure monsters lurking within. I waited for my eyes to adjust.

Suddenly, strange noises emerged from the depths of the darkness. My mind raced to identify them. I whipped around to face them, heart pounding, just as I realized what the growing clamor was—a large animal, breathing heavily, charging toward me.

Before I could react, an enormous, ferocious-looking German shepherd burst from the shadows, teeth bared, barreling straight toward me. With only ten feet between us, I froze in terror. The dog's muscles coiled for a leap. Just as I braced for impact, a thick, unseen chain yanked the dog back violently before it could lunge toward me. Undeterred, it whirled around to face me, barking wildly, repeatedly tugging at the chain as if its life depended on sinking its teeth into me.

I gasped and shuddered at the close call. It took a while to steady my nerves; my chest heaved with quick, shallow breaths as the shock slowly subsided. Once I regained a semblance of control, I hurried the rest of the way home, my heart still pounding. I was shaken but thankfully unharmed.

The next day, while strolling through the neighborhood, I spotted the German shepherd from a distance, walking with its owner on a tight leash. The dog barked at a couple passing by when the owner bellowed,

"Bear, knock it off!"

Bear. I chuckled to myself. *That's an apt name for him.*

Still fresh from my encounter the night before, I gingerly turned around and headed in the opposite direction before he could spot me.

Two nights later, I was back on my bike, riding home after another long day at work. As I came up to the house where Bear lived, tension mounted in my body. The streetlamp flickered faintly, casting long shadows over the road, and like before, the house remained shrouded in darkness. I got off my bike, and this time, I kept it between me and the house, heart pounding as I drew nearer, expecting the dog to emerge from the shadows once more.

And then, just as before, the growling began—low, threatening, and unmistakable. The rustle of movement in the blackness told me Bear was there, hidden until the last second. This time, though, I was ready.

The moment Bear burst from the pitch-black darkness, eyes fiercely locked on me as he rushed forward, I firmly yelled out his name: "Bear!"

The effect was instant. The dog froze midstride, his head cocking to the side, clearly confused. I could tell from the look on his face that he was trying to figure out how I knew him. As I repeated his name in an overly friendly tone, Bear noticeably relaxed, the aggression quickly fading and giving way to a calm demeanor.

For a brief moment, we both just stood there, wary but no longer enemies. And then, with a soft whine, Bear retreated into the shadows, leaving me standing alone on the darkened road, heart pounding but strangely calm and collected.

I stood there for a long moment, letting the rush of adrenaline taper off. As I made my way home under the quiet watch of the moon, replaying the encounter with Bear in my mind, a profound new understanding about fear came to me in an aha moment.

When we can name our fear, it loses its power over us.

I'll come back to that later in the story.

Let me backtrack a little and ask you, what is fear? Where does it come from, and what's its purpose? Before we can answer that, we need to cover some basics about what you and I are as human beings and how we function.

As human beings, we're like icebergs. Think about an iceberg. What you see jutting out of the ocean is only about 10 percent of the actual iceberg. The rest is much larger, hidden and unseen under the surface. It's the same with our minds. What you know (your conscious mind) is only about 10 percent of who you are and what makes you tick. The rest of you is hidden under the surface in the subconscious or unconscious parts of your brain.

Think about that for a minute. Ninety percent of what makes you tick is unknown to you.

To help you understand how much information that 90 percent represents, imagine a huge library lined with bookshelves, each filled to the brim with books—each containing information you've collected over your entire lifetime. Now imagine a thousand libraries, and you might be close to how much information your brain has stored. The information we're talking about comes from all the interactions you've had—with people, animals, spirit, places, and things—as well as books, movies, TV, magazines, and other forms of media; your experiences with personal trials and tribulations; and events that have happened to you and around you.

I believe that every moment, thought, and feeling we experience—whether we're aware of them or not—is being recorded, as are the effects we have on other people, animals, and plants—basically, the entire living ecosystem.

To bring it back down to earth, I'll give you another analogy. Imagine you have a dog. Let's name him Fido. You and Fido are taking a walk. Fido is on a leash. How much do you think Fido is cognizant of the world around him beyond the reach of his nose? How much does Fido know about you and what your thoughts and feelings are? Maybe more than you might realize, but nowhere near as much as, say, your spouse or best friend. Who controls his behavior while he's on a walk? You do, right?

Now imagine Fido represents your conscious mind's wherewithal. The other 90 percent? That's you—with the awareness of the world you have as a human being—pulling the strings to control the dog (or the leash, in this case).

That analogy is just a creative way of pointing out that, just because you're not consciously aware of what makes up the other 90 percent, it doesn't mean it isn't exerting influence over your life—in the way you think, feel, and act. Ever do anything rash, impulsive, irrational, or just not so good for you, and wonder why? Wish you could get better results in your life and wonder why you haven't? Hello, unconscious.

What does all this have to do with fear? Well, let's define what fear is: Fear is a natural emotional response to a perceived threat, danger, or harm—real or imagined. It's part of the body's survival mechanism, triggering the "fight, flight, or freeze" response to help protect you from danger.

As I researched fear, I came across a new word and some humorous definitions of fear that made me chuckle. Backronyms are a type of acronym created after the word already exists, in which each letter of the word is assigned a meaning or phrase. I found a number of them for fear: False Evidence Appearing Real, Forget Everything and Run, Face Everything and Rise, Feeling Excited and Ready, Failure Expected and Received, and Future Events Already Ruined.

On a more serious note, I'm sure we can all identify with how much fear stops us from living the lives we dream of and from being who we truly feel we are, especially in this day and age.

Fear, whether real or imagined (both having the same effects), feeds off beliefs we have about life and ourselves—born out of experiences we've had and the meanings we've associated with those experiences—and we're often unaware of them because they're hidden in our unconscious.

Here's a powerful example of how naming our fear can dramatically change our lives, taken from my experience working with a client in my private practice. Cathy was an attractive, intelligent, single woman who wanted to be in a relationship. The problem? She wasn't having any luck attracting a man into her life, and she couldn't understand why.

Whenever a person wants something but can't manifest it, I often suspect the origin of the problem lies in the unconscious. Sure enough, as I focused on her energy with my intuition, we uncovered fears she wasn't aware of—fears that were preventing her from manifesting a relationship. One fear had to do with an unconscious concern that she would lose herself and her aspirations if she got involved with someone. Her fear was justified because this scenario had played out more than once in her past, and as a result, a part of her didn't trust that she could have both.

We also discovered Cathy had a fear of being emotionally vulnerable. Both revelations surprised her. Consciously, she thought of herself as being open, empowered, and ready for a loving relationship. That was the image her ego had created to make her feel good about herself. The truth painted a very different picture.

You can tell when information comes from the unconscious by the element of surprise it brings the conscious mind. Cathy wasn't cognizant of these particular fears and was completely taken aback by them. But once she identified the fears, she immediately reasoned they had no substance or validity anymore. This is the power of awareness. Your logical mind realizes the absurdity of the reasons for the fears, and then the fears immediately dissolve.

Cathy had done some personal inner work since her last relationship and felt she had the tools and the wherewithal to navigate her fear's concerns when it came to relationships and the dance of intimacy they entailed.

I rounded out our session by removing energetic blocks around her heart and power chakras and then sent her on her way.

Several weeks after her appointment, Cathy called me to tell me she had met a man she was really excited about—a week after our session. Did that relationship turn out to be "the one"? Months later, she informed me it wasn't, but it was a great opportunity for Cathy to learn and grow beyond her fear, and a huge step in her progress toward meeting Mr. Right.

Can you see how Cathy's unconscious thoughts and feelings about intimacy and relationships were incongruent and in conflict with her conscious desire to meet someone?

Fears are often irrational, originating from the inner child part of us. Addressing them with compassion and understanding can mitigate their influence and completely change our trajectory through life.

While fear may sometimes seem omniscient, leaving us feeling powerless against it, much of its hold over us comes from not knowing what the fear is really about—the root, underlying reason.

By simply naming your fear—by identifying it—you can tame it. Fear thrives in the shadows of the unknown, gaining power the longer it lurks in ignorance and the subconscious. But once it's recognized—once we acknowledge it for what it is—it loses its grip on us.

Fear, like Bear when called out by name, stops growling, stops threatening harm, and steps back—freeing us to become who we truly are, and giving us the ability to live richer, happier lives.

19

The Invisible Clock

Sometimes, the most obvious things in life are completely invisible. I learned that wisdom, not during some mystical vision or life-altering ceremony, but while dashing through a crowded airport, trying to catch a flight.

Maybe it's because I'm kinesthetic or that I had an excess of energy as a kid, but I loved running. If I needed to walk somewhere, I would run instead, imagining I had superpowers coursing through my veins like The Flash as I sprinted down the sidewalk in a flurry of motion.

Later in life, as a competitive runner, my favorite places to train were off the beaten path, racing down narrow trails through the forest. I reveled in leaping over fallen tree trunks, weaving through the twists and turns, and flying past shrubs and trees. I pictured myself as a gazelle, darting wild and free with endless energy. Even now, the memory brings a smile to my face.

Maybe that's why I loved the Hertz Rent-A-Car TV commercials back in the late seventies and early eighties. They showcased the former football star O. J. Simpson and his magnetic persona (before his fall from grace).

With a winning smile, a briefcase in one hand, and a coat in the other, O. J. raced through the airport on his way to the rental

counter. The commercials featured him leaping over velvet stan-
chion ropes, hurdling over metal hand railings, and even jumping
over people's luggage, while a catchy jingle promoted Hertz's image
and the speed with which you could rent a car from them.

Those Hertz commercials were such a hit that they boosted
Simpson's status from sports star to bona fide celebrity. They even
gave rise to a phrase that stuck in the cultural psyche for many years.
If you had to run through an airport to catch your flight, you'd say,
I had to do an O. J. Simpson![1]

I've flown on plenty of airplanes and navigated countless air-
ports over the years, collecting a few of my own O. J. Simpson
moments—instances when I had to rush from one gate to another.
As much as I dislike the stress of racing against the clock to catch a
flight, there's a part of me that loves sprinting through crowds and
leaping over obstacles.

On one such occasion, I flew into O'Hare airport in Chicago to
get a connecting flight to Portland, Oregon, after my annual Christmas visit with my parents in Washington, DC. A late takeoff from
DC meant that I barely had time to catch my connecting flight. As
luck would have it, the next gate was at the far end of the concourse.

If you've ever been to O'Hare, you know it's huge, with walkways that seem to go on forever. This trip took place before the
advent of smartphones, and I wasn't wearing a watch, so I started
looking for a clock as soon as I stepped off the plane to figure out
how much time I had to get to my gate.

After wasting precious minutes searching in vain for a clock,
I approached a woman nearby and asked if she had the time. She
didn't, but the woman turned out to be a seasoned traveler who
knew the airport well. "There's a large clock hanging from the

---

1 That phrase is now a colloquialism that typically refers to getting away with
something, particularly something that is morally reprehensible or illegal,
often in a high-profile or dramatic manner.

ceiling in the concourse up ahead. It's just past the coffee shop on your left," she said with a quick smile.

It was in the direction I needed to go, so I rushed over to the spot she directed me to, scanning the area as I went. But it was nowhere to be seen. *That's strange*, I thought. *Maybe they moved it?* When I reached the coffee shop, I turned to a man standing at the end of the long line waiting to be served. I explained that someone had told me I could find a clock hanging from the ceiling near the coffee shop and asked if he knew where it was. The guy gave me a look like I was an idiot and, without saying a word, pointed to a large clock hanging from the ceiling twenty feet in front of me.

I stood there flabbergasted. Just like the woman had said, a large clock was hanging from the ceiling for all to see. It was plain as day. I stared at it, racking my brain to understand how I could have missed seeing it.

In that moment, I had my epiphany. I realized the reason I couldn't see the clock was because I was searching for an analog clock—a round face with hands and numbers lined up in a circle. I was so fixated on that mental image that I became closed to any other possibility.

You see, the clock in the airport was a large rectangular digital clock with bright, bold red numbers practically shouting the time. But to me, it might as well have been invisible.

I shook myself out of my daze and remembered why I'd been looking for it. I didn't have time to dawdle. I picked up my bags and ran through the airport, weaving in and around the throngs of vacationers and leaping over obstacles with a serious, I'm-trying-not-to-miss-my-flight look on my face. Whizzing through the airport wasn't the safest thing to do, but with some finesse and a whole lot of heavy breathing, I was able to catch my flight.

Once I got myself situated on the plane, I mulled over the experience. The whole thing struck me as strangely surreal. It wasn't like I was looking for a needle in a haystack—this was a massive clock. I couldn't shake how bizarre it felt, and it made me wonder whether there was an explanation for why it happened. Had anyone else experienced something like this? Did this kind of thing have a name?

I sometimes wonder whether multiple dimensions coexist, overlaying our reality Was it possible I had blinders on that prevented me from experiencing them—blinders that could be removed if I simply knew what to look for? What else around me, whether in this dimension or beyond, was I missing because I wasn't looking in the right way or for the right thing?

As I was writing this story, I searched the internet for answers.

Here's an intriguing fact I learned: Our vision doesn't originate with our eyes, nor do our eyes create the images we see. Light that enters our eyes is converted into electrical signals, which are then sent to the brain to be processed. It's the brain that constructs the images. Our eyes are simply tools the brain uses. In other words, sight is generated in the brain.

It made sense to my logical mind, but in that moment, as I read the words, it felt profound. It still does as I write them.

I also discovered there's a term for what happened to me at the airport. It's called *expectation bias*—the tendency to perceive or interpret information in a way that confirms what we already believe or expect, often on a subconscious level. If you expect your partner to disappoint you, you may focus more on what goes wrong and overlook positive actions. Or if you're told a wine is expensive, you might perceive it as tasting better—even if it's not.

We all have biases and preconceived notions that narrow our focus or blind us from seeing a different perspective, the truth, or even objects in plain sight—like a large clock at an airport.

I had another interesting experience showcasing how perception can render something invisible. One spring, while working as a produce clerk at a large health food store, I decided to shave my head. I'd been intrigued by the idea for a long time but didn't have the courage to make such a dramatic change to my appearance. Whenever I saw someone with a shaved head, I would ask them why they did it and then, with their permission, I would slowly run my hand back and forth over the top of their head, enjoying the soft, fuzzy texture.

I can't believe I'm writing this in my book for the world to read, but there was a period of time when I got my hair permed. (In my defense, it was my hairstylist's idea.) I have those pictures under lock and key, especially the ones with me sporting a perm *and* a beard. (pained emoji)

A year or so later, on a Saturday night, sometime around two in the morning, I was feeling bored and restless. I looked in the mirror, decided I was done with having a perm, and searched for some scissors. The only pair I could find were the tiny fold-out ones in my Swiss Army Knife. It took me a while, but I eventually cut all of it off. Once I was done, I shaved my head numerous times until I was as bald as could be. Some people look good without hair. I, unfortunately, wasn't one of them. In fact, I looked like I had just been released from prison.

But I'm digressing. What was fascinating, besides realizing how much our hair insulates our head, was that when I was at work, milling about the store, people who knew me would walk right past me—as if I weren't even there.

My experiences revealed just how easily perception can be shaped by expectation. We think we're seeing what's in front of us, but more often we're experiencing life through a filtered lens. If something doesn't align with our bias, we simply don't register it.

Another moment of awe—of seeing something with fresh eyes that left an enduring impression—came while my girlfriend and I were sitting in a row of chairs facing a stage. We had been together for a year, but as I turned to look at her, it was as though I were seeing her for the very first time. Whatever subconscious filters I'd been viewing her through seemed to dissolve. I sat there in quiet wonder, taking in an essence and beauty I hadn't noticed before. It made me fall in love with her all over again.

My epiphanies about perception served as invitations to peel back the illusion about reality—a reminder that reality is not fixed but shaped by what we expect to see. I wonder—what else lies hidden in plain sight? What magick and miracles are possible?

There was a popular bumper sticker back in the eighties that read QUESTION AUTHORITY—a resurgence of a popular phrase from the late sixties and early seventies. One day, as I was in my car, I chuckled when I saw a spinoff on the vehicle in front of me that read QUESTION REALITY. Maybe magick isn't really invisible. Perhaps it's been there all along, quietly waiting for us to notice, if only with fresh eyes.

20

The Sound of Silence

The plush cushions on my living room couch cradled me in a cocoon of coziness as I settled in for an hour of rest and relaxation. An oversized mug of hot cocoa rested on my lap while I scanned the expanse of my apartment. My gaze lingered beyond the kitchen, on the sliding glass doors looking out into the backyard. A large, tiered fountain gurgled softly, inviting neighborhood birds to frolic in its waters. Groups of hummingbirds, sparrows, finches, pigeons, and even the occasional hawk visited regularly. Getting lost in their bathing rituals and playful antics was always a joy.

The aroma of chocolate rose to greet me, beckoning me to indulge. I raised the piping-hot cup to my nose, its steam caressing my face as I leaned in, like a sommelier savoring a fine wine. I lingered in its rich bouquet for a long moment before carefully taking a sip.

The muted winter light filtered through my windows as I let my mind wander, anchored in quiet mindfulness. I savored the warmth of the cocoa and the hush of the moment, taking slow sips without breaking the stillness.

Fifteen minutes into my silent reverie, a jarring clangor unexpectedly reverberated from the kitchen, rudely interrupting my Zen bliss. It was the motor of the refrigerator shutting off. The suddenness of it surprised me, but what struck me deeply—and what led to my epiphany—was the stark contrast between the moment before and the moment after the appliance powered down.

There's more to silence than we realize.

I thought I was enjoying the serene quiet of the moment, but the reality was that the refrigerator was humming the entire time. Not only was it running, but it was loud. I was baffled that I could be unaware of so much noise, especially while sitting peacefully with my thoughts. I didn't realize it was making any sound at all until the appliance cycled off. The revelation—that visceral realization that something so substantive was going on without me even knowing—was strangely unsettling.

The experience prompted me to ask, *What is silence, exactly? How could I think my surroundings were quiet when they really weren't? How many other things were going on without my knowledge or awareness?*

So, I did what I always do when I'm writing about something that touches on a topic I don't know much about— I let my curiosity do some research.

First, I went to the major dictionary sources. I was surprised to discover that none of them fully captured the meaning. *Merriam-Webster*, along with several others like *Cambridge Dictionary*, *Oxford English Dictionary*, and *Collins English Dictionary*, lists several definitions that echoed one another, claiming that "Silence is a forbearance or absence from speech, sound, or noise; complete quiet."

What I learned in my research is that silence—the complete absence of sound—doesn't exist, at least not here on Earth. The closest thing to absolute silence happens in outer space. Why?

Sound is what's called a mechanical wave—a physical disturbance that moves through air, water, or solid material. The vibration it creates causes the molecules in whatever it's moving through to bump into one another, producing sound.

I found this interesting: In air, sound travels at roughly 767 mph or 1,126 ft/s at room temperature. In water, it travels faster—3,310 mph or 4,855 ft/s—because water molecules are closer together and transmit vibrations more efficiently. That's why whales and dolphins can communicate across vast distances underwater.

Sound moves fastest through solids, like steel, because their particles are tightly packed. This allows them to transmit vibrations more quickly and with less energy loss—an astonishing 11,200 mph or 16,445 ft/s. That's why if you put your ear to a railroad track, you'll hear a train coming long before it's audible in the air.

In space, there are no molecules—only a few particles per cubic yard—so there's nothing for sound waves to travel through. If you were floating in space with a suit on and someone exploded a firecracker a few feet away, you wouldn't hear a thing. (*Doesn't that fact just blow you away?!*)

Pure silence is dangerous. It can actually cause serious psychological and physical discomfort when experienced for too long. This was discovered through the use of a unique scientific invention: the anechoic chamber (pronounced an-ih-KOH-ik).

Anechoic chambers are specially designed rooms that absorb all reflections of sound and electromagnetic waves. The term *anechoic* literally means "without echo." These chambers create an environment free from both external noise and internal reverberations, making them ideal for highly sensitive acoustic and electromagnetic testing. The silence is so profound that you can often hear your own heartbeat, the movement of your joints, and even the flow of your blood.

Why is absolute silence so disorienting? Our brains rely on sound bouncing off surfaces to perceive the size of a space, orient ourselves, and maintain balance. In an anechoic chamber, those echoes are gone. People often lose their balance or feel dizzy, and it becomes difficult to localize sounds—even your own voice. Without background noise or external stimuli, many lose track of time. Some experience panic or claustrophobia, and with prolonged exposure, even hallucinations.

Here's an interesting bit of trivia: According to Guinness World Records, the quietest place on Earth is the anechoic chamber at Microsoft's headquarters in Redmond, Washington.

As for how I could be so unaware of the hum of my refrigerator, I learned that our brains are wired to tune things out for the sake of everyday functioning. Just ask any woman who's ever been in a relationship with a man—she'll confirm it.

Jokes aside, the silence we experience on Earth is actually full of sound. Much like with our sense of smell, where the brain gradually tunes out lingering scents, our auditory system engages in what's called auditory adaptation (or habituation). We filter out or suppress the perception of constant, repetitive, or nonthreatening sounds so we can better focus on new or meaningful ones.

I once had an experience that opened my mind (and my ears) to a heightened awareness about sound and silence. I was participating in a meditation class in which the teacher had us do a simple exercise. We were instructed to sit in silence for five minutes and identify as many sounds around us as we could. At the end of the exercise, we were asked to share our results.

I was genuinely surprised by how many sounds others in the group had picked up. I heard five. One woman listed over a dozen. She was a classically trained musician, and her education had taught her how to truly listen. It had never occurred to me that hearing was a skill—something you could actually refine and strengthen over time.

After the sharing was over, we were instructed to sit in silence again and repeat the exercise. On the second round, with my sharpened attunement, I was able to hear some of the noises I had missed the first time. This experience made me realize how much we unconsciously filter out each moment—and how mindfulness can increase our awareness and expand our perception of the world around us.

Just like the silence experienced in an anechoic chamber can be detrimental, so can the awareness of too many sounds at one time. I once had that surreal but excruciatingly painful experience. While sitting at an outdoor café, the sheer volume and chaos of hearing too many sounds at the same time was unbearable. Based on my experience, it wouldn't take more than twenty seconds for that to cause serious psychological harm. (You can read about my experience in the story "Panic Attack.")

I've always been fascinated by those moments when silence feels thick and palpable, like when walking into a quiet room. I find that unique quality soothing. It's so pronounced, it almost feels like a presence. That phenomenon actually has a name: sensory contrast. We're constantly surrounded by subtle background noise—wind, distant traffic, HVAC hums, electronics, voices in our surroundings, etc. When that vanishes, our brains notice its absence. Silence can actually feel loud because it's so stark compared to our normal environment, hence the oxymoron "deafening silence."

But silence is not a void, nor is it the absence of noise. Much like the constant drone of my refrigerator that I had stopped registering, the consistent hum of our mental chatter—an endless stream of thoughts, concerns, and distractions—becomes indiscernible background static—still present, subconsciously shaping how we feel and respond, even if we're no longer aware of it. Only when it suddenly stops, or when mindfulness sets in, do we realize just how loud it had been all along.

It is mindfulness, then, that opens the doorway to awareness—a gentle threshold between the clamor of the world and the quiet truth within us. When we're present enough to notice what we've tuned out, both around and within, stillness reveals itself—not as emptiness, but as clarity about the true nature of silence. And within that space, insight and healing are possible.

Stillness becomes a mirror, reflecting what's stirring beneath the surface, what we've been too distracted to see. The body softens. The breath deepens. And in that openness, we begin to notice what's often drowned out beneath the layers of our current awareness: a quiet nudge, a flicker of knowing, the faint voice of inner guidance.

21

When One Is Worth
More Than a Thousand

I love bread. Not the mass-produced squishy kind in plastic bags that sits on grocery store shelves full of strange ingredients with names impossible to pronounce. No, I'm talking about real bread: artisan loaves from boutique bakeries, crafted by hand with simple, natural ingredients that turn out a robust crust, tender, airy insides full of character, and an earthy, soulful taste.

I was lucky to grow up in six different countries as a child with cosmopolitan parents who loved to travel and savor the delights of gourmet cuisine from around the world. As a result, I had the good fortune to experience some amazing bread masterpieces from more than a dozen cultures.

Bagels have been favorites of mine too. I still remember the first one I ever had. I was six years old, tagging along with my family to visit my cousins in my dad's hometown of Long Island, New York. It's funny to think how something as simple as eating a bagel can get imprinted in your memory so deeply that you carry it forever. Of all the amazing trips and experiences I had in my youth—and remembering only a few clearly—you'd think I'd be able to recall something more consequential. But actually, it was such a scrumptious bagel, I'd go so far as to call the experience profound.

As I was writing this story, I stepped away from my computer to go into the kitchen and fix myself a snack for a short break. My wife happened to be sitting at the kitchen island, talking to a mortgage broker on the phone. We were planning to buy an investment property, and she was getting the details of a loan. Knowing I'd want to listen to what he was saying, she put the gentleman on speakerphone so I could join in the conversation. I immediately noticed a strong accent. Whenever I hear one my inquisitiveness becomes an itch I have to scratch, so I asked him where it came from.

"I was born and raised in Long Island," he answered. "That's where I'm talking to you from now."

What are the odds?! I mentioned that my dad was born and raised there as well, and after we exchanged a few words, I confided in him with a dramatic flair that I had had a religious experience in Long Island as a child.

"Oh?"

"Yeah," I said. "I had my first-ever bagel there. It was so good that as I was chewing on it, the skies parted, and I saw God."

We all let out a hearty laugh. I was kidding, of course, about having a religious experience and seeing God—but I wasn't about the bagel being so delicious. I still remember sitting at the dining table, feeling the texture of the crust as I held it in my hands, the smell of the dough as I brought the bagel close to my nose, and the chewiness of it as I munched on a bite.

Throughout my young adult years, I tried various kinds of bagels: poppy seed, cinnamon raisin, blueberry, cheese, whole wheat, banana walnut, and others. But nothing appealed to me more than a sesame bagel. It rose to become my favorite—especially halved, toasted, and slathered with salted, melted butter.

Just as my dad did, I would often eat my bagel while sitting at the breakfast table, perusing the morning paper or enjoying it as a snack while reading a good book.

I have nothing against multitasking—I do it all the time. But we pay a price for it. Because our attention is split between two or more things, we aren't fully present in the moment for either task. We can't absorb or fully appreciate each experience as deeply if we were solely focused on one.

Have you ever eaten popcorn or an orange while reading, and you absentmindedly reach for more while your eyes are on your book—only to realize, with a rush of disappointment and surprise, that you've eaten the last kernel or segment after your fingers search the bottom of the bowl? If you have, then you know what I'm talking about.

Here's an experiment for you to try: Be present and attentive while eating whatever it is you're eating. Take time to look closely at your food. Notice as many details about it as you can like texture, color, and shape. Bring your nose close and smell it. If you accidentally get food on your nose (like I often do) and you're with company, you can save face by borrowing a quote often spoken by my dad when he'd get food in his mustache: "Why let the mouth have all the fun!" Now compare that to the experience of absentminded eating while you're focused on doing something else—like reading a book.

I had a taste of that kind of experiment (no pun intended) at a Buddhist temple just north of San Diego one sunny afternoon. Every Sunday, the Deer Park Monastery opens its doors to the public to participate in a silent walking meditation, followed by a service and then a "mindful" vegetarian buffet lunch.

When lunchtime came, a monk spoke to all the guests, inviting us to try an experiment before getting up to serve ourselves the food.

"I encourage you to take about twenty-five percent of what you might normally put on your plate," he said. "Once you sit down, take small amounts and chew each mouthful thirty times before taking another bite."

I followed his instructions and was amazed at how long it took me to finish my food. Additionally, I felt full, even though I was only eating a small amount of vegetables and rice.

Another profound moment with food, and the subject of my story, came about one morning as I was absentmindedly inhaling a toasted sesame bagel while reading the paper for the news of the day. Suddenly, I inadvertently bit into one of the toasted sesame seeds. Flavor exploded in my mouth with fervor, saturating my tastebuds and my mind with a toasted sesame sensation. I was so enraptured by the experience that I put the paper down so I could enjoy it with my undivided attention.

I became completely absorbed by the rich aftertaste still unfolding in my mouth.

Wow! I couldn't believe one tiny seed could do that. I smacked my lips like I was a world-renowned sommelier tasting an expensive hundred-year-old wine. That's when I had my epiphany: One toasted sesame seed, if bitten into, is infinitely more flavorful than a thousand seeds swallowed whole.

As I sat in deep thought, a memory bubbled up into my consciousness. We all have instances etched in our minds, times when someone says something that stays with us for the rest of our lives. One of those moments for me was when I was participating in a personal growth workshop. The facilitator took the entire group outside and told us we could pick any object in our environment and use it as a tool for self-discovery. He taught that by asking pertinent questions of it, like "How are you a mirror for my life?" we could gain meaningful insights into aspects of our current circumstances or character.

The idea that we're like sesame seeds came to me. We are small, often overlooked, and going through life downplaying our significance. Yet the truth is, each one of us carries something pro-found within. Each of us holds a hidden richness—untapped depth waiting to be discovered. But if we rush through life, distracted and disconnected, that potential remains sealed—never awakened, never tasted, never experienced.

That single toasted seed reminded me that when we pause, when we bring our full attention to something—even something as simple as a morsel of food—it can reveal a world, a perspective, or a truth we've been too busy to notice. A moment of presence can stir the soul more deeply than a thousand moments passed by unnoticed.

There's something sacred in slowing down—in truly tasting life one bite, one breath, one seed at a time.

And in that sense, one can truly be worth more than a thousand.

CHAPTER 4

Profound but Emotionally Intense

22

Comfort Food Overdose

Pre's Trail in Alton Baker Park, Eugene, Oregon, is a popular bark trail for walkers and runners of all levels. Living nearby, I often made it part of my daily run.

One day, halfway through my run, I stopped at the part of the trail where runners usually gathered to stretch or socialize before their workouts. My legs were feeling tight, so I decided to stop for a quick stretch.

True to form, I struck up a conversation with a guy about my age who was warming up for his run. Since we had a lively banter going, we decided to hit the trail together. Over time, Nate and I became fast friends. He was a rugged outdoor enthusiast with a tendency to be brash, though he'd often surprise me with his quiet thoughtfulness and emotional intelligence.

But one conversation early in our friendship left me uneasy, questioning whether I really knew him—or if he had a few loose screws. I was a passenger in his car, and we were driving to a hiking trail just outside town for a run. At one point, he started talking about his little kid and how that child was feeling about some issue in his life. I knew enough about Nate to know he was single, and he had never mentioned having any children before. I went along with what he was saying, but in my mind, I wondered, *Am I riding in a car with a psycho? Am I going to make it home today?*

Okay, maybe I was exaggerating a little, but I truly didn't know what the hell he was talking about, and it left me feeling unsettled. I liked hanging out with Nate, but that interaction raised a serious red flag. I decided to wait and see if he showed any other signs of mental instability.

I knew a thing or two about what it felt like to be mentally off-balance, because, well, I had some version of it too, as a result of childhood wounds and the resulting yet-to-be-discovered trauma hidden in my subconscious. To help me navigate through my thoughts and feelings, I saw a therapist every week.

A month after Nate's eyebrow-raising comments, I had an aha moment in my therapist's office. During our conversation, she used the term *inner child*, which made me stop and ask, "Inner child? What's an inner child?"

The concept of the inner child has its roots in the early 1900s with Carl Jung, but the idea wasn't significantly expanded until the 1950s to the 1970s by therapists such as Eric Berne and Donald Winnicott. John Bradshaw's best-selling book, *Homecoming: Reclaiming and Championing Your Inner Child*, published in 1990, made the concept of the inner child a household term when he proposed that many adult struggles stem from unresolved childhood wounds, and that healing requires re-parenting the inner child with love, attention, and safety.

In a nutshell, the inner child is the subconscious part of us that still carries the emotions, needs, and memories from our earliest years. Like a real child living within us, it holds both the wounds of being hurt, ignored, or misunderstood, and the wonder of joy, play, and imagination. The therapeutic concept behind inner child work is that by acknowledging and reconnecting with those parts of ourselves compassionately, we can heal the emotional scars, creating space for deep healing and greater self-acceptance.

It was only after she explained what the inner child was that it dawned on me—Nate wasn't talking about a "real" kid that day in the car. He was talking about his inner child.

Through my personal healing journey and in my private practice as a massage therapist and shaman, along with helping men heal from sexual abuse, I've realized that we all have multiple inner children, each at different ages, influencing our thoughts, feelings, and behaviors. Like multiple personalities that pop in without warning, our different inner children can do the same, but without us knowing if we're not aware.

Imagine you're driving your car—focused and responsible while running errands on your adult to-do list. You're in control. But you're also feeling stressed, maybe worried about something. Somewhere along the way, you impulsively make a sharp turn into your favorite clothing store and walk out with bags of stuff you didn't plan on buying. How did that happen?

In that moment, a younger, impulsive part of you—maybe one that craves comfort, excitement, or validation—subtly reached over and took control of the wheel. You, the adult, were still in the driver's seat, but that part of you wasn't making the decisions. That's how our inner parts can work—quietly steering our actions from beneath the surface. There are countless ways our inner selves influence our behavior, but that's a whole other book.

Our inner children reflect our passions, creativity, and aliveness. But they also carry the pain of life—trauma, neglect, abuse, loss, sickness, and addiction. As adults, we can fall prey to using distractions like work, sex, porn, drugs, alcohol, food, shopping, and exercise to avoid feeling the pain. But when we do that, we close ourselves off from the positive aspects as well. Engaging in those distractions is an ineffective coping mechanism with potentially major negative consequences that can leave us emotionally frozen or disconnected.

As a teenager, food—or more specifically, simple carbs like

bread, ice cream, and pastries—became my source of comfort, my escape from the stress of navigating change and trying to figure out my life. I was a lonely youngster who felt like I didn't quite fit in, yet too scared to be vulnerable with others in the way I craved. Instead of connecting on a deeper level with others, I turned to food.

I had become a purist as a young teen, abstaining from junk food, alcohol, drugs, coffee, and anything else I didn't think was healthy. But as an older teen, living with friends of the family while finishing high school, I would sneak food into my bedroom that I normally wouldn't allow myself to eat, food I didn't want others to know I was eating, either, like pie, ice cream, and cookies.

The following year, I lived with a housemate who was gone frequently, so I had the house to myself. I would eat a nutritious meal, then sit in front of the TV gorging on sweets until I felt I was on the verge of throwing up. I didn't know what bulimia was back then, but I realize now that was a real possible outcome given my level of self-contempt. What saved me from going down that path was a profound emotional experience that led to a life-changing epiphany.

One night, I was consoling myself in my usual way—watching TV and stuffing my face with sweets, consisting of half a gallon of ice cream, two large slices of apple pie, a dozen cookies, and four slices of extra-thick toasted raisin bread slathered in butter.

At first, I was in heaven, cocooned from the harsh reality of the world, like a kid with his favorite treat. The satisfaction of eating all that sugar and carbs, though, eventually turned into self-disgust, shame, and guilt as I continued to put food in my mouth beyond what I knew to be enough. It always did. Comforting myself with food that turned into a hate fest was a vicious cycle I didn't understand and felt powerless to stop.

After eating everything but two slices of raisin bread, my stomach felt distended, stretched tight beneath my pants as if it no longer had room to contain anything. I unbuttoned my pants to relieve the pressure so I could make room for more. A sluggish heaviness settled in my core. The sweetness clung to the inside of my mouth, overstaying its welcome, now sickening instead of satisfying, my jaw tired from all the chewing. My chest felt compressed. I had to breathe more shallowly, as if the food had taken up space meant for oxygen. I could feel the slow, sticky churn of sugar and fat turning over inside me.

My hand shoveled another thick piece of toast into my mouth; I was desperate and longing for the comforting feelings I had at the start of my binge. I felt like throwing up, but I kept forcing food down my throat, lamenting that my binge was coming to an end. I was drowning in a pool of self-pity while vile self-loathing crouched, waiting for me to finish and growing with every mouthful.

As I raised my hand to my lips with another mouthful, I suddenly felt overwhelmed with a deep, profound sense of loneliness. It was as if a door to my subconscious had cracked open, letting out a cry for help. Feelings I'd long hidden under layers of sugar and carbs came rushing to the surface, drowning me in sorrow.

Tears cascaded down my face as an epiphany emerged from the floodgates of feeling. In that crystal-clear moment, I realized what I was doing; it was as though I had been lost in a long, unconscious stupor and suddenly came to. I was literally stuffing my feelings down my throat, cramming them down with food so I wouldn't have to feel them, while simultaneously trying to placate my inner child with desserts.

I stood in front of my young self, his innocence and vulnerability glowing brightly in the darkness I had surrounded myself with. As I looked into his eyes, I felt a profound connection as a beautiful wave of compassion welled up and washed over me for that child. I felt, to the core of my being, the love he needed.

When my nonverbal inner child pointed to my stomach, not in accusation but in supplication, I suddenly became hyperaware of the feelings in my body—the sick-to-my-stomach tightness, the bloating, and the heat flashes of sugar overload. In that alchemical exchange, I felt forgiven. But more importantly, I knew in that moment that I would never ever force food down my throat like that again. I still had to contend with my physical discomfort, but that night, I felt an inner peace I hadn't felt in a long time.

While I still turn to food for comfort, I'm free from the destructive behaviors of my past. Like an onion, I continue to peel away the layers of denial, learning what and how to heal, little by little—and sometimes by leaps and bounds—while making conscious choices for my well-being.

23

The Tiger Within

I am a survivor of sexual abuse. I was molested by several different men over the course of my childhood. Like many survivors, I completely suppressed all memory of the abuse as a way to cope with the trauma. If someone had told me at nineteen that I was a survivor of sexual abuse, I would've thought they were crazy. That's how powerful denial can be as a coping mechanism.

Everyone is in denial about one thing or another. There's plenty to be in denial about—but that's a story for another time. The issues we don't face—and our thoughts, feelings, and beliefs around them—get swept under the rug into our subconscious, where they're soon forgotten and remain hidden. The problem is, those buried truths still affect our lives—often in painful, self-sabotaging ways. It's a fallacy to think otherwise. This was certainly true for me in more ways than one.

If I hadn't opened Pandora's box and unearthed my memories, I might never have begun the journey that changed my life—and for that, despite the pain, I'm deeply grateful.

I learned in my years of working as a massage therapist and shaman that memories, thoughts, and emotions stored in the subconscious can be accessed through a myriad of ways—mindful touch, breathwork, meditation, conversation—anything that cultivates awareness or acts as a trigger. And when the timing is right, those hidden diamonds coated in tar can be discovered and released. Once they are, the journey of healing begins—often transforming a person's life. That's exactly what happened to me.

It all started one night when I was twenty years old. After a long, tiring day, the only thing on my mind as I walked through my front door was how good a shower would feel and how much I was looking forward to vegging out in front of the TV. My house-mate was out of town, and I was excited to have the whole house to myself.

I cleaned up, heated some leftovers for dinner, and made my way into the living room for an evening of binge-watching. I placed my dinner plate on the coffee table, turned on the TV, and plopped down on the couch. As I landed, my hands inadvertently fell over my genitals as if to cover them, and a voice inside my head matter-of-factly announced, *You were sexually abused.*

I sat there, stunned and puzzled.

Why would a thought like that suddenly pop into my mind?

One notable thing about the silent declaration is that it didn't feel like it materialized from my imagination. It was an announcement delivered from a voice I recognized—the voice, the mysterious messenger that I was learning to respect as wise counsel. I knew enough to take it seriously, but I was flabbergasted. I had no recollection of being abused and couldn't imagine it ever happening to me. The voice didn't offer any proof, so I was left to wonder whether I had actually made it up.

Over the next six months, I continued to receive impressions from my unconscious—sporadic glimpses, feelings, and flashes of memory about being abused. They surfaced at unexpected moments—while showering, pushing a cart through a grocery store, or driving in my car. They felt real yet offered no concrete evidence. Nothing definitive made it absolutely clear I had suffered that sort of violation.

In my ignorance and naivete, I found it hard to believe something like that could happen to a boy, and I doubted whether any of it could be true. I knew girls were being abused, but boys? I took the inner cues seriously enough to seek out the help of a psychologist, but that was short-lived and offered no answers. In hindsight, I realize I wasn't prepared to face the scope of what I had gone through and wouldn't be until I was ready—and until The Universe gave me the right conditions to face it.

The experience caught me off guard and struck with such power and depth, it sent shock waves reverberating through every part of my life. It became a defining event—one that not only initiated my healing but also reshaped the path I was on, ultimately transforming me into the person I was meant to become.

At the time, I was enrolled in a state-certified massage therapy program at the local community college. One of the curriculum requirements was to give and receive a number of massages outside of class time. Since I didn't own a massage table, I set out to buy one. After doing my research, I found a company two hours north of where I lived that built portable tables with the specific features and accessories I wanted. I ordered one over the phone and arranged to pick it up the following week.

I was thrilled at the idea of having my very own table and waited eagerly for the day it was ready, like a kid anticipating Christmas. When the time came, I drove up to the factory and met with Kirk, one of the business owners, who also happened to be a massage therapist.

We chatted about massage and the different techniques one could learn as I followed him through the factory to where completed orders were shelved. Kirk mentioned that he specialized in a particular form of bodywork and asked if I was familiar with it.

"Yeah," I replied. "I've heard of it but haven't experienced it."

I had read about the technique in school, and based on what I learned, it seemed too airy-fairy or superficial to be effective—

definitely not something I felt interested in learning to do or even experiencing. Not wanting to seem rude, I left that part out.

"Oh?" he replied. "You gotta try it! It's amazing."

Kirk pulled out my table, gave it a quick once-over, and opened it to make sure everything was in good working order. Before I could say anything, he flipped the table onto its legs and patted the top, inviting me to lie down and experience a taste of his work. I didn't want to be impolite, so I accepted his offer. I climbed onto the table and lay on my back, fully clothed.

What happened next not only surprised me—it surpassed my comprehension. Kirk took hold of my hand with both of his and stepped back, positioning my arm at a forty-five-degree angle from my shoulder. Then he gently swayed it in a rhythmic motion, periodically adjusting the angle. Not only did it feel good, but there was also a healing quality to the movement. Within sixty seconds, I entered a deeply relaxed state and hovered in and out of consciousness, like what sometimes happens right before falling asleep.

Less than two minutes into Kirk's demonstration, I heard a voice in my head. It was like I was Kevin Costner's character in the movie *Field of Dreams* when he walks through his cornfield. But the declaration I heard wasn't "If you build it, he will come." It simply whispered one word in a soft, wise tone: *Yes.*

The invisible messenger didn't have to say more for me to understand the meaning. It affirmed the power and healing quality of what Kirk was doing. It made me acknowledge that the technique I had written off as too foo-foo to be effective was far more powerful than I'd assumed—I had deeply underestimated its therapeutic value. The experience opened a door in my mind, one that needed to be opened for me to undergo one of the most profound transformations of my life.

Kirk ended my session and stepped back, keeping his eye on me, a look of satisfaction on his face as though he were an artist admiring something he had just created. I slowly sat up on the table and swiveled my legs around so they dangled off the edge, trying to process what had just happened. All I could do was marvel at the unexpected sense of calm I felt. I gathered myself for a moment, thanked Kirk for his time, and tucked the one-word message in my mind like a scribbled note in my pocket. Some part of me knew I would need it later.

As an intuitive person, I've learned there are signs in life—seeds planted by Spirit to help guide us along the way. These moments often act as catalysts, validations, forms of guidance, or encouragement, shaping the decisions we make or the paths we take. Signs are like landmarks or breadcrumbs, quietly nudging us in a certain direction. Sometimes they're obvious, but most often, they're subtle. Like omens, they can come in the form of a book, the timing of a song, something someone says, or, in my case, the name of a person. The ways Spirit communicates with us are endless.

The trick to recognizing signs is to first believe they exist and then cultivate the skill to perceive them. For some people, coincidences are nothing more than random events without meaning—simply because they lack the belief or perspective to see them as possible signs pointing to what they long for, or even to their destiny. I believe everything happens for a reason—even if we don't always get to understand or know what that reason is. What may appear inconsequential or "bad" may actually end up being crucial, and the very thing we need for our soul's evolution.

For example, when a name shows up in your life three or four times in a relatively short span and there's a clear sense of synchronicity in how it appears, it's a good idea to pay attention and consider whether the name holds a deeper meaning. Fortunately for me, I was paying attention.

Several months after I bought my massage table, I experienced low back pain that threatened my ability to work at my physically demanding nine-to-five job, as well as do massage. As I thought about who to see for help, one name stood out: Sylvia.

Sylvia was a massage therapist who specialized in the same technique Kirk did. I knew about her because her name presented itself three times after my interaction with Kirk. Two instances occurred when acquaintances mentioned her out of the blue, and the third happened when I came across her ad in a local alternative newspaper. Intrigued, I decided to make an appointment with her to see if she could help me with my lower back pain.

Sylvia was a tall, slender, middle-aged woman with a strong, quiet presence. Her eyes radiated a "don't mess with me" intensity that magnified her no-nonsense attitude. She was notably complex. While I felt a little intimidated by her, her compassionate, down-to-earth nature and the wisdom she articulated during our session put me at ease.

My first session with Sylvia went well. As a massage therapist myself, it was hard for me to fully relax unless I trusted the person's skill. But the moment she began working on me, I knew I was in good hands. Her touch was grounded and intuitive, and I quickly melted into the table. By the end, I felt a noticeable difference— enough to schedule a follow-up for a few days out.

When I returned for my second visit, I lay fully clothed on my back as Sylvia worked with quiet focus. Midway through, I noticed a faint tension begin to stir in my abdomen. At first, it seemed minor, nothing worth mentioning. But the sensation kept intensifying. Within minutes, it grew into a distinct pressure—as if I had gas, which I knew I didn't. As the discomfort continued, I finally spoke up.

Sylvia stopped what she was doing and asked me questions to better understand what I was feeling. After listening carefully, she determined that whatever was happening warranted her full attention.

She gently placed her hands above my belly button and instructed me to close my eyes, breathe slowly and deeply, and bring mindful awareness to the sensations I was experiencing. My chest gently rose and fell as I quieted my mind and concentrated on the distress I felt.

What happened next completely took me by surprise. After a few deep breaths, I slipped into an altered state. I was transported to another time and place, thrust into a repressed fragment from my childhood—a memory of being sexually abused.

I burst into tears, my body thrashing involuntarily on Sylvia's table as I tried to get away from the shadowy figure of a man forcibly holding me in his grip. My throat burned with each scream as my small body did its best to wrestle free from the horror of that experience.

Sylvia remained calm, standing beside me like a seasoned psychotherapist, offering words of encouragement and grounding support. Loud, primal sobs that would have once embarrassed me poured from my soul and erupted from my throat. Tears I never cried flowed freely and endlessly from the deep well of my inner child's heart.

Eventually, the convulsions in my body and the emotional storm tied to the memory began to subside. A small part of me registered the rhythm of my breath beginning to steady, the slowing beat of my heart, and my damp shirt clinging to my skin from a cold sweat. But most of my awareness was still suspended elsewhere, grappling with the enormity of what had just occurred.

As I floated in a cocoon of energy, cradled in a blanket of clouds, the mist in front of me began to swirl and take shape.

It was another vision.

A large metal cage with vertical bars, like one you might see at a zoo, appeared before me. Towering over eight feet tall and eight feet wide, it had thick, impenetrable bars spaced too closely for anything inside to escape. Gazing at me with piercing intent from behind the bars stood a massive tiger.

Our eyes met. His gaze held me—arresting, unwavering,

impossible to look away from. I should have been terrified, but instead, I felt a strange sense of being welcomed, safe, and in awe. His presence held me in reverent stillness, imbuing me with a quiet calm. His golden, luminous eyes expressed a deep sadness as if he too had just witnessed my ordeal. I became aware that the denial and fear that had kept me from facing my abuse were also keeping the tiger locked away.

I've been waiting for you, he said telepathically.

I instinctively understood who he was and what brought him to me in this profound moment. He was the embodiment of my masculine energy, and after years behind bars, it was time for him to claim his freedom—to mark the beginning of my incredible healing journey.

My masculine energy had been locked in that cage for most of my life—a cage I had built for him after being abused by men. As a child, I unconsciously decided that men were inherently perverse and that neither their power nor their intentions could be trusted. Though I was male, I wanted little to do with that part of myself— not when men were the cause of so much pain and suffering, both in my world and in the world at large. The effects of that belief ran deep—impacting my psyche, my emotions, and even the way my body developed and my appearance.

When I was an adolescent, I looked very feminine. I had fine facial features, long hair, and a high-pitched voice. People often mistook me for a girl. As you can imagine, it was painfully embarrassing. By my late teens, that assumption morphed into people often assuming I was gay.

But my willingness to face the truth about my past was about to set the tiger free. I watched in silent reverence as the padlock and chains that bound him shattered and fell to the ground. He glanced down at the floor and then back up to meet the look of my astonishment. A sly, almost imperceptible smile radiated from him as the metal door to his prison slowly swung open. His strength was palpable as he took his first step through the threshold of his long-awaited freedom.

And then, much to my chagrin and without any advance notice, the vision quickly vanished, swallowed by a swirl of fog-like energy. I stared after it, trying to will it back, but to no avail.

Resigned, I let go, turning inward to the fullness in my heart and mind. I lay quietly on Sylvia's table as I slowly reacclimated to reality. I was caught in a strange paradox—peaceful from the catharsis and release, yet horrified by the memory that had just surfaced. There was so much to take in and process.

Sylvia stood patiently, giving me the time and space to absorb my experience without interference. When I signaled that I was ready, she helped me off the table, and we debriefed the session. We scheduled my next appointment and said our goodbyes.

I walked out of Sylvia's office and into the world feeling as if I had been reborn.

Dramatic changes soon ensued after my encounter with the tiger. Within a couple of weeks, my body began to transform in noticeable ways. My jaw grew more square and defined, my voice dropped into a lower register, and my facial hair began growing more quickly. As time went by, I was also relieved to find that people no longer assumed I was gay.

Not long after my experience on Sylvia's table, I looked into local resources for survivors of sexual abuse. I was fortunate to find the services of a nonprofit organization that offered peer-facilitated support groups—one for those just beginning their healing journey and another for those further along.

The things I learned through the programs at the nonprofit shed profound light on sexual abuse and how it had affected me, helping me tremendously to heal and grow. The journey was incredibly challenging, marked by deep lows and occasional highs, but I felt fortunate to have that resource at a fraction of the cost of traditional therapy. Grateful for the support I received, I chose to give back by volunteering as a peer facilitator, leading support groups for other men taking their first steps toward healing.

For the next decade, I continued to discover instances of abuse. Like Matt Damon's character in the movie *Good Will Hunting*, I too believed these were my fault. I spent years peeling back the many layers to uncover and heal my inner child—the anger and rage, the helplessness and despair, the grief and sadness, and the subtle nuances of my victim mindset.

Over those ten years, I worked with more than two dozen therapists, explored various psychological approaches, and participated in numerous personal growth workshops designed to empower individuals.

Healing from sexual abuse is not for the faint of heart, but the rewards were profound and worth every ounce of effort. If you or someone you know is a survivor of sexual abuse, I encourage you to seek support. No matter how difficult or frightening the choice to heal may seem, you are far better off making that choice than continuing to minimize or deny the pain—especially if doing so means prolonging your suffering.

The staff at the nonprofit for survivors of sexual abuse often talked about the goal of healing: transitioning from "survivor" to "thriver." One of the ways they instilled a sense of empowerment was by displaying framed quotes on almost every wall. One of my favorites—and one I returned to often—was "The only way out is through."

My hope for anyone reading this who is suffering in silence: Free your inner self from its cage and let your beautiful, radiant self shine.

24

The Devil Came in Four

I am sometimes asked whether evil truly exists. While I still can't say for certain, this experience forced me to seriously wrestle with the possibility.

The next five paragraphs contain graphic details of a murder so brutal, some may find it deeply disturbing. Reader discretion is advised.

In the late hours of a spring evening in 1994, in the quiet town of Eugene, Oregon, four young men walked into a convenience store. They weren't there to browse or buy. Their minds were fixated on violence, driven by a cruel and malicious intent. Not only did they plan to kill the two female employees inside, but they had also premeditated the attack as part of a satanic thrill killing—not for money, not for revenge, but solely for the twisted satisfaction of inflicting violence on innocent lives.

The day of the attack, the men inconspicuously staked out the convenience store, watching and waiting. They took note of the number of employees present, whether there were cameras, and if so, where they were located. Once they were confident they could execute their plan without interference, they left—only to return later that night, just before closing.

Armed with a metal bar with a pointed end, a chisel-like hammer, a dumbbell, and a knife, the men stormed into the store and unleashed a brutal assault on the two female clerks. The man wielding the metal bar drove it through the skull of his victim, killing her instantly. The second woman fought desperately to protect herself, raising her arms and hands to block the relentless blows from the other three men.

Just as they were about to deliver their final deadly strikes, an unexpected sound cut through the horror—the entrance bell chimed, signaling the arrival of a last-minute customer. Startled, the attackers fled, leaving the second woman clinging to life. Miraculously, she survived, despite losing nearly half of her blood. Her desperate struggle to shield herself had saved her, but at a devastating cost.

A five-month manhunt followed before the four men were finally caught and brought to trial. Testimony revealed their deep involvement in drugs and death metal music, as well as their horrifying intent. They had planned to carve satanic symbols into their victims' bodies and use their blood to paint demonic imagery on the store walls—a grotesque attempt to terrorize the community.

When news of the homicide first broke, the town erupted in shock and outrage, appalled by the sheer savagery of the crime.

Though it dominated headlines for weeks and became the talk of workplaces and homes alike, I made a conscious decision to shut it out. I avoided the news, both in print and on TV, and refused to discuss it with others. Violence—whether real or fictional—had always unsettled me. Even scripted injustice and cruelty in movies and television could trigger something deep within me, stirring fear and an overwhelming sense of vulnerability. Those feelings weren't new; they were remnants of the traumas I had endured as a child. And when they surfaced, they didn't just bring fear—they awakened my rage.

Imagine the Hulk in the throes of fury, muscles coiled, fists trembling with the unbearable need to smash. That was me when rage took hold. I would growl loudly, every muscle in my upper body locking in tension, my clenched fists shaking uncontrollably in front of me, desperate to break something—anything.

The rage was intoxicating, a primal force that promised power but delivered only regret. It was my inner child's futile attempt to combat helplessness, but it came at a cost to my body. I almost always strained my upper torso or neck muscles when I let the fury consume me. To protect myself, I did everything I could to avoid triggers that might set it off.

While the city wrestled with the horror of the crime, I battled demons of my own. My attempt to build a private practice as a licensed massage therapist had failed. I was barely scraping by, juggling two part-time minimum-wage jobs, and renting a room in an elderly woman's house because it was all I could afford. On top of it all, I was nursing the grief of a recent breakup.

At thirty years old, I was embarrassed by my circumstances and ashamed of my inability to build the life I had envisioned—one filled with confidence, purpose, a decent income, and someone to share it with. I felt lost, adrift in a sea of failures, with no clear path forward. Days blurred together as I sank deeper into self-loathing, convinced I was hopelessly inept. When I wasn't at work, I either took refuge in my bed or berated myself relentlessly for being such a failure.

My landlady was a kind woman, but I dreaded the moments when she was home. Her presence meant I had to put on an act, feigning normalcy whenever I stepped out of my room, when in reality, I was unraveling inside. So, I welcomed the solitude on the days I had the house to myself.

One bright Sunday morning while my landlady was out running errands, I emerged from the self-imposed prison of my bedroom and made my way downstairs to the kitchen. Craving comfort, I prepared a cup of homemade hot chocolate, the rich aroma curling into the air as I stirred. Settling at the antique table in the open dining room, I wrapped my hands around the warm mug and took slow, savoring sips.

My gaze drifted to the living room—and landed on a sad sight. Stacks of overburdened cardboard boxes loomed in uneven towers, packed with papers and once-cherished belongings, now abandoned to a permanent purgatory between love and discard. The musty scent of cardboard clung to the air, thick with memories long forgotten. My landlady was a hoarder. The sheer weight of it all—the clutter, the stillness, the stagnant air—only deepened the heaviness pressing down on me.

I turned my focus back to the dining room. A bright stream of sunshine poured through the window, drawing my attention. Its soothing glow was a welcome respite, a small boon for my weary soul against the dark clouds looming over me. I shook my head at my desperation for anything comforting.

As I raised the mug to my lips, I pondered my predicament, searching for a way to improve my circumstances—to feel better about myself.

What can I do to add meaning to my life?

As if in answer, a memory surfaced from the depths of my subconscious, rising like a bubble through water, swelling until it burst—spilling its contents into my awareness.

It was a memory of a premonition I'd had at sixteen—one that had come true. That day, I was preparing to see my girlfriend for the last time before my family moved from Belgium to the other side of the world in Australia for my dad's job. As I gathered my things to leave for her house, a quiet certainty settled over me—a subtle but unmistakable feeling that something specific would unfold when I got there.

When my intuition played out before my eyes, I was awestruck, completely mesmerized by the experience. It wasn't just an eerie coincidence; it was a revelation. That moment ignited a fascination with intuition that would blossom later in life.

That memory triggered a cascade of others. In the years since that first revelation, my life had been peppered with random acts of serendipity and extraordinary moments of magick—events that pierced the veil between this world and the unseen world of Spirit. Each occurrence deepened my intrigue, making me wonder about my own psychic potential and whether I would ever develop it.

Up until that day, I hadn't—not since a fateful night from my college days abruptly ended my pursuit of psychic development. (You can read about that in the story "The Fourth Knock.") In fact, it would be another fifteen years before I had an experience that not only proved I could read people's energy at will but also reignited my interest in intuitive development.

As I sat at the table, reminiscing about the majesty and wonder of my past experiences, a powerful yearning stirred within me. Like a daydreamer, I imagined how incredible it would feel to use my intuition to help others. I had no reason to believe I could—but as I took my last sip, an idea took hold. Desperate for a sense of purpose, to feel better about life, I concocted a wild plan: I would attempt to contact the spirit of the woman who had been killed in the local convenience store homicide.

I had never done anything like that before, but what did I have to lose? Clutching onto the idea as if I had just discovered hope, I made my way upstairs to my room, seeking privacy.

Sunlight streamed through the only window of my sparsely decorated bedroom, casting a golden glow across the space—a beacon of my newfound sense of purpose. Its warmth softened the room's dreary atmosphere, lifting the mood of the musty floral wallpaper and the faded, threadbare carpet that had seen better days.

I scanned the room, searching for the best place to sit. None of the furniture was mine—the aged, ornate, antique iron bed, the rickety bedside table with peeling paint, the wingback chair with dog-eared fabric, worn like a well-loved teddy bear.

I gathered my yellow pad of paper and a pencil, then settled on the floor at the foot of the bed. I propped a pillow against the footboard's railings and leaned back, stretching my legs out in front of me. It wasn't the most comfortable spot, but after some shifting and adjusting, I found a position I could tolerate.

Meditation wasn't a regular practice of mine, but I did have some experience with it. As a massage therapist, I had trained myself to enter a calm, meditative state quickly while working with clients. And as a long-distance runner for over a decade, I had often slipped into the altered state known as the runner's high.

I closed my eyes and slowly deepened my breath, imagining my body releasing tension with every exhale. Breathing in calm. Breathing out stress. I visualized a cocoon of peaceful energy enveloping me as I sank deeper into relaxation.

After a few minutes, I called out to the spirit of the murdered woman, inviting her to communicate with me. I asked her to send me details that could help capture the men who had killed her.

As a novice, I assumed it would take at least half an hour of meditation before I could reach the mindful state needed to connect with the dead. So when her message came within minutes of closing my eyes, I was stunned.

Two pieces of information fluttered into my consciousness. My first thoughts were, *This must be my imagination—it's happening too easily.* And then, *There's no way I could communicate with a spirit from the Other Side this quickly.*

Despite my doubts, I opened my eyes and quickly jotted down the details. The first was a woman's name. I got the distinct impression that it was a nickname she went by. The second clue was the word *Cloverleaf.* Through subtle impressions, I was led to believe it was the name of a street in the Seattle, Washington, area—nearly three hundred miles north of where I lived.

My logical, rational mind waved red flags as if it had just spotted danger, then took center stage.

You don't seriously think you just communicated with a dead woman, do you? it sniped. *You're dumber than I thought. You know you just made it up, right? Five minutes of breathing and pretending to meditate, and now you think you can talk to the dead? Come on! You're just desperate to find meaning in your pathetic existence.*

Its words were harsh, but they struck with a persuasive sting.

I knew intuition often came in subtle tones, but this celestial development was on a whole new level. Did I really communicate with the dead woman's spirit, or was I finally falling off the cliff into mental instability? I sorely wanted to believe in the former. I offered my analytical critic a compromise.

What if I sat here for thirty minutes and tried again?

Suit yourself, it said with a cavalier attitude.

I shifted my weight, settled in, and closed my eyes, hoping to re-create the same state I had before. The soft sound of my breath flowing slowly in and out of my nose was the only sound I heard amid the silence that permeated the room. My thoughts drifted aimlessly like dust motes suspended in a shaft of light. Time grew abstract as I surrendered to the stillness.

When I felt I had sat long enough, I sent out a quiet request for more information—and waited. Nothing came. My inner critic loomed in the background, its dismissive stance unspoken but palpable. I let out a deep sigh, which mirrored my disappointment. Frustrated, I opened my eyes and checked the time.

Fifteen minutes?! I groaned. I was certain more time had passed.

I looked down at the scribbled notes on my pad. The urge to rip the page out, crumple it into a ball, and chuck it into the trash can across the room was strong. That critical part of me insisted I was chasing a pipe dream.

Instead, I carefully tore the section of writing from the rest of the page, folded it into a small rectangle, and stuffed it into my pocket.

The rest of the day and night, my mind circled back to my surreal encounter, replaying it over and over.

Let's say I did communicate with the murder victim, I mused. *How in the world was I supposed to verify whether she had a nickname?*

Even if I could track down a family member or a detective on the case, what were the chances anyone would give me the time of day? Who in their right mind would entertain a call from a complete stranger claiming to have spoken to the victim's spirit?

As for the name of the street, the year was 1994—long before Google's vast empire of knowledge was at anyone's fingertips—and years before I would even own a computer. Without an easy way to look it up, the mystery remained just that.

But no matter how much I mulled it over, I kept circling back to the $64,000 question: Had I really communicated with the dead woman's spirit, or was I simply so desperate that I had conjured up the entire experience in my mind?

As I headed into work the next morning, I still had no answers, just an endless loop of doubt playing in my mind.

My first job of the day was as a locker room attendant at a ritzy athletic club—a social hub for the town's well-to-do men and women. Polished cherrywood lockers lined the walls like silent witnesses as businessmen, lawyers, and doctors, draped in towels, lounged in comfortable armchairs. They read newspapers, discussed deals, and prepared for the day ahead, their conversations drifting through the air like murmured negotiations in an exclusive club.

My responsibilities as a locker room attendant were simple and monotonous: keep the sprawling locker room tidy and wash, fold, and stock the complimentary towels available for members. You'd be surprised how many grown men toss their used, sometimes disgustingly soiled, towels onto the floor for someone else to pick up—despite there being hampers strategically placed for their convenience. Or how one person could go through an absurd number of towels in a single visit. Cleaning up and restocking was a thankless, never-ending cycle, repeating itself throughout the club's open hours.

It was also a common sight to find the weathered innards of local newspapers strewn across the floor as if a generation of mothers had collectively gone on strike when raising their kids.

My inner critic thrived as I went about my daily duties. It whispered relentlessly that I had wasted my life, that this was proof of my failure, that I would never rise above this. Every discarded towel became evidence, every crumpled newspaper a reminder of my shortcomings.

The day after my ghostly encounter with the Other Side was no different. I walked into the locker room that morning to find towels and newspapers scattered everywhere. I gathered the myriad towels from the floor, tossing them into my wheeled cart before turning my attention to the loose pages littered across the room. I moved from pile to pile, item to item, bending down over and over to pick up the scattered mess.

With a rumpled bundle of papers in hand, I walked over to an end table and began tidying the stack so other members could read the papers. As I stuffed the pages back together, my eyes inadvertently landed on the paper at the top, drawn front and center to a boxed section with a few lines of copy—an article about the convenience store murder, headlined by a brief recap of the case.

Something compelled me to read it.

As I scanned the text in the box, the world around me disappeared. My breath caught. My body froze. One sentence leaped off the page, sending a shock wave through my body.

I gaped in disbelief. There, in black and white—next to the name of the murdered woman I had tried to contact—was a detail that made my heart pound. It stated that for most of her life, she had gone by a nickname.

The very name that had popped into my head the day before.

I reached into my pocket, my hands trembling with excitement. Carefully, I unfolded the piece of paper where I had scribbled the messages I'd received, hoping my mind wasn't playing tricks on me.

It was the same name.

I shook my head, awestruck by the synchronicity. What was going on? My logical mind scrambled for an explanation, but its reasoning clashed against an undeniable truth—I had no way of knowing her nickname.

Yet, there it was.

I had stopped believing in coincidences long before, after countless incidents of serendipity throughout my life. Still, part of me doubted my experience was real.

What were the odds?

My logical mind stuttered, grasping for a retort—but nothing it said could win the argument that this was nothing more than a meaningless coincidence.

In that moment, I made a decision. I was going to take the information I had received in my meditation seriously. The next step? A trip to the library.

The town's public library was within walking distance of the club. As soon as my shift ended, I would head straight there to see if they had a Seattle White Pages.

The moment I was free, I bolted out the door.

Too excited to walk, I ran the entire way, my pulse pounding with anticipation until I reached the one-story building. I stood bent over by the front doors, hands on my thighs, pausing to catch my breath, whispering a prayer that the library would have what I needed.

As I entered, the silent, reverent ambiance of the library filled my senses. I quickly scanned the area and spotted a middle-aged woman pushing a cart stacked with books. She was heading toward a series of aisles formed by tall industrial bookshelves filled with published works. I quietly but nimbly made my way to intercept her.

"Hi," I whispered, trying really hard not to yell out of excitement. "Do you have a copy of the Seattle White Pages?" I asked.

She nodded and pointed to an area on the other side of the library.

"The White and Yellow Pages are in that section past the sitting area," she said in a pleasant, professional-sounding voice. I turned my head to see where she was pointing and thanked her.

I strode quietly to a section of the library where several wooden tables and stiff-backed chairs waited for patrons to settle in with their reading material. Immediately beyond them stood rows of medium-height bookshelves, strategically placed to mark the end of the open space.

Impressive rows of large paperback copies of the White Pages and Yellow Pages for every major city in the United States filled the shelves, neatly arranged in alphabetical order. My eyes skimmed the spines until I found the one for Seattle.

I pulled the large, thick paperback from the shelf, made my way to one of the nearby tables, and plopped myself down into a chair.

I scanned the first page and frowned. The listings inside were organized alphabetically by resident name in bold print—not by address as I had hoped. If an address was included, and that was a big if, it was printed in a smaller, plain font, frustratingly difficult to read. With several hundred thousand residents in the area, the book had over one thousand pages, with each page having approximately four hundred listings crammed into four columns.

Squinting, I ran my finger slowly down each column, forcing my mind to register every line, afraid I might miss the one I was looking for. It was a tedious, arduous process.

I started with the first few pages, scanning methodically, but boredom and impatience quickly set in. Abandoning my original approach, I began flipping through at random, stopping on pages at whim, again running my finger over every listing. It took me less than ten minutes to realize how futile my search was. Looking for the name of a street felt like I was literally searching for a needle in a haystack.

Exasperated, I slapped the book shut. *There's no way this is going to work!* I stewed in frustration for a couple of minutes, then pushed my chair back, preparing to leave.

But before I could stand, I heard the voice.

This was a quiet, subtle whisper in my mind—one I would come to recognize over the years as counsel I should take seriously.

Try again, it said, in the faintest inkling of a thought. Its pleasant, matter-of-fact tone made me pause. I waited for it to say more, but it didn't.

Try again. That was all it said, yet the implication was clear—if I did, something good would come of it.

Based on experience, I had learned that this voice offered sage advice, the kind I should listen to. But my strong-willed, analytical mind wasn't about to give up control without a fight.

It let out a long litany of verbal diarrhea.

Are you seriously going to listen to that nonsense? Look at what it's asking you to do. Go through the entire book? All one thousand-plus pages? Do you even realize how long that would take? How tedious it's going to be—just to find the name of a street?

And let's not forget Murphy's Law, it added smugly. *If that street exists—and that's a big "if"—it'll probably be on the very last line you check. You barely made it through seven pages without wanting to tear your hair out. Do you really want to put yourself through that?*

My analytical mind continued its tirade as if I had committed a crime.

Come on. Be reasonable. It's a ridiculous idea. Go home and forget about it. Getting the name of a street while meditating yesterday? Total fluke. Even if you found the street in the White Pages, what exactly would you do with it?

Its argument seemed sound. But on the other hand, how could I doubt that I'd communicated with the spirit of the murdered woman after finding the article in the paper the way I did? If the message about her nickname was accurate, why wouldn't the name of the street also be a valid clue?

As I pondered what to do, I remembered a neat trick a friend had shared with me years ago over drinks. She'd said, "If you're ever struggling to figure something out in your life and need an answer, ask the Universe by opening a book."

"Ask the Universe by opening a book?" I repeated, unsure of how that would work.

"Take a book, preferably a self-help book, open it to a randomly selected page, place your finger somewhere on the page, and read whatever your finger is pointing to. You might be surprised by how relevant the words are regarding your question."

I tried it a number of times with interesting, even eye-opening results that led to an insight or bona fide answer to my question. But more often than not, what I read was completely irrelevant, making the practice feel like a silly waste of time. It was a bit of a crapshoot.

As I sat there, a thought crossed my mind. *Why not try this technique with the White Pages?* It was a compromise, satisfying both my analytical mind and my intuition. But more than that, it felt like a challenge, almost a dare aimed at Spirit that said, *Prove to me this is real.*

It was a crazy idea, but it grabbed me like a zealous scientist on the verge of a breakthrough. I grasped the edges of my seat, scooted forward, and pulled the White Pages closer. My plan was simple: Close my eyes, open the book to a randomly selected page, and then arbitrarily place my finger on one of the two pages in front of me.

My immediate challenge was tempering my excitement enough

to enter a meditative state. I took my eagerness by the reins like a cowboy driving a horse wagon. Instead of pulling leather straps, I reeled it in with a few slow, deep breaths, focused on calming my energy.

As my mind relaxed, an idea popped up. A hypnosis technique I'd learned from a movie.

It was from a scene in the 1991 film *Dead Again*, starring Kenneth Branagh and Emma Thompson. I remembered Kenneth Branagh's character hypnotizing Emma Thompson's character so she could recall a past life. He instructed her to imagine herself walking slowly down a flight of ten steps, each one drawing her deeper into a trance. His voice guided her through the process, step-by-step, leading her into an altered state.

What do I have to lose? I thought. *Let's give it a shot.*

I positioned the White Pages in front of me and rested my hands on my lap. Sitting up straight, I pressed my back into the chair, took a few slow, deep breaths, and visualized myself slowly and deliberately descending a staircase—ten steps down, deeper into relaxation with each one. I repeated the process several times, maintaining my slow, rhythmic breathing until I sensed I was ready.

Keeping my eyes closed, I reached for the White Pages on the table. I positioned my hands, peeled the book open, pressed it flat against the tabletop, and placed the tip of my index finger on a randomly selected section of the right-hand page.

I opened my eyes and leaned in close. Lifting my finger, I squinted at the tiny print.

I froze.

How is this possible? I gasped, my mind struggling to process the implications.

Listed where my finger had been was the address: 404 Cloverleaf Drive. No name, just the street address.

A surge of excitement exploded through me—like a die-hard

sports fan whose underdog team had just pulled off a miraculous, last-second victory. Every fiber of my body wanted to jump, yell, and throw my fists in the air. I whispered, "Oh my God," again and again as I shoved my chair back, shot to my feet, and clutched the top of my head with both hands. I paced back and forth, my pulse hammering.

"Oh my God, oh my God, oh my God!"

Then, without warning, fear gripped me. The odds of blindly landing on the one street name I was searching for—in a book filled with hundreds of thousands of addresses—were astronomically small. One in a gazillion, probably. Doubt crept in, its whisper planting a paralyzing seed in my mind.

What if you read it wrong? The print is tiny. Maybe you made a mistake.

I held my breath. I sat back down, pulled the book toward me, and leaned in, heart pounding. Eyes scanning. Fingers trembling. I double-checked the name.

And then I exhaled. A deep, shaky sigh of relief.

I was right. It did say 404 Cloverleaf.

For a moment, time stopped. I wasn't just holding a phone book—I was holding a bridge between worlds, a thin sliver of proof that something far bigger than me was at play. It didn't just feel uncanny; it felt otherworldly.

I had no idea what finding the address meant—or what to do next—but one thing was clear: I was onto something. The idea that I should call the police or try to reach the detectives on the case resurfaced.

And what exactly are you going to say to them? my inner pragmatist quipped. *Something like, "I spoke to the dead woman's spirit, and she gave me this address when I asked her for information that would lead to her murderers"?* The thought made me pause. I felt sheepish, realizing how strange—maybe even suspicious—that might sound to law enforcement. I conceded it wasn't a good idea.

For the next couple of days, I mulled over the string of events that had culminated at the library with finding the address on Cloverleaf. What, if anything, should I do next?

The homicide committed by the four men—who were still on the loose—was horrifying. To say I was concerned about what might happen if I crossed paths with one of them was an understatement. Terrified was more like it. But I was desperate to find a sense of purpose, and this felt like an opportunity that had fallen into my lap. Maybe even a chance to be a hero. How good that would feel!

The mystery surrounding the serendipitous clues scribbled on that small piece of paper was too compelling to ignore, so I made a decision. Everything seemed to be pointing in the same direction: I would drive to Seattle and knock on the door of 404 Cloverleaf.

Immediately, my mind went into planning mode. These were the days before GPS, so my first stop was a bookstore. I picked up three maps—one for Oregon, one for Washington, and one for the city of Seattle. I needed to be strategic and plot my route by hand.

Since there was a chance the address belonged to one of the killers, I figured it would be a good idea to pick out a disguise—something to protect my identity and create a ruse that hid the real reason I was knocking on their door. I brainstormed several possibilities. Pizza delivery guy? Pest control company rep? Insurance salesman? Grassroots campaign volunteer? I even considered Seventh-day Adventist.

I ran through various scenarios in my mind, rehearsing what I would say for each disguise and playing out different outcomes—including what I would do if things went south. I debated what wardrobe to wear and how to get my hands on whatever uniform I decided on. There was a serious element of danger in my plan, and as I thought it through, other questions surfaced. *Should I take a weapon? Do I buy a gun? Or do I take my ten-inch chef's knife with me?*

In the midst of all my planning, I had a significant realization.

It happened while I was sitting in the foyer of the club where I worked. It was lunchtime, and as I often did, I ordered my meal from the juice bar situated at one end of the room, then waited in a seating area by the reception desk.

To call the foyer a room was a misnomer that didn't do it justice. The club was housed in a historic downtown building, and the owners had spared no expense in creating a space of unparalleled beauty. The foyer was grand.

Ornate textured tiles, reminiscent of a golden age, graced the eighteen-foot ceilings. Rich cherrywood paneling lined the walls from floor to ceiling, while Italian leather couches, stately chairs, and richly stained wooden tables were arranged in tasteful clusters, defining the spacious layout. Designer décor, expertly placed, added the final touches to an atmosphere of refined aesthetics. Floor-to-ceiling windows on two sides completed the scene, offering panoramic views of the downtown bustle unfolding just beyond the glass.

The foyer was the main artery for members and the public to enter and exit the building. A large receptionist station—equally regal with cherrywood and granite—was strategically placed to monitor the club's comings and goings.

From my chair, I passed the time alternating between watching everything unfold—inside and outside the foyer—and masterminding my plan to scope out my lead on the convenience store homicide.

That's when it hit me. There was one very important detail I had completely overlooked.

My inner critic rolled its eyes, berating me for my lack of foresight. *How are we supposed to ID the killers if you don't know what they look like, you dummy?*

I didn't like being called a dummy, but I had to admit—it had a good point. How did I not factor that into my plans? I wondered how I was going to find out what the suspects looked like.

A minute later, as if on cue, a young man entered the foyer from the street, carrying a bundle of large, rolled-up sheets of paper. He strode up to the receptionist, his posture exuding purpose—like he was on an important mission. Something about his energy and the way this young man approached the receptionist piqued my interest.

I eagle-eyed him until he reached the counter, then cocked my head slightly, leaning in just enough to listen in on their conversation without making it obvious I was eavesdropping.

He explained to the receptionist that he was going around town putting up WANTED posters of the convenience store killers and was wondering if several could be posted somewhere in the club. The receptionist told him she would talk to management, but in the meantime, she would take them. He handed them to her, then did an about-face and marched out with the same determination he had when he arrived.

I couldn't believe my ears. I jumped out of my seat and hurried over to the receptionist, telling myself to temper my excitement—to avoid running.

"Did I hear that young man ask you if the club could post some Wanted posters concerning the convenience store homicide?" I asked, trying not to sound too conspicuous.

"Yup," the young woman replied, nodding in affirmation.

I asked her if I could have one of the posters, and she obliged. Unrolling it in front of me, I stared down at the images. Four mug shot sketches, one of each killer, glared back at me. Chills ran up and down my spine like lightning, leaving a trail of goose bumps on my skin. The synchronicity just kept happening. Things were starting to feel eerily strange, as if I were playing a role in a real-life supernatural mystery—one with a plot that kept thickening and unfolding right before my eyes.

Armed with the mug shots and everything else I thought I'd

need, I decided it was time to set a date for my trip. It was Thursday, and since I had the weekend off, Sunday seemed like the right day to venture north. I decided I would leave that morning, giving myself two and a half days to finalize everything before my trip.

The hours leading up to my trip were filled with a sense of purpose and excitement. But as Sunday crept closer, so did the unease.

I felt nervous. Worried.

The men involved in the robbery I was investigating weren't just reckless teenagers. They were cold-blooded killers—men who had committed heinous, unthinkable acts of violence. The closer Sunday approached, the more acutely aware I became of the danger in my choices. What was I getting myself into?

I revisited the idea of going to law enforcement. The thought of being dismissed—or worse, seen as suspicious—gnawed at me. What if they thought I was involved? What if, instead of helping, I became a suspect? I couldn't shake the fear that instead of solving a mystery, I'd become part of one.

Once again, I talked myself out of the idea and carried on with my plans.

Saturday came quickly. I was glad my wait was almost over. That morning, I joined a friend for a private gymnastics lesson. I had never taken a gymnastics class before, let alone a private lesson, but I've always loved watching gymnastics on TV. The idea of running and flying through the air and landing on something soft was exciting, so I took him up on his offer.

By the afternoon, my bags were packed, my car was loaded, and I had nothing left to do but bide my time. The wait was grueling. My nerves had nowhere to go, and the idle hours stretched before me, thick with anticipation.

I decided to watch a movie, hoping for a distraction from the anxious thoughts racing through my mind. I drove down to the local Blockbuster Video and wandered the aisles, scanning the shelves for anything that might capture my interest. My fingers skimmed over the plastic VHS cases until they landed on a noir psychological thriller titled *Black Rainbow*, starring Rosanna Arquette. Dark crime movies were never my thing, but something about the cover inexplicably pulled me in.

I flipped the box over and read the synopsis on the back. A strange shiver ran down my arms. The movie featured a psychic medium as the main character.

This can't be a coincidence, I thought. It was as if something— fate or maybe Spirit—had led me straight to this film. My pulse quickened. I hesitated for a beat, absorbing the eyebrow-raising synchronicity, then clutched the case tighter and made my way to the register.

I paid for the rental and headed home, my thoughts buzzing.

Black Rainbow is about a psychic medium, played by Rosanna Arquette, who travels from town to town, offering readings to group audiences from a stage. During one of these public events, she interacts with a woman in the audience. Rosanna's character reveals shocking details about the murder of the woman's husband—a man targeted by a hired gun for exposing corruption at a local company. The woman is stunned and confused because her husband is still alive. In the course of the story, it becomes clear that the reading she's giving isn't about the past—it's a premonition of the near future.

Her public reveal of the intimate specifics of the crime also lands on the ears of the killer himself, who, unbeknownst to her, is in the audience. She now inadvertently becomes his target in a deadly game of cat and mouse

Toward the end of the movie, the psychic medium uses her abilities to locate the killer's whereabouts. She notifies the police that he's hiding out at a local motel. In the very next scene, several law enforcement officers and a couple of detectives race into the front entrance, ready to capture him. They don't know what room number he's in, so as they barge into the lobby, one of the detectives yells out to the motel clerk, "Which room is Gary Wallace staying in?"

The clerk yells back, "He's in room 404!"

My heart almost leaped out of my chest as it thumped hard against my sternum. 404! The same house number I had found in the White Pages days earlier.

The sheer improbability of it sent a cold rush through my body. I shook my head as I struggled to grasp the meaning and significance of this timely scenario in the movie.

The unsettling feelings I had about pursuing the men, the creeping doubts that had taken root in my mind, swelled to an unnerving crescendo as I watched the plot unfold. The peril the psychic medium faced in the movie strangely mirrored the sense of looming danger I felt about tracking down the four men in real life.

I felt as if the Universe itself was warning me.

But if that is true, I asked myself, *why lead me with a breadcrumb trail deeper into the mystery that felt like destiny?*

The climactic convergence of this last scene in the movie instilled more awe in me, but it also fueled my uneasiness and growing doubt. Maybe the synchronicity I was experiencing wasn't meant to be interpreted as a confirmation to continue with my plans to knock on the door at 404 Cloverleaf.

Was I getting it all wrong? I couldn't come up with a definitive answer.

But that wasn't my only concern. There was another element fueling my distress. I couldn't put my finger on it, but something in the air around me felt sinister.

Was I becoming needlessly paranoid? I couldn't tell if it was just my imagination, but it made me wonder.

Was there an evil spirit that influenced the men to do what they did? And now that I'm on its trail, is that same spirit, like the hitman in the movie, plotting against me with the intention of harming me? Am I walking into a trap?

I couldn't shake the gut feeling that something bad was going to happen on this trip—something that would bring me pain. I tried to make sense of it, but no insights came. Though I had no idea what I might need them for, I felt compelled to throw a couple of therapeutic ice packs into the car before going to bed.

In addition to my uneasiness about the potential dangers of my trip, the movie heightened another strange and mystifying feeling. I struggled to find the right words because the sensation was difficult to grasp. The only way I can explain it is to say that I felt like I was becoming transparent—that my physical body was becoming less like matter and more like mist, slowly fading away between dimensions. The experience was deeply unsettling.

Until that point, I hadn't told anyone about the strange synchronicities, intuitive nudges, and inexplicable occurrences that had been unfolding around me—or my plans to follow the leads I received about the homicide. But that night, out of a growing sense of alarm, I decided to call my good friend Amanda, the woman I write about in "The DNA of Destiny." She was a mystic and healer, and I wanted to see what she thought. At the very least, I wanted someone to know what I was doing and where I was going in case I got killed.

Amanda had no insight into the strange sensation coursing through me, but the apprehension in her voice was unmistakable the moment I shared my plans.

"Are you sure you want to do this?" she asked. "I don't think it's a good idea." Her worry threaded into every word. Despite my deep respect for her instincts and the misgivings already circling in me, my resolve was unshakable. I needed purpose in my life, something to distract me from my problems, and this journey had announced itself loudly, unmistakably, and repeatedly. The divine timing, bordering on bizarre, that inspired me to drive up to Seattle was impossible to dismiss. Uneasy or not, I was going.

At 6:00 a.m. the next morning, I woke feeling like I'd been run over by a Mack Truck. The gymnastics adventure the day before had been a blast, but that morning, my body was paying a hefty price. Every slight movement elicited groans from muscles I'd forgotten existed, serving as a harsh reminder that I wasn't exactly a spring chicken anymore. I slowly stretched beneath the covers, grimacing as each stiff limb protested. Eventually, I floundered out of bed and eased into a long, hot shower. The soothing warmth provided temporary relief, but the lingering tightness made it clear that soreness wasn't leaving anytime soon. I made sure to bring extra water for the trip to help flush out all the extra lactic acid in my system.

By 6:45 a.m. on June 4, 1994, I was on the road, rolling out of Eugene in my tiny two-door 1986 Honda CRX hatchback, heading north toward Seattle. If you've ever driven from Oregon to Seattle, you know how lackluster most of that trip can be. The highway is wide, straight as an arrow, and offers little in terms of scenery or variety. Mile after mile stretched out in monotonous repetition.

Just north of Olympia, Washington, about three and a half hours into my drive, and with seventy-five minutes left to go, exhaustion suddenly hit me hard. My eyelids grew heavy, and my body felt drained. I struggled to stay alert as the dull landscape slipped past.

Why am I feeling so wiped out? I knew the gymnastics had something to do with it, but this fatigue felt unnatural at 10:30 in the morning.

I tried everything to shake it off. I rolled down the windows and stuck my hand outside, funneling cool air into my face and breathing deeply. I cranked up the music and sang loudly, then danced wildly in my seat, yelling like I was at a rave.

When that didn't work, I stretched, rubbed my arms and the back of my neck, lifted my hips to massage my butt muscles, drank water, munched on snacks, and twisted in my seat—desperate for anything to help me snap out of it.

My attempts to wake up helped a little, but none of them invigorated me for very long. Waves of lethargy only came back stronger, threatening to overpower my will to stay awake. My eyelids would slowly shut as if they had a mind of their own. Half a second would go by, and then I would suddenly jolt in a horrible panic at how close I came to falling asleep.

The temptation to close my eyes was overwhelmingly powerful. It felt surreal, as if there was something behind my drowsiness using a sweet, calming voice, encouraging me to give in, lulling me gently toward sleep.

Just let them rest for a moment, it cooed. *It's okay to let go. Doesn't it feel wonderful to close your eyes? You'll be okay, just rest.*

When I look back to that moment, I think about the old tales in Greek mythology about the sirens of the sea. Sirens were dangerous creatures, similar to mermaids, who had the ability to sing with voices so lovely that no one could resist them. Sailors would hear their call and be seduced into abandoning their ships by jumping into the sea, thinking they were jumping into the arms of a voluptuous beauty when, in fact, they were jumping to their deaths. As I drove down the highway, it felt like I was dealing with my own siren—a siren of the road.

Feeling deeply unsettled by my drowsiness, I decided to stop at the nearest gas station to rest and search my map for a more scenic alternative route—something less monotonous than I-5, which seemed determined to lull me into an accident.

Soon, a highway sign appeared on my right, marked clearly with a gas-pump symbol, announcing a station just two miles ahead. Relieved, I pulled off the freeway minutes later and parked in front of the convenience store. After grabbing a sandwich and a fresh bottle of water, I settled onto a picnic table bench overlooking a small grassy field, grateful for a chance to clear my head. Spreading my map across the weathered wooden table, I traced my finger northward until I spotted a smaller highway branching off not far ahead. It promised a more engaging route—one that would, hopefully, keep me alert and safe for the rest of the journey.

Once I finished my food, I cleared the table and lay on it for a quick catnap. I didn't manage to fall asleep, but after twenty minutes of quiet rest, I felt noticeably more refreshed than when I had first pulled in.

The fascinating thing about falling asleep at the wheel is that you don't know you've done it until you wake back up—that is, if you live to tell about it. Ten minutes up I-5 and another ten minutes on a quiet, winding two-lane highway, and it happened. Fatigue won. I closed my eyes for just a moment and dozed off.

Without my guidance, my car sped forward between 55 to 60 mph, traveling another quarter mile as if an invisible force had taken the wheel. Whether by luck or providence, no other vehicles were on the road as my car drifted across the double yellow line into the other lane. I would later learn that if I had gone just another quarter mile, I would have reached a major intersection—one where the likelihood of colliding with another vehicle skyrocketed. The damage could have been far worse. I could have hurt or killed someone.

After crossing into the other lane, my vehicle veered off the road and into the only gravel turnout for miles. The sudden crunch of my wheels over loose pebbles startled me awake.

It took me a moment to realize what was happening. My car was hurtling straight toward a massive wooden telephone pole. Time suddenly warped, stretching into slow motion. In that fleeting window, I took stock of my situation. In nanoseconds, I scanned my surroundings, evaluated my circumstances, and weighed my options. Stopping wasn't possible. The pole was too close, and I was going far too fast. To my left loomed a dense forest. To my right, the highway.

You're going to get into serious trouble if you turn left, my thoughts interjected. I imagined slamming into a tree, my car jackknifing into a spin, flipping several times before finally landing upside down—leaving behind nothing but a pile of broken bones.

Definitely not turning left, I thought.

I glanced to my right, searching for any sign of other cars. Getting back onto the highway was my best option, but it was a huge gamble. Trees bordering the road beyond the telephone pole blocked my view, making it impossible to tell if there was oncoming traffic. And there was no time to check my mirrors to see what was happening behind me. Once I committed to turning right, the slow-motion haze vanished, and I was thrust back into the rush of the moment.

I held my breath and turned the steering wheel to the right. The front wheels of my car spun furiously, digging into the gravel and launching a spray of stones as they searched for solid ground. I froze in panic as I felt the rear end fishtail, spinning the rear of the car to my left. My white-knuckle grip on the steering wheel grew clammy, and I instinctively squeezed harder. My eyes widened in horror—my plan wasn't working. My car was still on a collision course with the pole.

The roar of my two-thousand-pound car bulldozing through gravel filled my ears as the swerve's gravitational force pushed my head and left shoulder into the door. My upper body slouched into my seat, sliding downward as if gravity itself were pulling me through the floor. A sense of doom gripped my chest, squeezing the air from my lungs. The sheer dread of what was about to happen paralyzed me.

One moment, I was barreling toward the pole. The next, everything went blank.

I could have easily died that day. At the very least, I could have been paralyzed from the neck down, dictating this story into a recorder for someone else to transcribe instead of sitting in front of my computer typing it out myself. What saved my life was that I lost consciousness just before my car careened into the pole.

Statistics show that drunk drivers often survive their crashes with fewer serious injuries than their sober counterparts. The reason? Intoxicated drivers remain loose and don't brace for impact. Serious injuries occur when a person sees an accident coming and instinctively tenses up in anticipation. When the body fights against the momentum of the crash, the concentrated force increases the likelihood of catastrophic injury.

When my car crashed into the pole, my body was limp. My mind wasn't there to freak out. My body flopped around, held in place by the straps of my seat belt. The fact that my body was relaxed allowed it to evade some of the force of the impact rather than bracing for it and breaking.

That's not to say I escaped without harm. Because my car didn't have airbags, my chest slammed into the steering wheel, and my head and shoulder struck the driver's side door, leaving me with major soft tissue damage and a bruised lung.

What struck me as weird was that I didn't realize I had lost consciousness before the impact until the next day, when I was replaying the accident in my mind. It was a surreal, *Twilight Zone* moment.

After I passed out, my car broadsided the pole, smashing into the driver's side. The momentum launched the car off the ground, rolling it up and into the pole, crushing the roof to within inches of my seat's headrest. The car then slammed back down with a jolt so forceful that it bounced on its wheels, shaking violently before finally coming to a standstill.

I regained consciousness sometime after the car had come to a complete stop. How much time had passed, I didn't know. Disoriented, I slowly looked around to assess my situation. Blood was splattered on my dashboard, but I couldn't tell where it came from. I was badly hurt, but because of the adrenaline surging through my body, I was feeling only a benign amount of discomfort.

Instructions from CPR training over the years echoed in my

mind. Never move an accident victim unless absolutely necessary. Even small movements can cause paralysis.

I had no sense of time as I sat still, trapped in a daze of shock. I scanned my body with my mind. I couldn't feel my legs, and that terrified me. Did that mean I was paralyzed? I prayed it wasn't the case.

A low, electrical buzzing sound caught my attention. I listened closely, trying to figure out what it was. The noise was coming from the dashboard—or so I thought. I stared at the console, racking my brain, dumbfounded as to what could be making the racket. Then it dawned on me. It wasn't coming from the dashboard—it was coming from under the hood.

I held my breath and listened carefully. The engine wasn't running, but something electrical was. *Could it cause a fire?* I wondered.

My imagination ran wild, playing out the worst possible scenario in explicit detail. I envisioned a spark igniting a flame, the fire quickly growing as it fed on flammable liquids under the hood until it engulfed the entire front end of the car. I saw myself screaming, watching in horror as the flames crept closer, trapping me inside. I was helpless to do anything. My heart pounded as visions of the fire reaching the gas tank filled my mind.

I didn't know what was causing the noise or how real the threat of fire was, but the possibility terrified me. I was caught in a harrowing dilemma—reach for the key in the ignition and risk permanent spinal damage, or sit there and risk burning alive, praying someone would find me in time to save me.

I didn't like the odds. Sitting still, waiting for help, wasn't an option. I wanted to be proactive. I needed to know what my body was capable of, whether I could move or not in the event I had to.

First, I lifted my hands in front of me, one at a time. Relief washed over me—my arms worked. Carefully, I leaned my upper torso forward a few inches, keeping my head still, then settled back into my seat. No pain. No twinges. No indication of life-threatening injury.

But my fear of fire escalated with every passing second. I decided to take the risk. I stretched my right arm toward the key in the ignition, groaning with the effort. Pain flared through my body, making me hesitate. The fear of paralysis loomed in my mind, forcing me to move cautiously.

My hand was still six inches away when I realized I couldn't reach any farther. I had miscalculated how much force it would take. Deflated, I slumped back into my seat, debating my next move.

I was torn. I hated that my attempt to turn the engine off might cause paralysis, but my fear fueled an irrefutable sense of urgency about my predicament. I decided to try again. I pushed my concerns aside and strained forward with renewed vigor. This time, my outstretched fingers grasped the key. I quickly turned it counterclockwise. Relieved that I had mitigated a serious threat, I fell back into my seat and lost consciousness.

I awoke to the soothing sound of a young man's voice. He was a local EMT on his day off who had spotted my wrecked vehicle while driving by. He quickly turned around, pulled into the turnout, and ran to my car to check if I was hurt.

When I didn't respond to his questions and appeared unconscious, he called 911. Unable to open my door, he crawled into the back seat from the passenger's side and assessed my condition, speaking to me calmly until I came to. He introduced himself, urging me not to move. Then, in a steady voice, he asked, "Are you feeling any pain?"

Before I could answer, I blacked out. While I was unconscious, a crew of firemen and paramedics arrived on the scene. They quickly conferred with the EMT who had found me, checked my vitals, and secured a neck collar around my neck to minimize the risk of spinal damage as they prepared to remove me from the vehicle.

In an ideal situation, they would have taken their time, carefully extracting me from the wreckage with extreme caution. But my motionless body, slumped in the seat with deteriorating vitals, forced them to act quickly. They knew they were working within the "golden hour."

The term *golden hour* stems from World War I data collected by the French military, which showed that the survival rates of trauma victims dropped dramatically if they didn't receive critical care within the first hour.

Given that I was drifting in and out of consciousness, bleeding from what appeared to be a head trauma, and had been driving a car without airbags, the rescue team knew they had to get me to the hospital as quickly as possible.

That was easier said than done. The driver's side had taken the brunt of the impact when I collided with the pole. The mangled metal of the door clung stubbornly to the crumpled frame, refusing to budge no matter how hard the firemen pulled. After multiple failed attempts, the captain barked an order for his men to grab the generator and "Jaws of Life" from the fire engine.

The Jaws of Life is a massive, high-powered set of hydraulic pliers used by fire departments to free people trapped in wreckage. Once everything was in place, they fired up the generator, its growl breaking the tense silence. One of the firemen took control of the tool, positioning it against the door while the others stood back, watching and waiting. With a mechanical roar, the powerful jaws clamped onto the twisted metal, prying the door away from the frame inch by inch.

The steel groaned and buckled under the relentless force, but it refused to give. He tried several times, and on his last attempt, the driver's side window shattered from the pressure, sending a spray of glass fragments into his face. I was later told that because he hadn't worn protective eyewear, a shard of glass injured one of his eyes.

Concerned about my condition and the time slipping away, the captain called for Plan B. They would have to pull me out through the passenger side. It was far from ideal—more difficult and far riskier—but they had no other choice.

My rescuers squeezed into my tiny car, made even smaller by the collapsed roof. The cramped space forced them into awkward, uncomfortable positions as they prepared to extract me. There was no room for gentle maneuvering. With a sharp count, they lifted me from my seat and heaved me onto an unforgiving spine board stretcher. The strain of their efforts was evident in their labored breaths and terse voices as they shouted instructions, coordinating each movement with precision.

Pain shoved its way into my cocoon of unconsciousness, jarring me awake. I groaned, trapped in a half-conscious stupor, as the men hauled the stretcher over the center console and out the passenger door. Before I was completely free from the wreckage, I blacked out again.

The EMTs strapped me onto the spine board, secured me to a cot, and wheeled me into the back of the ambulance. As the doors slammed shut and the siren wailed to life, we sped to the nearest hospital—fifteen minutes away.

At some point during the ride, a jolt from the ambulance hitting a rough patch on the narrow highway snapped me back to my unpleasant reality. The adrenaline that had spared me from pain was wearing off. My upper torso and ribs seized in a crushing spasm, wrapping me in an unforgiving vise. My body's natural tightening response was meant to protect me from further harm, but with every breath, the pain grew unbearable.

It was too much to endure. I passed out before we reached our destination.

I came to again as they wheeled me into the hospital. Disoriented, I furrowed my brow, trying to focus my eyes, my brain struggling to make sense of what I was seeing. It took a long moment, but then it finally dawned on me. The perforated panels overhead, punctuated by glaring lights, were the ceiling. I was being wheeled down a hallway, deeper into the bowels of the building. I couldn't move my head, but I could only assume they were taking me to the emergency room.

No one spoke a word to me as they maneuvered the gurney to a halt, the silence broken only by the metallic clank of the wheel brakes locking into place. I lay still in my groggy state, waiting, wondering what would happen next. Muted voices hummed in the background, but I couldn't make out the words.

Eventually, a young man's face appeared within my line of sight, peering down at me. He identified himself as the off-duty EMT who had been the first to find me at the accident scene. Soft-spoken and steady, he filled me in on everything that had happened—from the moment the firemen and ambulance arrived to the moment I was driven away.

"Where were you headed," he asked. "Do you have any family I can contact for you?"

I mumbled I was heading up to Seattle, thanked him for his help, and told him he could call my parents. He scribbled down their number, bade me well, and disappeared. That was the last time I ever saw him.

I later learned that when he called my parents, it was my younger sister—who happened to be visiting them at the time—who answered the phone. But instead of asking if she knew a "Keno" who had been driving to Seattle, he got my name wrong and asked if she knew a "Keith."

When my sister replied that she didn't, he promptly hung up.

My mother happened to be in the room when the call came in and asked my sister what it was about. As soon as she heard that an EMT had asked about a "Keith" driving to Seattle, she instinctively knew it was me.

With a mother's unshakable concern, she immediately started calling every hospital in Washington, desperate to confirm if it was me and to find out if I was okay. But hospital after hospital gave the same answer—there was no record of my admission.

Convinced the EMT had been calling about me, my mom's desperation escalated. She redialed the last hospital she had spoken to, her voice urgent as she pleaded for help. After explaining the situation, she begged them to check again.

The gentleman on the other end of the line paused, then offered a possibility.

"There's a military hospital in the area. If your son's injuries were severe enough, and that was the closest hospital, they could have taken him there, even though he wasn't in the military." Out of empathy, he offered to call the hospital himself to find out. She hung up and waited in anxious suspense.

Minutes later, the phone rang. The same man was on the line, his voice steady. He confirmed that I had indeed been in a car accident and had been taken to the military hospital. Then, with quiet reassurance, he added, "Your son is alive."

Meanwhile, I was in my own private hell.

After being wheeled into the hospital, I was left alone, strapped to the hard plastic spine board. The rigid surface pressed relentlessly into my body, kicking my pain into high gear.

I tried shifting my weight in small, agonizing increments, hoping to lessen the pain. Each adjustment brought fleeting moments of relief before the pressure built up again, forcing me into an endless cycle of repositioning and suffering.

Time ticked away mercilessly as I waited for someone—anyone—to help me.

What the hell is going on?! I wondered. I could hear voices murmuring in the background, but I was beginning to think I had been forgotten. It felt like they were treating me as if I had come in with a sprained ankle—not life-threatening injuries.

Was I in the middle of a zombie apocalypse? My imagination ran with the thought, plucking a scene straight from a horror movie. A dimly lit hospital, eerie silence, medical staff shuffling mindlessly down the hall—had they all been turned? Had everyone been infected, leaving me to fend for myself?

Summoning what little strength I had, I rasped into the abyss.

"Hello, hello?" I croaked. "Is anyone there? Can someone tell me what's going on?"

A disembodied voice responded, its tone indifferent. "We're waiting for an X-ray tech to take you for X-rays."

As if on cue, a gruff middle-aged police officer approached and positioned himself so I could see him. His expression was stoic, revealing his indifference to my pain as he hovered over my body.

"Were you driving under the influence of alcohol or any substances that might impair your ability?" he asked, his tone flat.

I told him I didn't drink or do drugs and that I hadn't taken anything that would have affected my driving.

"I'm waiting for your blood test results to verify that," he replied, his voice cold, hardened—as if I were already guilty of a crime.

Then, shifting gears, he grabbed his pen from his shirt pocket, flipped open his writing pad, and asked me about the accident. When I told him I had fallen asleep at the wheel, he looked up from his pad.

"Falling asleep at the wheel is against the law in the state of Washington," he stated nonchalantly.

I stared at him, disbelief mixing with frustration. *You're seriously giving me a ticket for falling asleep at the wheel? It's not like I did it on purpose!* That was the polite version of the thoughts running through my head. Instead, I asked him how much the ticket was.

"Two hundred dollars."

It felt unfair, but I chewed on the news silently. I had more pressing concerns. Satisfied he had done his job, the officer disappeared from my sight.

After what felt like forever, the X-ray tech finally arrived. I assumed getting X-rays would be a simple, painless process. I was wrong.

To get a clear picture of my chest injuries, they had to position my arms at my sides and forcibly pull them down toward my feet to bring my shoulders down—holding that position until the image was taken.

The intensity of the pain caught me off guard. A howl tore from my throat, reverberating through the small room, followed by a series of moans and groans as the agony settled in. Minutes later, the same guy who had pulled on my arms reappeared. I let out another groan as he winced apologetically.

"I'm so sorry," he said. "We have to retake the X-ray. The first one wasn't clear enough."

When they wheeled me back to wherever I had been before the X-rays, the cop was waiting.

"Your blood test came back clean," he said flatly as if he had expected a different result. Then, without so much as a nod of acknowledgment, he placed my ticket by my side and walked away.

Eventually, after what felt like an eternity, I was moved to a hospital room where they hooked me up to an IV drip and monitoring equipment. I was in stable condition, but because my vitals had flirted with the red line between life and death, the nurse checked on me every fifteen minutes. I didn't feel like I was dying, but apparently, I wasn't out of the woods yet.

Hours dragged by as I drifted between bouts of sleep, pain, and boredom. Morning faded into late afternoon, and for the first time since the accident, I realized I was hungry.

Until that moment, the thought of food had been repulsive. My body had been too focused on survival to care about eating. But now, something had shifted. I sensed that eating would help me heal, so I rang for the nurse.

Thankfully, he arrived quickly.

"It's Sunday, so the cafeteria's closed today," he said when I asked about food.

"Is there anywhere I can get something to eat?"

"There are some vending machines down the hall. I can see what they have."

"No, that's okay," I said. "I want to check what they have for myself."

He gave me a look. With a tone of authority mixed with concern, he countered, "I don't think getting up right now is a good idea. You got banged up pretty badly."

I wanted to move around—to feel my body in motion, to gauge the extent of my injuries for myself. The only way to do that was to get out of bed.

He didn't stand a chance against my Scorpio stubbornness or my persuasive reasoning. When he realized I wasn't going to take no for an answer, he sighed and helped me out of bed.

Intense pain radiated from different parts of my body, merging into one loud siren of warning. I steeled myself against it. The adage "When life gets hard, the tough get tougher" rattled through my mind.

As a competitive runner, I had learned to coexist with pain—the kind that comes from pushing my body and mind beyond what I thought I was capable of. But this was a whole new level. This wasn't the pain of endurance; this was the pain of damage. I stifled my groans as best I could, lest the nurse change his mind.

I hobbled down the hallway, stopping every few feet to rest. Every movement was harder than I'd anticipated, but at least I was free from the confines of the hospital bed.

Two lonely vending machines stood in a sterile, empty nook off the walkway, next to a cheap-looking couch that looked like it had never been sat in. I scanned their dimly lit interiors and found a dismal selection of junk food. The best I could manage was a dry salami sandwich on squishy, bleached-white bread.

I fumbled with the packaging, my fingers weak and uncoordinated. It was tougher to open than it should have been, a frustrating reminder of how little strength I had. As I wrestled with the plastic, I realized just how hungry I was. My body needed nourishment, whether I liked it or not.

The sandwich was disgusting, but I forced myself to swallow as much of it as I could.

"It's a wonder anyone gets well in a hospital," I half muttered to myself.

I found the nurse waiting for me. By the way he studied me, I could tell he was assessing my gait, trying to determine whether he had made the right choice in allowing me to walk on my own. Satisfied that I wasn't about to collapse, he helped me back into bed.

I lay there for the next hour, sorting through my options. I was miles from home with no way to get there, but one thing was certain—I needed to get out of the hospital.

As bad as the sandwich had been, it had done its job. I felt stronger. And the stronger I felt, the more convinced I became that leaving was my best bet for recovering faster. It took some effort, but I managed to persuade the hospital staff to discharge me.

I used the hospital phone to make some calls and secured a place to stay with a six-degrees-of-separation kind of connection who lived within a reasonable distance from the hospital.

Brad was a friend of the son of the elderly woman I was renting a room from. He happened to be a nurse, and he and his family graciously took me in for a week, nurturing me back to enough health for me to be able to head back home.

At first, I could barely move, confined to bed for several days as my body struggled to recover. Each small shift sent waves of pain through me, making even the simplest motions an ordeal. But gradually, I regained enough strength to sit up, then to stand, and finally to hobble around, each step a reminder of how much healing I still had ahead of me.

As the days turned into weeks, I reflected on everything—the accident, the recovery, and the uncanny series of events leading up to that day.

Then, one day, the enormity of my entire ordeal hit me like a bolt of lightning.

Out of the blue, my mind raced back to that fateful day—the inexplicable drowsiness, the car's seemingly guided path to safety, and my near-miraculous survival. I replayed the details in my head: my car careening toward danger, my frantic efforts to avoid the collision, the crunch of gravel beneath my tires, and coming to after my car had stopped.

I thought about the off-duty EMT who had found me, his timely intervention, and the first responders who followed. It was as if invisible hands had orchestrated my survival—ensuring I lost consciousness in the nick of time and that help arrived within the critical "golden hour."

A surge of emotion overwhelmed me as a profound realization took hold. I should be dead—or at the very least, paralyzed. Given the severity of my accident, my being alive was a proclamation: a miracle.

The cocoon of shock that had shielded me from the full weight of the experience finally unraveled, leaving me raw and exposed. A sob erupted from deep within, my whole body shaking as the reality of what had happened came crashing down with staggering intensity.

But there was more.

This wasn't just a random accident—it felt like a confrontation between forces beyond my comprehension. The devil had come in four that night at the convenience store—four young men motivated by hate and violence who brutally slaughtered innocent lives without mercy. What compelled them to act so atrociously? Had an evil spirit manipulated them—something with dark and diabolical intent? And worse . . . had I drawn its attention? Had my prying into its sinister business placed me in its line of sight? Was the accident an attempt to silence me?

If so, it almost succeeded. Almost.

I knew this wasn't just survival. It was a divine intervention—subtle, deliberate, and unmistakably timed. The synchronicities that had led me here were not anomalies. Whatever forces had intervened—Spirit, angels, ancestors—I could feel their hand in protecting my life.

The idea that evil could reach into the lives of the living raised questions I wasn't sure I wanted answered. But if angels could intervene, why not spirits with far darker intentions? It's a topic for another conversation.

What mattered most was that I had been saved. The fact that I survived made one thing abundantly clear: I was being given another chance. A tidal wave of gratitude surged through me at the realization that I was spared an untimely death. It was pure euphoria, the likes of which I had never experienced before. Tears came—not because I feared death, but because in that moment, I felt and understood deep in my soul how sacred life truly was. I had taken it for granted until I realized how close I came to losing it.

I didn't emerge from that accident with a new sense of purpose or a sudden calling to serve. Life didn't transform overnight like a Hollywood movie. But I knew with every fiber of my being that something—or someone—had intervened. I had been protected. Preserved. As the magnitude of what happened sank in, a deeper question surfaced. It wasn't just a matter of how I survived anymore.

It was why.

25

The White Light

My body felt broken, and my will to live was just as bruised as I stepped into Mikayla's office. She was the bodyworker I had chosen to help me recover from the soft tissue damage in my upper torso and neck and the deep bruising in my ribs—injuries I sustained when my car slammed into a telephone pole at fifty-five miles per hour. It had been three months since my first appointment, and I was still limping into her treatment room. My body was healing, but I wasn't mentally prepared for the reality that full recovery would take another three months.

While I was grateful my injuries weren't life-threatening or paralyzing, the limitations were debilitating. So many things that once brought me joy—hiking, bike riding, running, dancing— were suddenly completely out of the question. Even the simplest movements, the ones most people take for granted—bending down to pick something up off the floor, lifting a glass of water, climbing stairs, or breathing without discomfort were either difficult or impossible for me.

And then there was the pain—unyielding, insidious, ever waiting. It lurked beneath the surface of everything I did, turning every breath, every shift, every movement into a potential ambush.

I could have taken pain medication, but I didn't. Bound by my die-hard purist philosophy, I chose to endure it, knowing my body would heal itself with the help of alternative forms of healing, without reliance on drugs.

At an early age, as I got into competitive running, I embraced the belief that my body was my temple. I fueled it with healthy foods and steered clear of alcohol, soda, coffee, and drugs. I also rejected allopathic medicine, avoiding aspirin, muscle relaxers, or anything that might mask pain rather than address its cause.

Pain isn't pleasant, but I think it has its place in our lives. I see it as a messenger that something isn't right in our body or in our life. In the case of my car accident, the pain served as a barometer for how well I was progressing in my healing journey, and it highlighted what my physical limitations were. It also kept me from doing something that might make my injuries worse.

With that said, I proactively sought out alternative forms of pain management. What Spirit orchestrated to help me was beyond my wildest imagination. You can read about it in detail in my story "The Power of Intention."

Even though my pain was sometimes exhausting, it was nothing compared to the mental anguish I endured. I had two part-time, minimum-wage jobs that weren't leading anywhere, my attempt to start a private massage therapy practice had failed before the accident, and I was single—with little to show or offer to any prospective love interest. Shards of hopelessness cut deeply into my lonely heart.

I tried to console myself with the tools I had—methods to manage my emotions, like reframing, repeated affirmations, and prayer. Whatever I knew, I tried, hoping to quiet the storm within me. But nothing could cast away my inner demons as I hobbled toward recovery.

I was suffering through depression. It wasn't the first time, and like all my previous episodes, I attributed it—rightly or wrongly—to my circumstances, to the weight of my thoughts, and to my struggle to manifest a better life.

Mental health experts declare that depression is a mental illness, a disorder of the brain. I didn't want to admit to myself that I had a mental disease. I knew antidepressants were an option, but I didn't trust that pharmaceutical companies—or the doctors who prescribed them—fully understood the risks linked to these powerful drugs. I longed for the peace of mind they promised, but my distrust, coupled with my commitment to alternative medicine, kept me from taking them.

Instead, I continued searching for relief in ways that aligned with my beliefs. For my physical pain, I tried herbal topicals, acupuncture, meditation, heat and cold, and the specialized bodywork Mikayla offered.

She performed her routine check-in to assess my progress, then left the room so I could get ready. I undressed down to my underwear and shuffled over to the massage table. Even the simple act of getting under the covers felt like a struggle. I winced as I gingerly maneuvered onto my stomach, shifting my weight until I found a tolerable position—one I could hold without aggravating my pain.

Once I was situated, an overwhelming exhaustion bore down on me with the weight of an avalanche. Fear and a crushing sense of doom wrapped around me as I thought about my uncertain, dismal-looking future. I felt like a failure and had no idea how to turn my life around. As I lay there, waiting for Mikayla, a dark thought crept in—I secretly wished my life would end.

The perfunctory knock on the door pushed my despair back into its shadow. I took a slow breath and called out, "I'm ready."

Mikayla was the epitome of prim and proper. Everything about her—from the way she dressed to the carefully curated décor of her office—was polished and precise. She wasn't the warm and fuzzy type, but she was highly respected by her peers for her skill and expertise. While I wished my recovery would move along more quickly, I appreciated Mikayla's intuitiveness and skillful hands.

When Mikayla asked me to roll onto my back, I knew the session was drawing to a close. The end came far sooner than I wanted. The calm I felt during my hour-long reprieve was slowly replaced by the suffocating weight of all my problems. There was no escaping my reality. The dark, persistent lust for ending my pain by ending my life resurfaced—ravenous, undiminished, and unwilling to loosen its hold.

Mikayla finished up the session and left the room so I could get dressed. "Take your time," she whispered as she closed the door, completely unaware of my inner turmoil.

I shut my eyes and lingered on the table, clinging to whatever bit of respite I could steal from the clutches of my private hell. In quiet desperation, I searched for a lifeline—anything to push back against the shadows of despair circling me with outstretched claws.

Then, in an instant, with my eyes still closed, it happened.

From the right side of my periphery, a sudden flash of light ignited and streaked across the backs of my eyelids like a shooting star, traveling at supersonic speed. It was as if I had a front-row seat to a panoramic screen with a breathtaking 180-degree view.

Before the light reached the other side, time suddenly slowed to a glacial crawl—like a special-effects scene from *The Matrix*. I don't know how I knew, but I had a deep, unshakable sense that the light I was witnessing was part of the same described by those who have had near-death experiences—the loving, all-knowing brilliance that greets and shepherds many as they transition into the spirit world.

At the same time, I was left with a distinct impression: I wasn't supposed to see this. Someone—or something—had made a mistake. It was as if, for a brief moment, a hidden door had been left ajar, allowing me an unintended glimpse of something beyond this dimension.

As I lay on Mikayla's table, the part of me desperate for an end to my pain saw an opportunity. Without hesitation, and before my mind could grasp what was happening, my soul leaped toward the body of light, reaching with both hands.

In the flash of a nanosecond, the illumination resumed its lightning speed. But before it could rocket away, I latched onto its coattails. In an instant, the light vanished into the ether, carrying my soul away, leaving my body on the table. Then, nothing. No thought, no emotion, no sensation. I simply ceased to be.

Mikayla later recounted what had transpired next. Outside the room, Mikayla stood in the hallway, waiting for me to call her back in. Minutes passed—longer than usual. Knowing that clients sometimes dozed off at the end of a session, she knocked gently on the door.

"Keno, are you getting up?" she asked politely.

When I didn't answer, she knocked again, this time with more determination. Her voice grew louder. "Keno, are you awake? Are you getting up?"

Silence.

Mikayla cracked the door open and called my name again. When I still didn't respond, she hesitated, then poked her head around the door and peered inside. The room was large and dimly lit, but she could make out my body lying on the table exactly as she had left me.

Thinking I had simply fallen asleep, she approached the table cautiously.

"Keno?" she called out, her voice uncertain.

Then she saw me.

Her heart slammed against her chest. My skin had taken on an unmistakable shade of blue. Breath caught in her throat as panic surged.

She rushed to my side and grabbed my shoulders, shaking me violently.

"Keno, wake up! Wake up!"

I remained unresponsive.

She moved to the head of the table, pressed her ear close to my mouth, and listened—praying for a breath.

Nothing.

Her hands trembled as she shook me again, her urgent commands turning to frantic pleas. "Please, Keno, come back!" she screamed, her voice breaking.

Her mind raced. The enormity of the moment was paralyzing. Pressure mounted in her chest, a wave of fear swelling inside, threatening to pull her under. Nothing in her training or life experience had prepared her for this. She fought to steady herself, to find a foothold in the chaos or a single clear thought to grasp onto.

She placed her hands on my body. My skin was cold against her clammy palm.

"BREATHE, DAMN IT!" she yelled.

As if by the sheer force of her will, my chest gently rose and fell.

She froze, staring at my upper torso, her own breath caught in her throat. Then, my chest rose and fell again. A mountain of relief crashed over her as she watched life return to my body. One small breath gave way to another, then another.

Her body shuddered as the fear that had threatened to consume her began to subside. She drew in a deep breath, and the muscles in her body released tension she hadn't realized she was holding. The terror of this nightmare loosened its grip, and for a fleeting moment, she took comfort in knowing she had narrowly escaped disaster.

But the relief was short-lived.

Aside from the rise and fall of my chest, I showed no other signs of life.

Panic surged again. She grabbed hold of me and shook my body, repeatedly calling my name, her voice rising with a mixture of fear, anger, and fragile relief. When that didn't work, she leaned closer, scanning my face, desperate for any sign that I would wake up and free her from this nightmare.

During Mikayla's ordeal, I heard nothing, felt nothing, and knew nothing of what was happening around me. I simply drifted in a lifeless, timeless void. I felt weightless, formless, and unanchored to anything.

When consciousness came, it was microscopic at first—a whisper so faint it barely existed. It took some part of me a while to realize someone was calling my name. The voice seemed to travel an immense distance to find me, poking tiny holes in the veil of stillness that held me.

Hearing my name set something in motion. A slow pull. A gradual return to consciousness, gently drawing me back to my body. My soul moved like a wisp of smoke slipping through a long, narrow duct. At first, I floated lazily, caught in an invisible current. But the closer I got to my body, the faster I traveled—until, suddenly, I was thrust forward, flung out of the conduit, and snapped back into my body.

My muscles, bones, and organs felt foreign, unrecognizable. My brain was like a computer without a keyboard or mouse—active but with no way to control anything. Confusion clouded my thoughts as I struggled to grasp where I was and what was happening.

After what felt like an eternity, I regained limited control of my extremities. One leg bent slightly at the knee as my arms groped through the air, moving as if submerged in thick molasses. I couldn't tell if my eyes were open or shut. Mikayla spoke to me, but I couldn't respond. My mind slowly formed words, but my lips moved without a sound.

Then, suddenly, Mikayla grabbed my lower legs and yanked them over the edge of the table, forcing me to sit up. My feet dangled above the floor as she shoved a tiny paper cup of water into my hand, gripping my wrist to make sure I took hold of it. My fingers instinctively curled around it. Without a word, she briskly gathered my clothes, shoved them at my side, and stormed out so I could get dressed.

I carefully slid off the table onto my feet, swaying as if I were in a drunken stupor from anesthesia. I took several tentative steps, as unsteady as a baby learning to walk, before my legs buckled. I dropped to my knees on the carpeted floor, struggling to keep hold of the water but spilling it as I collapsed into a semi-controlled fall.

There was a knock on the door and a familiar voice. I wanted to answer, but my tongue wouldn't move.

A moment later, Mikayla swung the door open to find me sprawled on the floor in my underwear. She strode over, plucked the empty paper cup from my hand, and fired off a barrage of sharp, demanding questions.

"What's going on with you?!" she snapped, her frustration slicing through the air like a blade.

I fought against the paralysis gripping my vocal cords. With a Herculean effort, I managed to force a response. When the words finally staggered out, they made no sense.

"Ask me what my name is."

Mikayla stood there, frozen, as if she couldn't believe what was happening. She covered her eyes with her hands, then slowly dragged them down her face and neck, like an iron trying to smooth away invisible tension. Her arms dropped to her sides. She drew in a breath, let it out with a weary sigh, and seemed to summon the strength to respond. Her voice cracked under the weight of the moment. "What's your name?"

"Keno," I replied. As the words left my lips, a flood of tears suddenly poured down my face like the bursting of a dam. "I want my mommy!" I cried, like a Freudian slip. I had regained enough coherence by this time that when those words flew out of my mouth, I was mortified. I was a thirty-year-old man, but in that moment, I was a grief-stricken child lying on the floor sobbing uncontrollably. Was I embarrassed? My ego certainly was. I feared I was also losing my mind.

Mikayla knelt beside me, clearly appearing lost, overwhelmed, and bewildered. She did her best to keep her wits about her, but she was completely out of her element. As my sobs subsided, I signaled that I was okay—at least enough to get dressed.

But everything that had happened—the shock of finding me lifeless, the panic, the helplessness, and the weirdness of my catharsis—had pushed her beyond what she could handle. I didn't expect anyone to know exactly how to respond to something like that, but I wasn't prepared for what came next. As she abruptly stood to leave, her voice cut through the air, hot and sharp.

"If you want to die, do it somewhere else."

I knelt on the floor, flabbergasted, my face flush with shame. My logical self understood her response; she was scared and overwhelmed, but her words hit hard, leaving a wound I was in no condition to process. I collected myself as best I could and left her office without meeting her gaze or uttering a word. It would be the last time I went to her for treatments.

But it wasn't the last time we would meet.

Mikayla was a member of the social club where I worked, and as a result, our paths inevitably crossed over the next few months. Each encounter carried the same uncomfortable tension: the fleeting glances, the deliberate avoidance of eye contact, and the silent heaviness of unresolved issues from our final appointment.

I didn't want it to be that way between us, but for months, I couldn't summon the courage to face her or the unresolved tension directly. After running into her several times, though, the discomfort of avoidance became more uncomfortable than the idea of talking to her. I decided to reach out. I emailed her and asked if we could meet at a local coffee shop to talk openly about what had happened and hopefully find closure.

Mikayla fidgeted nervously with her coffee cup as she sat across from me. We forced ourselves to meet each other's gaze, tentative at first, but gradually easing into honesty. She began by apologizing for her harsh words, expressing regret for her lack of empathy and composure.

"I was terrified and so far out of my comfort zone. Nothing I've done in all my years of practice had prepared me to deal with something like that."

She apologized again, then acknowledged that what happened in my session had been a significant growth experience for her. It forced her to examine her role as a healer—and how she could have done a better job of holding a safe space for me. Despite how frightening it was to find my lifeless body on her table, and the emotional ordeal she went through afterward, she recognized that she was now a stronger, more grounded, and more compassionate person because of it.

Mikayla looked down at her hands for a moment, her jaw working through questions she wasn't sure she should ask. As if to mark her newfound courage, Mikayla met my eyes and asked, "What happened to you once I left the room?"

It had been months since my session. I was in a better place now, but as I reflected on that time, I felt the lingering vestiges of my former pain and a familiar vulnerability around sharing my deepest secret. Even so, I told her everything. I owed her that. I spoke about my suicidal depression and the struggles I was going through that contributed to my sense of resignation. I shared how the white light appeared, what I understood it to be, and how I grabbed onto it in an effort to escape my life.

Mikayla sat silently, absorbing everything I said. When she was ready, she shared with me, in vivid detail, what it was like for her when she walked into the room to find me unconscious and blue—how she felt frightened, helpless, overwhelmed—and the things she did to try to revive me.

Her words surprised me with their raw honesty. Hearing what she went through gave me a deeper appreciation for the fear and pressure she had felt. For the first time, I saw the situation through her eyes—and with that, something inside me softened. There was no blame left between us, only two people doing their best in an impossible moment.

We had finally acknowledged the pain between us, and by doing so, we released it. We cleared the air graciously and parted ways on amicable terms. As for where I went and what I experienced while I lay unconscious on Mikayla's table, I sadly don't know. I awoke with no recollection, and to this day, the where, why, and what transpired remains a mystery. Life is like that sometimes. Or rather, the mysteries remain mysteries most of the time. I imagine I'll get to find out when I cross over and have my life review. For now, all I can do is chalk it up to the inner workings of the spirit world being beyond the grasp of my finite understanding . . . elements of the master plan none of us are privy to.

I wish I could say that my experience with the white light marked a turning point—that I had been gifted some profound revelation or wisdom while unconscious, some insight that propelled me toward a better life. That would have made for a great Hollywood ending. But there wasn't. Far from it. No sudden epiphany. No profound healing. No shift in mindset. Things did eventually get better, but not before they got worse—and not for several difficult months.

My suicidal depression continued, gnawing at my resolve like lions closing in on a weary, desperate antelope with nowhere to turn. My choice to isolate and keep my struggle a secret came at a heavy cost.

To make matters worse, not long after my final session with Mikayla, my landlord gave me notice to move out. Unable to find anything I could afford in the short time frame I was given, I became homeless in the dead of an Oregon winter. I spent hours each day sitting in my car, sinking into my misery, trapped in an endless cycle of despair, contemplating not just if I would end my life but how.

Unbelievable as it sounds, I was still trying to start a massage practice during all of this, renting a room a couple of days a week at a chiropractor's office. When the office shut down for the night, I let myself in and slept in the treatment room. The chiropractor soon found out and put an end to it.

As if that weren't enough, another blow followed shortly there-after. A letter arrived at my workplace from a lawyer on behalf of a client I had borrowed money from, demanding that I repay a $2,500 loan I had fallen behind on. It felt like life wasn't just beat-ing me—it was kicking me while I was down.

When I look back at that time in my life, it's a wonder I survived.

What I've learned is that Spirit will be there for us in hard times, but it can only do for us what it can do through us. When we allow ourselves to be vulnerable and receptive to help, we open the door energetically for both Spirit and other people to come to our aid. Spirit can do a lot more with an open heart and mind than it can with the ego's need to look good, be right, or strive for perfection.

When I hit rock bottom and didn't think I could take it any-more, I threw out a lifeline by confiding in a person I barely knew.

James was a middle-aged man, new to town and from Hawaii. When I met him, he was facilitating a small group for those inter-ested in learning how to channel energy for healing and manifesta-tion. An acquaintance of mine, who was a member of the group and knew of my interest in such things, asked if I wanted to join. When I found out that it was free, I took advantage of the opportunity— and attended their next meeting, just days later.

Over the next two weeks, I became mesmerized by James's cha-risma and enigmatic presence. He had a confident yet unassuming demeanor and freely shared his insight. Taken by his warmth and wisdom, I asked if we could meet privately, and he agreed—without charging me a dime.

The first time we had a private session, we sat in his living room, facing each other. With my gaze averted, occasionally stealing glances to see how James was reacting, I told him everything—that I was living out of my car, barely making ends meet with my menial jobs, and contemplating suicide.

James listened in silence, holding space for me without judgment as I bared my soul. When I was done, he paused, letting my words settle. It was a lot to take in, but he didn't miss a beat. Gently yet matter-of-factly, he acknowledged my courage and said, "I think some energy work will be of great benefit to you. I can sense that your energy is blocked. Would you like me to work on you?"

When I accepted his offer, he rose from his chair and stood beside me, his hands hovering over different parts of my body, channeling energy, focusing mainly on my heart chakra. After a few minutes, he stepped back.

"The work I just did should initiate an inner shift of mind and heart," he said.

I didn't experience anything from his energy work, but I did feel incredibly free as a result of sharing my innermost thoughts and feelings. It felt like a heavy burden had been lifted from my shoulders.

Beyond that, I didn't expect our session to change anything in my life or have a lasting impact. So I was profoundly amazed by what unfolded the very next day—events that would bring a significant shift in my life emotionally, mentally, physically, and spiritually. One of the jobs I had was working at an upscale health and social club as a locker room attendant. It was a tedious, thankless job—one I was embarrassed to admit having. But it gave my life structure and opportunities to socialize, helping me hold onto my sanity while I struggled to find my way.

Among the club's many services was massage therapy. Because of its popularity, a team of six therapists was on staff to meet the demand. Only one had full-time hours while the others worked part-time.

The next day at work, I learned that the head massage therapist—the one with the full-time schedule—was leaving to pursue a private practice. The handful of other therapists had first dibs on his time slots, but miraculously, none of them wanted any of his hours. They all had other commitments and responsibilities.

I had tried unsuccessfully in the past to start my own practice but was still interested in doing massage, so I applied for the position. A couple of the therapists on staff knew me and vouched for my skills as a massage therapist. Those recommendations made all the difference. I was hired the following week and walked into a busy, ready-made practice.

My living situation was still dire, but that changed the same week when I set aside my pride and confided in one of my best friends that I was living out of my car. She was shocked. After a brief conversation with her husband, they graciously offered to take me in until I was able to get my life together.

Could the brief energy work that James did, removing my energetic blocks, have made that much of a difference? It's hard for my logical, left-brained self—steeped in an old-school, mechanistic worldview—to fathom, but I believe it did. The countless experiences with energy I would come to have in my future practice proved it.

We focus so much attention on our physical bodies without hardly acknowledging the fact that we have energy bodies too. Heck, we *are* energy. The link between our physical and energetic bodies is an intimate one. Heal the energy body, and the physical body heals. Heal your thoughts and emotions, and both bodies benefit.

With a new job and a renewed sense of purpose, my circumstances and the trajectory of my life finally improved. But the transition was anything but easy. The roots of my depression ran deep, and healing took time. I had spent so long carrying the weight of my pain and shame that learning to live without it felt unfamiliar.

More than 20 million Americans suffer from depression. It spares no one, despite fame and fortune.

Ever heard of Michael Phelps? Michael Phelps is the most decorated athlete in Olympic history, with twenty-eight Olympic medals, twenty-three of them gold. He's fit, articulate, handsome, successful, and admired the world over. What more could you want in life?

Yet would you believe that in 2012, immediately after winning six medals, he spent several days in his bedroom in a deep depression? He didn't eat, barely slept, and at his lowest point, he even contemplated taking his own life, having lost his will to live.

When I read that in an article, I wondered how that could be? Here was a guy who seemed to have it all, yet he was suffering from depression. My reaction highlights a common misconception—that depression only affects those who are lacking something in life. There are a multitude of factors that can trigger depression—medical, psychological, spiritual, and environmental, to name a few. In some cases, depression isn't the root issue but rather a signal that something deeper needs attention.

Despite its prevalence, depression continues to carry a terrible stigma. If you're suffering, I urge you to seek help. I can almost guarantee it will make you feel better. Confide in someone you trust, then find the form of support that resonates with you.

Michael Phelps is still alive, in large part because he chose to open up to friends and family about his internal struggles. He eventually sought professional help as well. By speaking out and sharing his experience, he has not only made a profound impact on others but also helped himself in the process.

A teacher from my days at massage school once shared a quote that has stuck with me ever since: "Pain is inevitable; suffering is optional." Michael Phelps suffered in silence for years. He turned to drugs and alcohol as a way to cope with life and his mental and emotional struggles. I was shocked to learn that he's had two DUIs.

Could he have avoided all that suffering? Yes.

Someone once asked Michael why he didn't seek help sooner. His answer was simple: "I wasn't ready."

I think if Michael were to dig deeper for an answer, he would have said something like—and I'm putting this in my own words—"I was too scared to be vulnerable. I felt ashamed of my depression. I didn't want to risk looking bad or weak, and I feared how people might judge me."

"Pain is inevitable; suffering is optional." When Michael Phelps was willing to face the pain and uncertainty of opening up, his suffering began to subside. The same is true for you, no matter what is fueling your depression. Admitting your pain is the first step toward healing. Confiding in someone you trust is the next.

You don't have to carry this alone. Speak your truth. Let someone in. Ask for help—even if it feels scary, even if you don't know where to start. It won't just make you feel better—it could save your life.

26

Panic Attack

Sleep. It's supposed to be a bastion of rest and rejuvenation—a time for the body to repair, the mind to organize, and the spirit to renew. In the stillness of night, the brain weaves memories and untangles emotions, clearing away the clutter of the day.

But sometimes, there are fears and unresolved conflicts that can't easily be processed during sleep, and when they rise to a boiling point, they set off powerful alarms in the brain that signal a deep unrest that goes beyond the scope of sleep.

Nocturnal panic attacks are one of those alarms—sudden, overwhelming episodes of fear that strike during sleep—jolting you awake and shattering the peace of night with severe physical symptoms accompanied by sheer terror. People often wake up convinced they're having a heart attack, dying, or losing their mind.

Few experiences are more unnerving. I know because in March 2023, I had one. It shattered my sense of safety in the world, turning my life into a waking nightmare.

But that's not where this story begins.

Throughout 2021 and 2022, I took a sabbatical, living off the inheritance left to me by my parents. During this time, I dedicated myself to several meaningful pursuits: writing this book, developing my psychic and mediumship abilities, and studying to become a financial coach through an online self-study program.

By the end of 2022, I was worn thin from stress. My inheritance was nearly depleted, and I wasn't making any money yet. Although I had made progress on my book, it still felt far from finished.

My ambition to become a professional psychic was derailed by my relentless perfectionism—a trait that filled me with dread and self-doubt before every practice reading or class. The self-imposed pressure squeezed out any joy, turning what should have been an exciting pursuit into a burden. Even with notable success, the weight of my own expectations created so much anxiety that it ultimately led to my decision to give up on the idea.

Meanwhile, my aspirations to become a financial coach were squashed under the weight of low self-confidence and a heavy dose of impostor syndrome, given that I was teaching from personal experience and self-study rather than a formal degree. Doubt impeded my progress until, eventually, I abandoned that dream altogether.

Though my wife had a well-paying corporate job, my lack of earnings created tension between us. It strained both our finances and our relationship. Despite my unconventional mindset, I wasn't immune to equating my self-worth with financial prowess or contribution, and the weight of not having either took a toll on my psyche.

Then, in the fall of 2022, the tenant renting a furnished property I owned in Maryland informed me that she was facing financial hardship and wouldn't be able to pay the full rent each month. I could have evicted her, but she was a single mother with four children under the age of twelve, and her own mother—who had been living with her—had recently passed away.

Much to my wife's chagrin, I decided to let her stay. She was working on securing a government-funded loan to buy her own home, so I chose to give her some time until that happened.

In hindsight, I wish I had given her notice. Trying to collect rent became a constant source of stress, and the pressure of covering two mortgages took its toll. The mental strain escalated to the point where, one morning, as I rolled over to get out of bed, my entire back went into spasm. The pain was so excruciating and sudden that I screamed, sending my wife running from the other side of the house.

Sweat dripped from my forehead as the spasm loosened its grip, leaving me trembling in its wake. The fear of the pain was enough to hold me hostage, convincing me that the wrong move could send me back into that agony.

I braced myself, shifting toward the edge of the bed with painstaking caution. Every movement was a negotiation, a silent plea to my own body not to betray me. My mind quivered in protest as I lowered my feet to the floor, my breath coming in measured, shallow inhales and exhales. With both feet finally under me, I waited, feeling cautiously optimistic—I had managed to get out of bed without another spasm. I told myself it might just have been a one-time thing.

I inched my way toward the nearby bathroom, each movement calculated, my breath shallow with anticipation. I eased myself onto the toilet, careful not to shift too quickly. A wave of relief washed over me, and I let out a long sigh. But the moment I adjusted my weight, a violent jolt seized my back, locking my muscles in a vise of agony. I lurched forward, clutching the wall, a raw, guttural cry tearing from my throat.

Back issues were not new to me, although the intensity of my spasm was a rare occurrence. As you can read in my story "Healing Back Pain," I knew that my back spasms were not due to a physical injury, obstruction, or pinched nerve. They were psychological in nature.

I ambled slowly to my office and searched through my small library for the book that had changed my life many years earlier, a book written by a doctor in New York, Dr. John Sarno. His widely acclaimed yet highly polarizing work with patients suffering from severe chronic back pain changed many lives for people the medical community had given up on.

I dusted his book off my shelf and shuffled through the pages, looking for the list of affirmations his clients, and I, had used as a tool to help overcome back pain. Once I found the page, I recited them and meditated on them several times a day to bolster my belief that my spasms were indeed a psychological issue and not from something structurally wrong with my back.

From my past experience, I knew it to be true, but in that moment, and for the next few days, it was a daunting task to silence the voice of my logical, empirical mind, which was convinced that there was something physically wrong with my back based on the spasms and pain.

Despite my awareness, I felt victimized by a cruel cycle of torment: a cunning adversary lying in wait, haunting my every move with the fear that it could strike without warning, inflicting its searing pain on me.

Within a week, though, and without medication, I broke the cycle of spasms. At first, I moved cautiously, wary of triggering another episode. But in the second week, my confidence in the belief that nothing was wrong with my back, and my efforts to address my emotions, erased the need for the pain, allowing my body to return to complete normalcy.

The ordeal, however, became the catalyst for reclaiming my peace of mind with my tenant. In February 2023, I served her a thirty-day notice to vacate.

Hoping for a fresh start, I listed the house for rent, in search of better tenants. But the property's remote location—in a small, economically depressed town on Maryland's eastern shore—made finding renters difficult. After a month of fielding inquiries, no-shows, and applicants with spotty credit, I reconsidered my options. With the housing market running hotter than ever, I made the decision to sell.

When I flew to Maryland in mid-March to ready the house for sale, I wasn't prepared for the state my tenant had left it in. I was distraught to find it not only filthy but riddled with damage: Most of the furniture was either broken or ruined, the walls were scarred, the landscaping was dead, and there were countless other issues needing repair. My heart sank. It was clear I'd have to extend my trip and line up the help I needed to get the house in shape to list it.

It was all too much for me to bear. On my last night at the house, I jolted awake at 2:30 a.m., drenched in sweat, my heart hammering against my ribs as if trying to escape. My chest tightened, every breath shallow and labored, as though the air itself had turned against me. Wet, clammy sheets clung to my body, smothering me in a suffocating embrace. My limbs trembled, tingling with a strange, electric numbness.

Am I having a heart attack?

Panic surged through me like a tidal wave, drowning out all logic. My thoughts spiraled, desperate and disoriented, grasping for a lifeline in the darkness. I had never felt so powerless, so utterly horrified—at the mercy of something unknown yet terrifying and overwhelming, gripping both my body and mind.

I pulled the damp sheets from my body and struggled to roll out of bed. Finally, my feet pressed against the cold floor. My hand fumbled across the nightstand, searching blindly for my phone. I was still gasping for air, my pulse racing as the keypad lit up. I stared at my phone, my finger hovering over the numbers—ready to dial 911.

But then, I hesitated—my breath still uneven, my thoughts a tangled blur. As the seconds ticked by, clarity slowly found its way through the haze. I realized it wasn't a heart attack—it was a panic attack.

Desperate to shake the terror from my body, I opted for a walk. I threw on my clothes and stepped out into the cold, damp night, hoping the movement and crisp air would settle my panic. The local hospital was only a couple of miles away, I told myself. I'd call them if I needed to.

I wandered the dark, silent streets, bundled in my winter coat, feeling like the sole survivor of an apocalypse. The world around me felt hollow, the emptiness pressing in, my footsteps and breath the only sounds breaking the stillness. *This is just a stress response*, I reassured myself, but the fear was raw, clawing at the edges of my mind, threatening to consume me. I whispered a prayer, hoping to get through the experience unscathed—but as I would come to learn, it would take more than prayer to pull me through.

I roamed through the night like a zombie—exhausted, numb, and barely aware of my surroundings—until my body refused to go any farther. Back at the house, I stripped off my clothes and stepped into the shower, letting the hot water warm away the chill that had seeped into my bones. I changed the sheets, and by 4:30 a.m., I crawled back into bed. Curling into a fetal position, I rocked myself in an effort to push the dread away, until finally, I drifted into a restless, uneasy sleep.

The months that followed were some of the hardest of my life. Without my wife's support, I probably would have committed suicide. My sympathetic nervous system, responsible for the body's fight-or-flight mechanism, was stuck on high.

Like a hypersensitive, defective smoke detector, my mind shrieked at the faintest hint of danger—even if it wasn't real—with no way to shut off the warning. I would feel a sensation in my body, like muscle tension in the back of my neck or phlegm in my throat, and my mind would seize on it as a threat, triggering a wave of irrational anxiety that logic couldn't override.

The fallout was ruthless, bringing a barrage of physical, emotional, and mental challenges I had never faced before.

Once anxiety took hold, it continually set off what professionals call the Panic Cycle. It's a vicious pattern that starts with a physical sensation. The mind zeros in on it and overreacts with fear out of a sense of danger, causing more anxiety that then magnifies the sensation. As a result, the stronger sensation then drives the anxiety toward panic. It's a total mindfuck. (Pardon the language, but experiences this bad require strong expletives.)

Desperate for answers, I turned to the internet, scouring dozens of articles and videos, trying to understand what was happening to me and how to make it stop. I researched the sympathetic and parasympathetic nervous systems and their roles in the panic cycle, hoping that knowledge could offer me a way out.

I watched countless YouTube videos from therapists, absorbing a multitude of coping skills. In addition to my personal research, I met virtually with two mental health counselors and a business coach each week. Though he wasn't a therapist, he was a spiritual person I had started working with before my panic attack, and when he learned what I was going through, he offered his own insights, using techniques he believed might help me heal. While they were sometimes helpful, I eventually decided to stop seeing all of them.

I also scheduled a virtual session with three different practitioners—one with a shaman, one with a psychic, and another with a healer. None of them made a difference.

Desperate for relief, I tried a number of things: massage, acupuncture, eye movement desensitization and reprocessing (EMDR), and CBD, a natural, nonpsychoactive compound from the cannabis plant. I explored meditation, emotional freedom techniques (EFT), and countless other techniques I found online—methods designed to activate my parasympathetic nervous system to relax my body and quiet the physical sensations my mind imagined as threats. Several people also suggested I try marijuana.

Massage and acupuncture proved unbearable. In my state, I

either spiraled into anxiety attacks midsession or lay there in fear, dreading the next wave of panic that could come at any moment.

The EMDR used by one of my therapists unraveled into something closer to an exorcism, leaving me deeply unsettled. After researching marijuana, I saw too many risks and decided against it. And the CBD that was supposed to calm me? It only made me jittery.

Some methods proved more effective than others. Certain strategies worked at times but failed me at other times. None of them could fully silence the persistent anxiety. My search for lasting relief continued as I felt determined to find something—anything—that could finally break the unforgiving cycle of misery.

Then, in the first week of April, I stumbled upon a video on YouTube produced by panic specialist Michael Norman. I immediately signed up for his self-study course on panic attacks. After completing the program, I bought a package of three one-on-one virtual sessions.

I'll never forget the work we did together. While I won't go into all the details, if you suffer from panic attacks, I highly recommend reading his material and working with him one-on-one. You can learn more at www.panicfreetv.com.

One technique Michael endorses—backed by scientific research—is intentional hyperventilation done over an extended period of time. Studies show that if a person practices hyperventilating for eight to sixteen minutes—fifty seconds at a time, with ten-second breaks between intervals—there's a strong chance of eliminating panic attacks. I learned that the purpose of voluntary hyperventilation is to mimic the sensations of a panic attack. By deliberately re-creating the physical experience, you confront the fear head-on rather than run from it. The goal is to retrain your brain to recognize that, while these sensations may be uncomfortable, they're completely harmless—and nothing to fear.

When I first read that hyperventilating for over eight minutes could stop my panic attacks, my immediate thought was, *There's no way I can do that.* The idea of deliberately triggering those sensations with rigorous breathing felt unimaginable.

But I was desperate. And with Michael's encouragement, I gave it a shot.

In the comfort of my home, I barely lasted ten seconds before needing a twenty-second break, and even then, I could only push through three rounds—just thirty seconds in total. That's how terrifying the process was for me.

Michael understood panic and anxiety on a personal level—he had battled them himself. That firsthand experience gave him a deep understanding of the struggle, along with a set of techniques he had used to help others break free.

But in our first two sessions, nothing seemed to stick. No matter what we tried, the fear wouldn't loosen its grip. Every strategy felt fleeting, slipping through my fingers the moment panic took hold.

During our third and final session, Michael focused on my fear of hyperventilating, knowing it was my best shot at healing. That's when he made an unexpected suggestion: We'd do it together, right then and there over the call, from my home office.

My gut reaction was to refuse—I wasn't comfortable with that. But with his steady coaching and persistent encouragement, I finally took a leap of faith.

As we began, Michael explained a crucial element of the process: shifting my mindset from fear to excitement. Both states of mind can create similar sensations in the body. By training the mind to associate the sensations of hyperventilation—and, by extension, panic—with something positive instead of something negative, I could begin to break the cycle.

To my surprise, with Michael's voice urging me onward from my computer speakers—and with him hyperventilating alongside me—I managed to push through two full minutes, breathing in thirty-second reps with fifteen-seconds of rest in between.

Encouraged by his support and armed with the recording from our third session, I committed to the practice every night. For nearly two weeks, I hyperventilated on my own, pacing around my office, exaggerating my movements like an impassioned rapper performing onstage as if to drive the breath deeper.

As I listened to the recording of Michael and me breathing together, I focused—not on fear, but on excitement, just as he had encouraged me to do. After a few reps, I would burst out loud with exclamations of "Way to go!" "Yeah!" and "I'm kicking ass!"—jumping and prancing around the room, waving my arms through the air like I was running on ten cups of caffeine.

I started with thirty-second reps, taking ten-second breaks between each, gradually working my way up to five minutes. Hitting that milestone fueled my confidence. When I reached the ten-minute mark, everything changed. I increased my reps to fifty seconds with ten-second breaks, continually extending the amount of time—each session pushing me further than I ever thought possible.

On the tenth night, I hyperventilated for eighteen minutes in fifty-second reps, maintaining ten-second breaks between each. The experience was both terrifying and exhilarating.

Terrifying because I felt some of the same symptoms I had during my panic attack, and I was afraid the hyperventilating could suddenly trigger a real episode.

But I felt exhilarated because I knew something fundamental was changing about my relationship with panic attacks. I was no longer at their mercy.

The freedom I felt from conquering my fear of hyperventilating and the confidence I felt knowing that I could stand up to the bullying of a panic attack was priceless.

Though I never experienced another panic attack, I had hoped the work I did with Michael would break the vicious cycle of anxiety I was ensnared in within the three sessions, like it had with others. But unfortunately, it didn't. As helpful as my private sessions with Michael were for panic attacks, I couldn't afford to continue working with him one-on-one.

I still suffered from generalized anxiety disorder, and it was ruining my life. My nervous system remained so unhinged that by the end of April, even talking or writing about my experience with anxiety would trigger an attack. It felt as if my own mind had turned against me. Any attempt to manage the anxiety only seemed to intensify it, as though my brain perceived my efforts to quell its reaction as a threat.

My experience mirrored a common message emphasized in many of the resources I found on panic and anxiety: Resisting made it worse. Experts recommended embracing the experience—leaning into it without trying to change it.

That sounded great in theory. But in practice, it felt nearly impossible and only left me feeling helpless and angry at my inability to let go.

My struggle with accepting my anxiety reminded me of a powerful metaphor I'd learned years ago. It's called the "monkey trap"— an illustration of how holding onto something can keep us stuck in victim mode. The concept perfectly encapsulated my dilemma.

The idea originates from a traditional method used in certain cultures to catch monkeys. A box with a small opening on one end and a piece of fruit inside is placed on the ground. The hole is just big enough for a monkey to slide its hand through.

However, once the monkey grabs the treat, its clenched fist becomes too large to pull back out through the hole. This simple trap is effective because the monkeys become fixated on the piece of fruit, refusing to let go, and therefore remain trapped—held captive by their own stubborn attachment.

Like the monkey, my instinct was to grip harder to escape the anxiety, but all that did was make things feel worse, trapping me in the cycle of torment. Talk about torture!

The relentless stress I was under created a host of other issues.

One morning in May, I woke up suddenly at 2:00 a.m. with my chest on fire. Fear shot through me like an electric current. It didn't feel like a panic attack, and so my first instinct (again) was to think I was having a heart attack. My mind scrambled, scanning my symptoms in search of an explanation. I sat up, my pulse hammering as I struggled to get my bearings. I swung my feet over the side of the bed and froze, listening to my body. *Should I wake my wife and have her drive me to the nearby urgent care, or would it be smarter to call 911?*

I got up, pressed my hands to my chest, and paced the dark room, my heartbeat a frantic drum against my ribs. Each second stretched unbearably long, but as they passed, so did the intensity of the pain. The fear lingered, but it was loosening its grip. *Maybe I'm not having a heart attack after all.*

Quietly, I made my way through the darkness to my office, massaging my sternum in an effort to ease the discomfort. It might not have been a heart attack, but the worry of what it was still gnawed at me, given the intensity. I fired up my computer and sat at my desk, searching online for answers. Everything I read suggested there was one culprit: acid reflux.

As it turned out, that's what I had. From that night on, acid reflux was another ailment I had to deal with. I researched ways to address it. Lifestyle changes, dietary adjustments, and medical treatments were all the recommended steps to manage and reduce the symptoms. I chose the first two, opting not to take any medication after what I read about them.

Our bed had a motorized frame, so elevating my head during sleep to prevent stomach acid from rising into my throat was an easy fix. I also tried to avoid trigger foods like citrus, spicy dishes, alcohol, chocolate, and tomatoes—*try* being the operative word. I reluctantly curbed my habit of eating close to bedtime.

I chose not to take any medications, but I did schedule an

appointment with a gastrointestinal specialist to rule out anything serious.

While the acid reflux dampened my mood, leaving me feeling victimized by life, its effect on me dimmed in comparison to another condition I developed called globus pharyngeus—a sensation of a lump or tightness in the throat that mimics a physical obstruction. This feeling, often linked to acid reflux, would strike without warning and trigger waves of anxiety.

Adding to my distress was the periodic buildup of mucus that accompanied the globus sensation. It clung to my throat, making me question my ability to swallow and feeding a fear of suffocation.

In addition to the globus and mucus, I also experienced physical sensations that made swallowing difficult, inevitably setting off my anxiety alarms. At times, the symptoms became so severe that my throat muscles spasmed, momentarily making it literally impossible to swallow.

Over a short period of time, my challenges with swallowing forged an unintentional association between eating and anxiety. My mind became convinced that eating was dangerous, and as a consequence, my anxiety would escalate every time I ate.

As you can imagine, eating became something I dreaded. I had to force food into my mouth. Because swallowing solid food was too intimidating, the only way I could eat was to puree all my meals.

As if my fear of swallowing weren't enough, the constant nervousness I felt also killed my appetite. In just three weeks after my initial panic attack, I lost 15 pounds. Within another couple of weeks, I would lose another 5 pounds. At 5'11" and 160 pounds, losing that much so quickly had a profound physical and mental impact. My clothes sagged on my frame as if they belonged to someone else. When I stood naked in the bathroom, eyeing myself in the mirror, I was struck by what I saw. I barely recognized the man staring back at me.

Sharp edges framed my face, and my cheekbones jutted out,

giving me a gaunt, sculpted look. My eyes—once familiar—now seemed hollow and distant. I wanted to look away, but I couldn't. I stared, mesmerized by a morbid fascination, tracing the way my ribs pressed sharply against my skin with each breath. My waist, already slender, had shrunk even more, evoking images of those pioneer women in old photographs, their corseted frames impossibly small.

This was me now—stripped down, raw, and fragile, like I had just stepped out of a concentration camp. My body was no longer mine; it was something I was trapped inside, something I was slowly losing control over.

Every glance at the mirror reminded me of the fear that kept me from eating, the anxiety that coiled around my throat like a vise every time I tried to swallow. I became obsessed with my weight, stepping on the scale three to five times a day, bracing myself for how much more I might lose.

Another consequence of my condition was a heightened sensitivity to stimuli like noise and touch. Since what I was going through put a strain on my wife, I made an effort to do normal activities with her, even when it was difficult—such as attending an outdoor concert or eating at a restaurant.

But these outings were rarely normal. When we ate out, I had to get up and leave the table multiple times. Nervous energy would build up in my body until it felt like I was going to have an anxiety attack. To stave off an episode, I'd excuse myself, leaving my wife to sit alone at the table while I retreated to the bathroom, hoping I could be alone to literally shake off the panic, pace back and forth, or talk to myself out loud. Other times, I'd step outside to walk around—the change of scene and the movement offering my only relief from the pressure building inside me—until the tension subsided.

One night, while dining at an outdoor café, I was suddenly bombarded by an amplified barrage of everyday sounds—cars driving by, birds chirping, pots clanging in the restaurant kitchen, leaves rustling. Sounds that were normally faint and distant were somehow sharp and loud as if the world had been turned up to full volume. I could hear every conversation at every table, all at once. As I gazed at the people seated nearby, I could even hear them breathe! It felt like I had suddenly gained Superman's power of hearing—but instead of a gift, it was a curse.

The experience reminded me of a scene from the 2013 film *Man of Steel*, when General Zod, played by Michael Shannon, experiences sensory overload while fighting Superman on Earth after his helmet is damaged. With his hearing suddenly exposed to Earth's countless unfamiliar and unfiltered noises, Zod is overwhelmed by the onslaught of sounds—his agony raw, his disorientation absolute. That's exactly how I felt—drowning in a sea of noise, every sound stabbing at my senses, leaving me no room to breathe. It threatened to drive me insane.

Thankfully, the episode lasted only about ten seconds, but those seconds felt like an eternity, my distress amplified by not knowing what was going on and whether it would stop.

Bedtime became another time and place for my anxiety to thrive. Despite being exhausted from the constant struggles of the day, the idea of going to bed offered no comfort. Lying or sitting still would sometimes lead to feeling trapped, which, if I stayed with the feeling for too long, would lead to panic.

If I became aware of the touch of the sheets or the weight of the blanket and dwelled on them for too long, the sensation of feeling confined would increase, pushing me closer to panic. If our small dog tried to snuggle beside me, I'd have to move away—otherwise, it could trigger panic.

The less sleep I got, the harder it was to defend myself against my all-consuming anxiety. Desperate for sleep, I resigned myself to taking trazodone, a strong medication meant to force my body into sleep. Even then, I'd wake up two or three times during the night, missing out on the rejuvenation I so desperately needed.

The nighttime, once my favorite creative time of day, became something I feared. A sense of purpose and a multitude of distractions during the day helped buffer the impact of my anxiety, but the night was a different story.

I dreaded the hour when the light slowly faded into darkness. With fewer ways to occupy my mind, the night became the domain of my unhinged self—a time when my defenses weakened, leaving me feeling exposed and helpless.

In April, amid my financial woes, my house in Maryland went on the market and sold quickly with a strong offer and a handsome profit. Even with that good news, it did nothing to ease the unyielding grip of my anxiety. Whatever hellish monster had taken hold of me showed no sign of letting go.

My wife watched in dismay as her husband steadily deteriorated, both mentally and emotionally. She believed the key to my recovery was having a sense of purpose—something to keep me occupied, focused, and earning money.

Then one day, with a brutal dose of tough love, she gave me a stern talking-to, telling me it was time to be a man and pull myself together. Her words hit hard. In the moment, I thought they bordered on abusive. But as difficult as they were to hear, her harsh truth sparked something in me. It helped me begin the climb out of the grave I had fallen into.

Determined to push me forward, she convinced me to sign up as an Uber driver. She also urged me to turn my love for dogs into an opportunity by promoting myself as a dog walker, and to put my fix-it skills to use as a handyman, advertising on local social media, which I did.

Staying busy and earning some money offered brief distractions from my inescapable anxiety, but the effort to be productive was often grueling and far from foolproof.

One day, while driving for Uber, two young women in their early twenties climbed into my car. As they chatted and laughed, my fragile mind interpreted their joy as ridicule, convinced they were mocking me and how pathetic I was for being an Uber driver.

I couldn't bear the thought, igniting a surge of anxiety that I struggled to contain. Although I delivered them to their destination safely, it took an immense effort to hold myself together.

There were several times I'd have an anxiety attack while driving, but thankfully, this didn't happen very often while driving Uber passengers. However, on several occasions while running errands, I had to pull over during an anxiety attack and wait for it to subside, trying every trick I knew to calm myself.

My wife understood that everything I was doing to earn money was just a temporary fix. In her eyes, I needed something more substantial—something I could be proud of.

Desperate for a solution, and without telling me, she reached out to a friend in May who worked at a recruiting agency, hoping to find me a job at the company where he worked.

"They might need someone to assist with onboarding new employees," her friend said. "Let me check, and I'll get back to you."

Hoping this opportunity would work out, my wife sat me down and admitted what she had done. After some discussion, I reluctantly agreed to accept the offer—if the position was still available. Since I had never handled onboarding before, I took the initiative to research the role's responsibilities online.

A few days later, my wife received a call from her friend.

"I'm afraid that opportunity isn't open," he said. "But I'll keep my eye out for him in case something else comes up."

By the first week of June, things slowly began to improve. I started drinking calorie-dense milkshakes and pureed soups loaded with heavy cream to gain weight, eventually putting on five pounds.

While Uber driving wasn't lucrative, it helped me focus outward instead of constantly obsessing over my problems. I found some enjoyment in driving people around, especially when they were up for a conversation. When I wasn't driving, I spent time walking dogs and getting paid for tackling the occasional handyman job in nearby homes.

Then, on the Friday and Saturday of June 10 and 11, everything fell apart. Physical sensations and muscle tension triggered a panic cycle, and for two days, I was consumed and tortured by relentless, debilitating anxiety. Nothing I tried decreased the intensity of the fear or discomfort. The weight I had painstakingly gained vanished, and the physical and mental torment left me feeling disheartened, defeated, and frustrated. The despair was so intense, I found myself wishing for a way to end it all.

By Sunday, I was beginning to seriously think that ending my life was the only way to escape my living hell. I was keenly aware that suicide would devastate my wife and family, and ultimately, I knew it wasn't what I really wanted. I just wanted the torment to end. I fervently prayed for relief.

Just when I thought it couldn't get any worse, I had what I would call a nervous breakdown later that week. I found myself consumed by darkness, a mere shadow of my former self, floundering in a morass of pain, confusion, and self-pity.

I couldn't see it in the midst of my crisis, but in hindsight, I realized I had been crossing an invisible threshold. It was a universal transition we all experience at one time or another, embodied in the yin-yang symbol. In essence, this symbol teaches that light and dark are intimately connected—one cannot exist without the other. It also reveals a profound truth: Light only emerges after the deepest darkness. Perhaps that's why so many who hit rock bottom suddenly find the will—or the way—to change their lives.

It was during my deepest darkness that my own moment of light appeared—bringing with it two miracles that not only saved me but forever changed the course of my life. Both miracles were brought about by my wife's efforts. Both were born out of a deep sense of desperation, with my life hanging in the balance.

The first miracle was that she insisted I take an antidepressant. She ultimately forced my hand.

I've never been a pill popper. My body was my temple by the time I was thirteen, and I didn't believe in taking pills for any kind of pain, from headaches to severe accidents. I was especially wary of antidepressants.

I had a laundry list of reasons why. I didn't trust that doctors truly understood these medications, I believed depression could be "fixed" through holistic methods, and I'd read or heard about too many instances of antidepressants not working. Most of all, I didn't want to admit I had a mental disorder or carry the stigma of that label.

In addition, much of the literature I had read said it could take up to six weeks before I would feel any benefit from taking an anti-depressant. It seemed pointless since I didn't think I could make it another two weeks, let alone six.

Somewhat begrudgingly—but also out of respect for what my wife had been dealing with—I started taking 10 mg of escitalo-pram. I'll come back to what happened shortly. But first, I need to tell you about the second miracle.

On Friday morning, June 16, my wife received a phone call. It was her friend from the recruiting agency.

"There's an opening for a contract role as a recruiter for the company," he said. "They want him to start on Monday."

While this was wonderful news for my wife, I was terrified. My mind was tangled in turmoil and self-doubt—I couldn't fathom pulling myself together to function, let alone step into a job in a field I had no experience in.

Whenever my anxiety became too much over the course of my ordeal, I often turned to the pool in our backyard for comfort.

Being submerged in the water offered a brief respite from my anxiety. There was something about the weightlessness and the silence beneath the surface that brought a momentary sense of peace.

After the call, I slipped into the water's depth and prayed. I reached out to my mom like I had done so many times as a kid—when she was alive—whenever I needed emotional reassurance.

"Mom," I pleaded out loud. "What should I do? This feels like too much for me to handle."

I moved slowly, mindfully in the water, taking deep breaths and listening for any guidance as I prayed and meditated for an answer. I also reached out to any spirits that had a vested interest in my well-being, calling on them for help. But like so many prayers, they went unanswered. I was left to make the decision on my own.

Like a mother bird nudging her chick from the nest, my wife urged me to take the job. After several conversations and hours of agonizing over it, I took a deep breath and a leap of faith, and accepted the offer.

Though the transition into a new job was anything but easy, that phone call and the opportunity felt like a significant moment of synchronicity—a miracle. I struggled to concentrate and still battled anxiety, but I couldn't deny the profound impact of having a "real" job—and how it reshaped the way I viewed myself and my life because of it.

As for the first miracle? Within just a few days of taking escitalopram, I noticed a marked improvement in how I felt. It was like night and day. *Was it a placebo effect?* I wondered. I didn't care. I was simply overjoyed to feel more like myself for the first time in months.

That said, feeling better didn't mean I was cured. I still felt anxiety and needed to keep up with my daily self-care regimen, but it was less intense, and things began to stabilize.

The mental fire alarms that once malfunctioned constantly went silent. My appetite returned, and I regained all the weight I had lost—eventually gaining an extra ten pounds. My acid reflux and globus fell dormant, and my sleep patterns normalized, allowing me to eventually wean myself off the sleep medication. After several months, I felt I could trust that the anxiety spells wouldn't completely overtake me again.

Even now, a year and a half later, anxiety occasionally wells up within me, a reminder of those tumultuous days. When it happens, I get scared, wondering if it will hijack my sanity and drag me back down that dark rabbit hole. But it never does. Though uncomfortable and unsettling, it always passes—and I come out the other side intact.

At one point, months later and under the care of my primary-care physician, I slowly weaned off escitalopram. But in early 2025, after experiencing a scary surge of anxiety like a wave that echoed past episodes, I decided to start taking it again, and continue to this day.

Reflecting on my experience, I see how close I came to being consumed by my anxiety—to the brink of losing everything that I thought defined me. The path to recovery wasn't linear or easy, but it was transformative. Every setback felt insurmountable at the time, yet each one shaped the resilience I carry today.

The miracles of that fateful Friday weren't cures; they were catalysts. They didn't erase my struggles but gave me the impetus to face them. Healing is not a destination but a process—one that requires patience, courage, and a willingness to embrace even the darkest moments. After all, light cannot exist without darkness.

Life's goal isn't to avoid falling, but to find the will to rise—no matter how many times you stumble. My journey taught me that while the darkness can feel endless, the light always returns if you remain open to it and keep moving forward.

If you're reading this and struggling with your own darkness, know this: You are not alone, and you are stronger than you think.

Miracles—or that spark of hope that propels you forward—may not come when or how you expect. But if you hold on long enough, they will. And sometimes, the greatest miracle isn't something that happens to you—it's realizing you have the power to create your own light through humility, self-compassion, and the courage to ask for—or accept—help.

CHAPTER 5

More Awe-Inspiring Moments

27

The Narnia Tree

The winter morning chill seeped through my down jacket as I hurried across campus toward the café in the student union. The damp mist hanging in the air and a heavy shroud of low-hanging clouds deepened my irritability.

I was a first-year student at the University of Oregon. With an early morning break between classes, I was rushing to grab food before my low blood sugar turned me into a wreck. Too many hours without eating left me running on fumes, my gnawing hunger threatening my mood like a trapped animal, cornered and ready to lash out.

If I don't eat, I become emotionally hypersensitive. Small irritations that normally wouldn't faze me add up and rattle my cage. The experience sometimes makes me wonder if I'm on the spectrum of autism because my sensory sensitivities can spike so intensely, and the world feels overwhelming.

As I made a beeline to the student union, my agitation inched toward a full-blown meltdown—not a pretty sight.

I knew this feeling would pass once I ate, but in the moment, logic didn't stand a chance against my hangriness. I scolded myself. *You did this. Will you ever learn?* Then, in a desperate attempt to stave off a blowup, I soothed my inner child, hoping that would be enough to keep him from unraveling. *Food is coming. Just hold on. Not much longer, I promise.*

The cement walkway beneath my feet wound past the Museum of Art on my right, leading into a large, parklike area where criss-crossing paths cut through fields of grass dotted with maple, cedar, dogwood, birch, and fir trees.

As I made my way, one pine captured my attention. It towered against the moody winter sky, its silhouette crisp with full branches fanning out in a perfect, gradual taper from top to bottom, like something out of a Christmas storybook. The lowest limbs swept the ground in a broad, majestic reach, reinforcing its stately presence.

Something about it felt regal, as if it were aware of its quiet majesty. The surrounding trees clustered nearby in still reverence—like courtiers before a queen. A pristine bed of grass lay beneath it, further accentuating its grandeur.

Any awareness of the cold or my hunger vanished like my breath dissolving into the winter air as I walked by, mesmerized by its presence.

The tree stood a good three hundred feet away, yet I heard its request as clearly as a whisper in my mind.

Hello. Could you come here, please?

I halted in my tracks, tilting my head as I cast a quizzical gaze toward it.

Wait . . . did that tree just speak to me? Am I hallucinating from hunger?

Yes, it's me, she said, answering my unspoken thought.

I say her because, though the tree made no sound, her telepathic message carried the essence of a woman's voice—soft yet strong, a tenor filled with warmth, kindness, and intelligence, and seasoned with the wisdom of ages.

Would you do me a favor and pick up the trash around my trunk? she asked politely.

Riveted, I veered off my path and made my way toward her. A tree was talking to me. Of course I had to go.

Ever since I was a kid, trees—especially pines—have held a special place in my heart. Give me a forest of pine over an ocean any day.

As a long-distance runner in my youth, there were times I'd stop mid-run in a forest or park, drawn to a tree that caught my attention. I'd wrap my arms around its sturdy trunk and meld my mind with it—like Spock from *Star Trek*—sending it healing energy and loving thoughts.

As I stood in our quiet embrace, I'd tilt my head back, tracing the rough bark upward to where its branches swayed, not from the wind, but because it was alive. I soaked in the view with a sense of wonder, imagining what it might be like to be a tree and to live its life.

I had always believed trees are sentient beings, worthy of respect and dignity, but never did I imagine I would one day carry on a conversation with one.

And yet, here I was, face-to-face with a tree that was speaking to me.

Eons of growth had made her branches wide and thick, completely hiding her trunk from view. I paced around her, searching for an opening, but after coming full circle, there was none to be found.

Standing at her side, I assessed how I would enter. I tried to pull apart her boughs gently, but they were too thick and unwieldy. The twigs and tendrils had woven together like an intricate web of limbs. It was clear that a delicate approach would not work.

Feeling sheepish about what I was about to do, I glanced around, hoping no one was watching.

"Sorry for the ungentlemanly entrance," I murmured, thrusting my hands through and forcefully pulling apart the layers. Grunting with the effort, I leaned in and lunged forward, squeezing through headfirst, like a mouse burrowing into a hole far too small for its body.

Halfway through, I lost my balance and tumbled forward in what felt like the start of a somersault, momentum carrying me until my foot snagged in an entanglement above me. I pitched downward in a comical freefall, landing on the back of my shoulder with a thud that forced a moan from my chest. A spray of dead needles showered over me as a grand finale to my theatrical comedy of errors.

My body dangled from my trapped foot, torso twisted, while my upper back and head touched the ground.

That must have looked ridiculous, I thought, hoping there were no witnesses.

For a long moment, the rapid heaving of my chest was all I could hear. I remained still, focusing on calming my breath as I mentally scanned my body for any injuries.

Fortunately, the layers I wore, along with my puffy down jacket and the thick blanket of pine needles, cushioned my fall. Once I determined nothing was hurt, I turned my attention to my ensnared foot.

Out of respect for the tree, I attempted to ease my foot free. I tugged gently, but nothing gave. I shifted my weight, adjusted my angle, and tried again. After a few attempts, I realized I would have to use more force. I pursed my lips together as I let out a deep sigh. I braced for the effort, then yanked harder, prompting another shower of needles. I whipped my face to the side, but not before several needles landed in my mouth. I sputtered and coughed, flicking my tongue in a desperate attempt to expel the bitter, papery needles. I spat several onto the ground, wiping the rest from my lips with the back of my hand.

Despite my effort, my foot remained wedged in place, locked in a vise grip. My mind conjured up worst-case scenarios—starvation, amputation, or worse yet, suffering the humiliation of being found in such a ridiculous predicament.

The problem was, given the height of my foot and the angle I was dangling from, there was nothing for me to grab onto for leverage. It made pulling with real strength nearly impossible.

Still, I tried again. Twisting and jerking my leg, I thrashed my foot in frantic, disjointed kicks, hoping to pry it loose. But the more I struggled, the more tired I became. My movements grew weaker, my breaths more labored, and doubt crept in—what if I couldn't get free?

As an athlete, I had plenty of practice confronting defeatist thoughts—the kind that could have kept me from winning or even trying. *Perseverance pays off* is one of the most important lessons I've learned in my life—so after a brief rest, I kept kicking, each heave more desperate than the last, until finally, with one all-or-nothing wrench, my foot tore free, falling to the ground with a muted thud.

After catching my breath, I slowly got to my feet, steadying myself as I rose, then brushed the needles from my hair and clothes. When I finished, I glanced around, surprised to find enough room to move about freely. A billowy blanket of decades-old pine needles lay dead and crunchy beneath me, forming a neatly defined circle around the tree's trunk. The rich, slightly pungent scent of earthy pine filled my nostrils.

A hush thickened the air, reverent and still, like the silence inside an ancient cathedral. Magisterial light—unlike the winter hues outside—streamed through the branches in softened rays, casting everything in a dreamlike glow. There was something magickal about the space. It felt otherworldly. The feeling struck me so powerfully that I imagined this must have been how young Lucy felt when she first discovered the enchanted world of Narnia in C. S. Lewis's *The Lion, the Witch and the Wardrobe*.

As I looked at the ground, my ethereal bliss turned to dismay. In one section, litter was strewn everywhere—candy wrappers, soda cans, beer bottles, cigarette butts, and an assortment of junk-food packaging. It wasn't just a few stray pieces either; it was enough to make the space feel defiled, as if people had used it as a dumping ground without a second thought. It was a silent testament to how little people thought of nature. A hollow feeling spread through my chest, my stomach tightening as I took in the scene. Disgusted, I got on my hands and knees, determined to remove every trace of humanity's inconsideration.

I pushed the cigarette butts into the soda cans, crushed everything down, and stuffed as much as I could into my pockets. But there was too much. I stared at what still lay on the ground, and I grimaced. The only remaining option was inside my jacket. The last thing I wanted was garbage pressed against my chest, but I wasn't about to leave it behind. With a sigh, I unzipped my coat and carefully crammed the rest inside.

When I was done, I moved toward her trunk, delicately easing my way through the stillness of her innermost branches until I was close enough to touch her. I reached out, placed a hand on her body, and closed my eyes, holding my hand there with deep reverence. Silently, I expressed my overwhelming gratitude for the extraordinary experience I had just been given and offered an apology for the people who had disrespected her space.

Just as I was about to say goodbye, I received another message.
Come this way, she beckoned.

Surprised and curious, I backed away and let her guide me toward a spot at her base that was less accessible—an area where I hadn't noticed any trash. At first, I saw nothing. Then, bending down for a closer look, I spotted several quarters, dimes, and a few scattered pennies, half buried in the bed of needles. I crouched to pick them up and remained there, letting the enormity of what had just happened sink in.

I sat in the quiet embrace of the moment, a deep warmth spreading through my chest as if an unseen presence had wrapped me in light. The air felt charged with something sacred, and I let it settle over me, relishing its divine purity. It felt as though I had been blessed by God herself.

My breath came slowly, drifting in delicate plumes, as I turned the coins over in my palm, listening to their faint metallic clink. Resting there like tiny relics, their worth suddenly felt far greater than their value.

At the same time, I was still trying to wrap my mind around the experience. I mean—Jesus—I had just communicated with a tree. But what struck me just as much was that this tree had a presence so distinct, so unmistakably sentient, that I instinctively thought of her as a she. And then, as if that weren't astonishing enough, she had expressed disdain for the trash around her trunk and asked me to clear it out. And now, as if rewarding me for my efforts, she had led me to money—something she clearly understood would matter to me.

This raised a profound question: Do all trees possess an intelligence capable of grasping the intricacies of the human world? Do they feel emotions and understand values? The implications were both staggering and heartbreaking.

I've always felt deeply saddened by the vast number of trees that have been cut down—especially in Oregon, where I lived for over twenty years, and where logging and timber extraction shaped the economy for far too long.

Logging sounds so harmless, doesn't it? But after my experience, I saw it for what it truly was—a form of slaughter.

Maybe one day, as a species, we'll wake up and recognize the plant kingdom for its true nature: a realm of living beings deserving of our respect. That's my hope.

I imagine most of us take trees for granted. I know I have. But as this story illustrates, trees are far more than inanimate objects or mere timber for consumption. Perhaps now, after reading about my experience, you'll feel inspired to stop by a tree, place a hand against its bark, or even wrap your arms around its sturdy trunk—taking a moment to acknowledge it with reverence.

Chances are, it will sense your thoughts, feel your kindness, and appreciate your attention. And who knows—maybe you'll even have your own extraordinary encounter, one that leaves you touched by the divine.

28

Summer Buzz

Summers in Eugene, Oregon, are usually the kind you dream about—pleasantly warm with plenty of golden sunshine and no humidity; the air is so refreshing that stepping outside feels like you're entering paradise. That's why most homes built in the fifties, sixties, and seventies weren't equipped with air-conditioning. But there are a few days when the sun beats down mercilessly, driving temperatures into the high nineties, and those without air-conditioning find themselves longing for relief.

I lived in one of those homes, and on a scorching Sunday morning in 1986, when I was just past my teens, I found myself in that camp. After nightclub dancing into the early hours of the previous night and collapsing into bed at 4:00 a.m., I woke five hours later in a groggy haze, as if nursing a hangover—despite not touching a drop of alcohol.

I dragged myself out of bed, took a cool shower, and spent the next couple of hours knocking out weekend chores. By the end of it, despite the satisfaction of getting things done, I was as cranky as a toddler kept up long past their afternoon siesta.

The heat had grown stifling by then, intensifying my need for a nap. Having finished my chores, I stripped down to my underwear, tossed the blanket off my bed, turned on the oscillating fan, and slid under the top sheet. The soft cotton felt cool against my skin as I burrowed my face into the plush, downy pillow.

A deep sigh escaped my lips as I sank into the comfort of being horizontal again, reveling in the joy of it. The fan, however, did nothing more than offer a fleeting hint of relief, and my sheets quickly lost their crisp coolness. Even though I was exhausted, I was soon tossing and turning, irritated by the damp stickiness of my body against the now-clammy sheets. I tried adjusting the fan so it blew directly on me, but that became just as annoying and uncomfortable, so I grabbed the top sheet and flung it aside, hoping that would help. I rolled onto my stomach and waited for my fatigue to win out over the heat.

My restless mind had finally settled when I heard the familiar sound of a fly buzzing overhead. It was like a noisy biplane circling a field, scouting for the perfect landing spot. I kept my eyes closed, praying the fly wouldn't notice me.

A moment later, my hopes were dashed. I felt the slight tickle of it landing on my middle back. I twitched, sending it airborne. It circled once before relanding near its original spot. Determined to keep my fragile, right-before-I-fall-asleep composure, I slowly waved my hand behind me to shoo it away. The fly took off, did a flyby, and then promptly landed back on my upper torso.

When I was a kid, I used to kill insects without a second thought—sometimes for fun, sometimes because they looked scary or because I feared they might hurt me—like the time a venomous spider bit me behind the knee, causing me excruciating pain after the venom had spread.

As a teenager, I made a conscious decision to stop killing them indiscriminately. I developed a deeper awareness that acknowledged them as sentient beings with their own uniqueness and a right to exist.

The only exceptions I make are mosquitoes determined to drain my blood and, occasionally, ants that invade my home. There may be others, but you get my point. I don't kill insects just for the heck of it. If I don't want them where they are, I catch them and take them outside.

This fly was definitely testing the conviction of my peace treaty with insects. After a few more frustrating rounds of cat and mouse—and some choice words—I scrambled out of bed, wrestled with my shirt and shorts like a drunkard, and chased the fly around the room, frantically waving my arms and roaring like a tiger to corral it out into the hallway and far away from my bedroom.

After I finally succeeded, I stumbled back to my bed, hoping I could find peace at last. Why I didn't bother closing the bedroom door afterward, I don't know—call it sleep deprivation or heat exhaustion. Not long after I laid back down, I heard the familiar buzz reenter the room. Within seconds, we were back at it, playing out our routine like a scene from a Saturday morning cartoon.

"This time you're really pissing me off!" I yelled as I leaped out of bed like I was possessed by a demon. The fly was both smart and fast, darting past my swats like a seasoned combat pilot.

I must have looked like I was auditioning for a cameo on *The Three Stooges* as I chased that fly around. I ran after it from the bedroom, down the hallway, and into the living room. We sparred there for a minute before I chased it through the dining room and into the kitchen.

The fly was always one step ahead of me, stoking my frustration into a frenzy. My manifesto about not killing innocent insect life was obliterated by my fuming rage as I continued my efforts to kill the intruder disrupting my peace.

The fly deftly evaded my swats in the kitchen and escaped. I gave chase back through the dining room into the living room and then back into the kitchen. By this time, I was practically frothing at the mouth with indignation. If you've ever seen Wolverine when he gets mad and starts thrashing his enemies, then you know how I was feeling.

I bent over in exasperation and fatigue, hands on my thighs, panting for air. When I stood up, I saw the fly perched on an upper cabinet, shoulder height, just a couple of feet away. I slowly crouched down, striking a pose reminiscent of Bruce Lee—fists cocked, ready to do damage, watching the fly intently to see if I could determine what direction it might fly.

As I stood there, brimming with ire and righteous fury that this persistent little creature had the gall to disturb my much-needed rest with what felt like premeditated intent, a memory of an intriguing book surfaced in my mind—one I had stumbled upon not long ago at the local new age bookstore—titled *Talking with Nature* by Michael J. Roads. In it, he shares his discovery of an ability to commune—intelligently and articulately—with the souls of plants, animals, and even rocks and rivers.

As I thought about the profound nature of his ability, my anger subsided. And when it did, I had a moment of clarity. I didn't really want to kill the fly. What I wanted more than anything was to take it outside and set it free.

As soon as that thought passed through my mind, I heard the voice—that wise and loving guide who always showed up unannounced in moments ripe with transformative significance. In a gentle, omniscient tone, it encouraged me to extend my hand and offer to carry the fly to freedom.

My logical mind scoffed. I imagined it smirking, ridiculing the notion that the fly would hop onto my hand and allow itself to be carried out the front door like it was being chauffeured.

I couldn't argue much with that line of reasoning—it made complete sense. But I also had enough experience with that inner voice to know better than to dismiss its suggestion outright.

The challenge was knowing whom to listen to. The voice was always subtle, easy to overlook, while my logical mind was loud and insistent. Both were persuasive in their own way. I took a deep breath and tried to quiet the noise in my head.

What do I have to lose? I thought. *It would be really cool if the fly did hop on my hand.* Despite my doubt, I spoke—both out loud and telepathically—to the fly. In a loving tone, steady with conviction, I said: "I will extend my hand to you, and if you hop onto it, I promise to carry you safely outside where you can fly free."

I then extended my right hand palm down—slowly but with confidence—toward the little guy, who hadn't twitched once since landing. A moment passed, and then, much to my surprise, it hopped onto the back of my hand. I held my breath in disbelief.

This is just a coincidence, my skeptical intellect sneered. *It'll fly away as soon as you move.*

I figured I had nothing to lose by trying. I began walking slowly toward the front door. To my amazement, the fly stayed put.

It's only staying there because you're walking like my ninety-year-old grandmother, came the retort from my intellect.

To test out its theory, I quickened my pace, racewalking to the door. It didn't move.

I opened the front door and then, with my left hand, I grabbed the screen door handle and pressed the button to release the catch. But instead of opening, the screen door held firm, and I crashed straight into it—startled and stumbling like a comedy act, trying to keep my balance. Fortunately, neither I nor the screen door was hurt.

I quickly gathered my composure, fully expecting the fly to be gone. But to my shock, it hadn't budged. Not even after all that ruckus.

I carefully opened the screen door and stepped onto the stoop, into the freedom of the afternoon air. The fly remained—no twitching, no walking, no flying. At first, I thought maybe I had killed it as a result of my mishap with the screen door.

I moved the fly closer to my face and saw it twitch as if to say, *I'm okay.*

Full of wonder and awe at the mystique of what was happening,

I found myself asking if I had really communicated with this fly, or was this just a once-in-a-lifetime fluke?

Then, I received a telepathic message—not in words, but as a feeling.

Thank you for helping me.

Stunned that this fly was communicating with me, I silently replied, *You're welcome.*

A mix of astonishment and disbelief washed over me, quickly followed by shame. This fly, which I had moments ago treated as a worthless pest, had suddenly become a fellow inhabitant on our planet—different from me but entitled, nevertheless, to respect and the grace of goodness.

I offered up an apology: *I'm sorry for my anger—all the swats, the chasing, the frustration. I was going to kill you, and I deeply regret it. I'm grateful you let me help you. Thank you for this moment, for the chance to connect with you. It is a sacred gift that fills my heart with joy, and I will always carry this experience with me. Thank you for trusting me to take you outside.*

The fly lingered for a few moments in my silent reverie as if acknowledging our interspecies synergy. Then, it twitched a farewell and jettisoned into the sky. I tracked its flight for a few seconds as it swept upward in a wide elegant arc, disappearing into the vastness of the summer afternoon—like a cinematic ending to a profound movie.

I stood still, letting it all sink in. I replayed the interaction in the theater of my mind, marveling at the sanctity of the experience. Not only did I feel good for helping the little guy, but—holy shit!—I had just communicated with a fly, and it was intelligent! There were no words to describe that kind of private exaltation.

As the magick of the experience faded, the heat suddenly brought me back down to earth, reminding me I was still standing outside. With a deep breath and a long sigh, I turned to step back inside.

A dreamy smile lingered on my face as I fell back onto my bed. An ordinary day fraught with fatigue and frustration had become transcendent—my attempt to kill a fly had transformed into a profound, life-altering connection. I closed my eyes, feeling a wave of ecstatic grace wash over me—not just for the fly, but for myself and the awareness that allowed me to have this kind of magick in my life.

Just before drifting off, I whispered, "Thank you, little friend," knowing this experience would be etched in my memory forever.

29

Butt of a Cosmic Joke

"Oh, that's so gross!" I squawked dramatically, grabbing the remote, aiming it at the TV, and pausing the movie. I turned to look at my best friend and housemate, Sara, seated in her cushy chair nearby. She laughed at my scrunched-up face, my tongue sticking out like I'd just bitten into a lemon.

It was a lazy weekday afternoon, and we were sprawled out in the living room, watching *Kiss of the Spider Woman* on DVD. Released in 1985, the film stars William Hurt and Raul Julia as two prisoners sharing a jail cell in Brazil during the country's military dictatorship of the 1960s through the '80s.

The movie focuses on the conversations and interactions between the two cellmates and the unlikely bond that develops. Without giving away too much of the plot, there's a scene where Raul Julia's character, a political prisoner, is poisoned by his jailers. After eating a meal handed to him in his cell, the toxins hit him hard.

We see him writhing in pain. His cellmate, played by William Hurt, tells him a story to distract him. Suddenly, a sharp cramp seizes him, and he realizes he's about to lose control of his bowels. He strains to reach the bucket they use as a toilet, but it's too late.

The poison has induced a severe case of diarrhea, and he soils himself. Humiliated, he slumps to the floor, legs sprawled in front of him.

The next scene is what made me stop the movie and cry out in revulsion. William Hurt's character volunteers to clean his cellmate, tending to him with quiet compassion. He removes the man's filthy pants and, without hesitation, wipes him clean with a towel.

I turned to look at Sara.

"There's no way in hell I would do that!" I exclaimed. "I would rather die!"

Sara chuckled. Being older, more mature, and seasoned by years as both a firefighter and paramedic, she'd seen her share of the grotesque and the gruesome. The thought of wiping someone clean didn't faze her the way it did me.

I opened my mouth wide and made a gagging sound as I pretended to stick my finger down my throat. Sara just shook her head and rolled her eyes. When I was done with my charade, I turned the DVD back on, and we continued watching the movie.

They say the universe has a sense of humor. If I didn't believe it then, I was about to.

Ten minutes later, our movie was interrupted by a fervent knock on the front door. I looked at Sara.

"You expecting anyone?"

"Nope," she said. "But it sounds urgent."

I stopped the movie, jumped off the couch, and strode to the door.

Standing on the other side of the screen was our neighbor's eight-year-old son, Kevin. He was one of four boys, raised by a single mother. Sara and I had a friendly-neighbor relationship with the family: casual waves, occasional chats with Julie, their mom, and periodic visits from the younger kids looking to play.

Kevin, the eldest, was different. A quiet introvert, he mostly kept to himself. We rarely saw him, and when we did, it was only in passing. Seeing him now, standing on our stoop alone, I couldn't help but wonder—what had brought him here? As I studied his face, I could see he was distraught. I swung open the screen door and asked him what was wrong.

He looked at me with an expression I haven't forgotten all these years later—anguish and shame were etched across his face. Tears burst from his eyes and tumbled down his cheeks as he explained that he had walked home from school to find no one there. The house was empty, and he had no way to get inside.

He told me he had to go to the bathroom—badly—but felt too awkward asking someone he barely knew to use their toilet. So, he decided to wait. Unfortunately, he waited too long. Between sobs, he admitted, mortified, that he had pooped in his pants.

Without hesitation, I invited him in. I ushered him into the guest bathroom and instructed him to step into the bathtub. I grabbed a few towels from the nearby linen closet and knelt beside the tub.

My heart swelled with empathy as I looked at him. The poor boy held his head down, avoiding my gaze as he sat fully clothed, legs out in front of him, tears still streaming down his face. I wanted to hug him, to console him, but we didn't have that kind of rapport—and I knew he wouldn't feel comfortable with that.

His plight struck a chord. As he sat there, dejected and humiliated, a long-forgotten memory surfaced—one from when I was about his age, a moment where I too had suffered the sting of intense embarrassment.

I was racing my green Schwinn through a park in a foreign country where I hardly knew the language, trying desperately to keep up with my older brother and his friends. They had invited me to join them, only to leave me in their dust, despite my pleas to wait.

Fearing I might lose them, I made a split-second decision to cross a street they'd traversed minutes earlier—without properly checking for traffic.

The moment I jumped the curb, I was committed. When I landed in the street, I realized just how foolish and idiotic my decision was. A car I hadn't seen hurtled toward me.

Panic seized my body. I froze, instinctively clutching the brakes to a full stop, my feet planted like cement as the car's hood loomed closer.

The driver's quick reflexes brought the car to a screeching halt just feet away. My body trembled. A wave of warmth ran down my legs. I had peed my pants. Not a little. A lot. A dark stain spread across my jeans like a badge of stupidity.

I still remember the humiliation as the passenger—a plump, middle-aged woman—jumped out to check on me. When she saw I was unharmed, she hugged me tightly and thanked God I was okay while the driver, a stern-looking man, glared at me from behind the wheel.

Kevin's expression mirrored what I had felt that day. I knew exactly what he was going through.

"Kevin," I said gently, "I know you're feeling embarrassed. I once peed in my pants in public, so I get it. I'm going to take your pants off and clean you up, okay?"

He nodded slowly, still avoiding eye contact. I started with his shoes, but the laces were knotted. Rather than struggle with untying them, I gently held each leg and pulled them off, one at a time. As I did, I spoke softly, reassuring him, letting kindness bridge the space between us. Then came the pants. Kevin's jeans clung tight. When they finally slipped off, I gasped inwardly. The mess had escaped his underwear, streaking his legs and coating the inside of his pants.

Under normal circumstances, the smell and sight would've made me gag—but in that moment, I was channeling Mother Teresa. *So, this is what it must've been like for her*, I thought, *tending to the sick and poor.*

As I knelt there, washing away the mess with a hand spray, I was struck by the cosmic synchronicity—and the irony. I had just watched a scene in a movie that I swore I'd rather die than endure . . . and here I was, living it ten minutes later. I shook my head in disbelief. What were the odds? And more importantly, what was going on here? Was I the butt of a cosmic joke? (Pun intended.)

I pulled the shower curtain closed and instructed Kevin to undress fully while I took his soiled clothes to the laundry room. I grabbed some sweatpants and a T-shirt from my room and left them on the bathroom cabinet as he finished up his shower.

When he emerged, we heard the sound of his mom's car pulling into the driveway. Before I could walk him out, he bolted—dashing through the living room and out the door like a thief on the run.

I followed him to the front stoop and caught a glimpse of him sprinting across his yard to greet her. After a quick wave hello, I went back inside to clean the bathroom.

The room still carried traces of what had happened—a damp towel on the floor, the faint scent of soap mingling with something less pleasant, Kevin's underwear, and the remnants of his accident in the tub. I sprayed everything down and wiped away the last of it, feeling deeply blessed by the experience.

My heart swelled as I thought about the vulnerability on Kevin's face—the way the shame had softened into something quieter, infused with gratitude that needed no words.

The whole experience felt divinely orchestrated. I couldn't help but marvel at how seamlessly the Universe had lined everything up—from renting the movie, to the moment we sat down to watch it, to the scene from the movie, followed by my melodramatic statement and Kevin's arrival.

As I was writing this, the phrase "All the world's a stage" drifted into my mind. I didn't know its origin, so—being the curious sort—I looked it up. Turns out, it's from Shakespeare's *As You Like It*, written around 1599:

All the world's a stage,
And all the men and women merely players;
They have their exits and their entrances;
And one man in his time plays many parts . . .

—*As You Like It*, act II, scene VII

It felt like Kevin and I were two souls in a play, directed by unseen forces that wove through our lives with impeccable timing—and, sometimes, a flair for the dramatic.

Our scene may have centered on Kevin's misfortune, but it was much more than that. It was a teaching moment for me: a lesson in empathy, the potential for character transformation, and the grace that comes when you stop thinking about yourself and simply respond with love.

I finished tidying up and rejoined Sara in the living room. As the movie resumed, I sat back and sent a silent prayer of gratitude to the heavens—for their cosmic, curtain-call blessing in disguise.

30

Hot Coals

"You're going to do what?!" I blurted, gripping the corded phone against my ear.

It was the fall of 1988—a time when cell phones were rare and the internet was still a distant dream. My long-distance girlfriend in Southern Oregon had just dropped a bombshell so outrageous, I needed to hear it again to make sure I hadn't imagined it.

"I'm going to walk on fire," she said as casually as if she were inviting me to dinner. "Want to do it with me?"

I couldn't help but burst into laughter at the sheer absurdity.

Jennifer was a beautiful, blue-eyed free spirit with a singing voice that could only be described as angelic. We'd first met years earlier when she performed at the Unity Church I attended in Eugene, Oregon. Her music—uplifting, soulful, and deeply inspirational—struck a chord with me. That night, I went home with her newly released cassette album, a treasure I would play almost every day.

At the time, I was facilitating support groups for male survivors of sexual abuse. Her lyrics, filled with hope and healing, resonated so deeply that I often played one of her songs at the end of each weekly session. The music touched the hearts of these men profoundly, often bringing tears to their eyes.

I thought she'd like to know the impact she was having, so one day I decided to write her a letter, telling her how much her music meant—not only to them, but to me as well. That letter sparked a friendship that soon blossomed into a long-distance romance.

Once the shock of what she said wore off, it didn't really surprise me. One of the things I liked about Jennifer was that she was into personal growth and alternative healing.

I leaned back on my couch, letting her words settle in. I knew people did fire walks with the motivational guru Tony Robbins. But I believed those people were different—that they possessed some special quality I didn't have. Never in my wildest dreams did I imagine myself doing it. Nor did I want to.

Jumping out of an airplane with a parachute? Risky but imaginable.

Walking on coals burning between 1,000 and 1,500 degrees Fahrenheit? That was just plain dumb and dangerous. The only buns I liked toasted were the ones on my hamburgers, thank you very much.

After a long pause, the only thing I managed to say was, "What on earth is possessing you to do that?"

Unfazed by my slightly sharp response, she went on. "I'm organizing a team-building workshop to foster a sense of community in my town, and a fire walk will be the centerpiece," she explained. "A friend of mine who's a life coach runs these kinds of events regularly, and I've invited her to facilitate one for us."

I told her flat out that I didn't think it was a good idea and that there was no way I'd be walking on hot coals.

She tried to persuade me to change my mind, but I was dead set on my answer.

When I heard the disappointment in her voice, I quickly realized how important it was to her and how much of a downer I was being. Not wanting to rain on her parade, I promised to make the three-hour drive down to support her while she did it.

"How does Saturday night, two weeks from now, sound?" she asked.

I was free, so I penciled it into my calendar.

Two weeks later, when I entered the community center where everything was taking place, about fifteen people were already seated in chairs, all facing the front, where a tall, attractive woman in a flowing satin gown stood addressing the group.

She was outlining the schedule and final details for the evening.

I quietly took a seat in the back, listening as she guided the group through a calming meditation.

Afterward, she led them through a series of interactive exercises meant to build teamwork, foster a sense of belonging, and cultivate mindfulness—all in preparation for the climactic fire walk at the end of the evening.

Even though I remained an observer, I couldn't help but get caught up in the allure and excitement of the night. The air buzzed with anticipation as the participants prepared for the ultimate test of will and faith.

As the group stepped out into the chilly fall night for the next phase, we were greeted by the hypnotic rhythm of drums. Three men perched on bar-height stools struck their drums with their palms in a steady, pulsing cadence. Nearby, an eight-by-twelve-foot bed of glowing red coals stretched out before us, its heat radiating into the crisp air. Led by the facilitator, the group gathered close to the heat for further instructions.

We were encouraged to grab a shovel and stoke the fire—to feel its intensity up close and truly grasp just how hot it was. I took a shovel and, out of curiosity, stepped forward. The blistering heat licked at my skin as I turned a few pieces of burning coal before quickly retreating. It was hotter than I'd expected.

When it came time for the main event, the facilitator explained how to proceed. The instructions for fire walking were simple: Step up to the firepit's edge, ask your body if it's ready and willing, and if you get a yes—walk across.

The facilitator demonstrated first. She stood at the edge, paused for a moment, then gracefully walked the entire length of the fire, her flowing gown brushing the tips of the flames.

I stood dumbfounded as if I had just witnessed a miracle. My mind struggled to comprehend how she hadn't gone up in flames. It was an incredible sight, made even more surreal as one person after another stepped up, closed their eyes as if in prayer, then opened them and walked across the coals as if they were strolling through a pleasant meadow.

At one point, three young girls, no older than nine or ten, lined up side by side at the edge of the fire. Holding hands, they walked across together, even pausing to spin in a circle, giggling, before stepping off the coals as if they had just finished a game of hopscotch.

When it was Jennifer's turn, I stood at the other end, holding my breath, silently praying she'd make it across unscathed.

I watched as she effortlessly walked across as if she were floating, her expression serene but intensely focused. When she stepped off the coals, triumphant, she came straight to me and wrapped me in a long, soulful hug.

Then, pulling back, she grasped both my hands. Her face glowed with excitement, and her eyes sparkled with joy.

"Come with me to the fire," she said. Her angelic voice carried a hypnotic, unshakable confidence I couldn't resist. The air around her swirled with magick portents and possibilities. As if in a trance, I followed her to the edge of the glowing embers. We stood together, facing the hot coals, hands clasped, and eyes closed.

I asked my body if it was okay to cross as if I were invoking some ancient rite, a sacred incantation calling on something more powerful than words alone. Jennifer squeezed my hand as if to ask if I was ready. I met the thrill of her gaze with fire in my eyes.

Together, we took a leap of faith, surrendering to the hot coals like a sacred offering.

Suddenly, intense heat surged around us, the air pungent with earthy aromas of burning wood, flames licking at our feet. But I felt no fear. The embers beneath us felt like oversized popcorn—crunchy, uneven, and strangely soft in places. It was oddly satisfying.

When we reached the other side, I let out a scream of disbelief into the deep starry sky, then hugged Jennifer tightly before jumping up and down like an ecstatic child.

Walking on fire is a total mind blow. (What I really want to say—what truly captures just how profound the experience was—requires the *F* word. But I opted for something more polite for my story.)

There's just no other way to describe it. The experience messes with your perception of reality. Your mind is convinced that what you're doing should cause excruciating pain—yet somehow, you emerge without so much as a blister.

After my first fire walk, I was hooked. The experience was so incredible, so uplifting, so surreal—it felt more like a stroll through a peaceful park on a sunny Sunday morning than a trial by fire. I couldn't wait to go again.

But the most astonishing part came during my third and final attempt—and what I discovered the next morning.

As I reached the halfway point on my third try, I felt what I could only describe as the fire biting my foot—a pain as sharp as a wasp sting.

When I reached the other side, I examined the bottom of my foot. Sure enough, there was a large red burn and a sizable blister quickly forming. It hurt but not unbearably—probably because my body was still riding high on adrenaline.

The real shock came the next morning. When I got out of bed, the blister and burn mark were completely gone—no trace whatsoever that they had ever existed. None!

For days, I couldn't stop replaying the night in my mind—the heat rising from the bed of fire, the impossible feat of walking across it (no pun intended), and the overnight disappearance of my burn and blister.

It felt like I had crossed, not just a fiery trail, but a threshold between worlds—where logic surrendered to something far greater. What had once been merely an event on my calendar became a moment of transcendence—one I would carry with me long after the embers had cooled.

31

The Power of Intention

I was lucky to be alive after my car accident in the summer of 1994, but my body felt like it had gone twelve rounds in the ring with a heavyweight champion. Every movement sent a jolt through my battered frame. Recovery trickled in like the drip of an IV, a relentless reminder that healing is a slow and grueling process and not the flood of relief I dreamed or hoped for.

Months dragged by, yet my only progress was trading in a painful hobble for a labored walk. Sleep offered no escape. I wrestled with discomfort, shifting positions in a futile attempt to find relief. The throbbing never let up; it was a cruel companion that greeted me every morning.

I was unhappy with my life before the accident, and the state of my body only made my life worse. Difficult tasks felt insurmountable while even small ones reminded me that I was locked in an incessant cycle of pain. Depression seeped into everything, like ink spreading through water, dulling my energy, clouding my thoughts, and dimming the light inside me.

Any sane person would have popped pills for relief, but as a purist, I refused every offer of allopathic drugs, even in the immediate aftermath of the accident. There was a stubborn kind of clarity in needing to feel what was happening in my body—to understand its limits, to know precisely what I could and couldn't do. Pain, as difficult as it was to endure, wasn't an enemy to be suppressed; it was a messenger, a gauge of my progress, guiding me through the fragile terrain of recovery.

Intense discomfort was something I learned to tolerate from my days as a competitive runner. I courted it, leaning into the hardship during training, knowing that the strength and endurance needed to win races were forged in the effort. Pushing beyond my physical and mental limits cultivated the grit that helped me through recovery.

Did I wish the pain wasn't there? Of course. But I was only open to alternative healing methods—so long as they were natural and effective. I was already getting weekly bodywork sessions, but I wanted something more, something that might speed up my recovery. So, I sent out a request to the Universe, like putting a message in a bottle and throwing the bottle in the ocean. What I didn't expect was the form in which the answer would arrive.

Running into Olivia at the health food store seemed unremarkable at the time—just one of those mundane moments we assume holds no real significance. But the next day, and again weeks later, I came to realize just how pivotal that meeting was, setting off a chain of events weaving its way through my life like a thread of destiny.

Olivia was a slender, soft-spoken woman in her fifties, with long brown hair that fell past her shoulders. I had seen her before at the health food store I frequented, but our exchanges never went beyond brief, polite hellos.

That day, however, we were standing side by side, reaching for the same vegetables in the produce section. I tend to talk to strangers—it's just part of who I am—and I couldn't resist this opportunity. I made an offhand comment about the produce, and just like that, we were talking. What started as casual small talk quickly shifted, and before I knew it, I was telling her about my accident, the persistent pain I was living with, and my aversion to allopathic painkillers.

She listened intently, her expression thoughtful and her presence surprisingly grounding. Then, with quiet certainty, she said, "I have something natural that can help with your pain."

I blinked, taken aback. "You do? What is it?"

She explained that she was a distributor for a multilevel marketing company that sold magnets—magnets that, according to her, had the power to heal.

I stared at her, certain she had to be joking. Healing magnets? I had never heard of such a thing. Even with my open mind, the idea hovered on the edge of absurdity.

"I've got one in my car," she said, motioning toward the parking lot. "Let me grab it for you. I'm happy to lend it to you so you can take it home and try it."

I practically rolled my eyes in skepticism. *A magnet? Really?*

A few minutes later, she returned, holding a peculiar-looking device. It was a small, rectangular plastic container with a lid. It housed two round, knobby magnets fixed in place. She brushed her fingers over them, demonstrating how, even though secured, they rolled freely within their casing. Then, she handed me the contraption to examine for myself.

I turned it over in my hands, running my fingers across the magnets, satisfying my instinct to touch and test, while skepticism and curiosity waged a quiet battle within me.

"Roll these magnets over the painful area for several minutes before you go to bed," she instructed, her tone confident, as if healing magnets were just another part of everyday life.

Olivia had initially struck me as an intelligent woman, but now I wasn't so sure. She handed me her card, and with that, we parted ways.

At least there wasn't a hard sales pitch, wild claims, or long-winded stories, I thought—just a simple suggestion and a business card.

That night, with an I-don't-have-anything-to-lose attitude, I followed Olivia's instructions. I rolled the magnets over my side and back, targeting the areas that hurt the most, for about ten minutes before bed. When nothing happened, I felt foolish for even considering the idea that magnets could heal me.

The next morning, I swung my legs over the side of the bed and stood up—without wincing, moving more easily than I had in months. To say I was shocked would be an understatement. No hesitation. No sharp jolt of pain. If you'd asked me to quantify the change, I would have said my pain had diminished by about 75 percent.

I picked up the phone and called Olivia immediately, my hands trembling with giddy excitement.

"You won't believe what happened!" I exclaimed, recounting my experience as if I was the recipient of a miracle.

Olivia took the news with the calm of someone who had heard it all before.

"Tell me more about these magnets," I exclaimed. I was so intrigued and awestruck by my results that I signed up to become a distributor for the company that produced them.

The company offered an entire line of magnets and required every new distributor to attend a three-day seminar. While I was eager to get started, I wasn't exactly looking forward to the event. I expected a tedious sales presentation and couldn't imagine sitting through three full days of lectures. At one point, I even reconsidered my decision to become a distributor because of it.

But with Olivia's encouragement—and her assurances that it wouldn't be a three-day corporate spiel but more of a personal growth workshop—I signed up for the next seminar. It was two weeks away, in Portland, a two-hour drive north of where I lived.

The seminar turned out to be far better and more engaging than I anticipated. The event didn't spend much time on the company, its products, or how to sell them. Instead, it focused on self-development and empowerment. It was a nice mix of engaging lectures, experiential exercises, personal reflection, and group activities.

At around noon on the second day, we all sat facing the stage as the facilitator gave a presentation on success and what it takes to achieve it. The journey to success, he said, could be summed up in a formula with two components: intention and the "how"—meaning the method you use to reach it.

"Think of a goal that seems impossible," he said. "One you don't know how to accomplish." Then he instructed the audience, "When it comes to success, rate the importance of intention versus knowing how, using percentages."

He then posed some options. "Would you say that the formula for success is fifty percent intention and fifty percent knowing how? Thirty–seventy? Or one hundred percent knowing how and zero percent intention? What do you think?"

He gave everyone a few minutes to write down their answers. When the time was up, the facilitator shared his perspective. He surprised me by stating that the formula for success was 100 percent intention and 0 percent knowing how. His argument was that if there was even a trace of hesitation or doubt in someone's intention, there was room for failure—especially when facing a challenge that required stepping beyond one's comfort zone. You could be clear on what to do, but if you weren't willing to act, then it didn't matter how much you knew.

It reminded me of the familiar adage, "Where there's a will, there's a way."

I sat in my chair, captivated by the facilitator's thought-provoking presentation. He walked over to his podium, looked over some papers, and then announced a seventy-five-minute lunch break. I had been mesmerized by his words, but the moment the presentation ended, my attention shifted inward—and I felt the sharp pang of hunger.

When I started competitive running in junior high, I embraced the belief that my body was a temple and that I should care about the kinds of food I fueled it with. By the time I was fifteen, I had stopped drinking soda and eating at fast-food restaurants, choosing whole, less-refined foods instead. I also avoided coffee, alcohol, cigarettes, and drugs.

Because there weren't any restaurants near the seminar location, the company arranged for some food to be provided on-site. After looking over their lackluster selection, I decided to strike out on my own. I threw on my jacket to stave off the autumn chill and got in my car. The seminar was being held in a bleak industrial part of Portland that I wasn't familiar with, but I was confident I could find something with all the time we had been given.

The first five minutes were spent driving through an endless horizon of drab buildings in all shapes and sizes, and not a single sign of food. Not that I'd want to step inside a restaurant in this area, though. Ominous plumes of varying colors spewed into the overcast skies, making it feel like I was driving through a set from the movie *Mad Max*.

I felt sure I was going to find something down the road, but a couple of things were working against me that added to my concern. The first was that I was directionally challenged—I don't think I could have told you which way was north or south, even if my life depended on it.

The second was that this was the fall of 1994. While GPS had been invented, it didn't become a common feature in most vehicles until the early 2000s. I didn't have a map of the area, so I was practically driving blind. Out of an abundance of caution, I decided to stick to the main roads and not make too many turns.

After another five long, uneventful minutes, I started getting antsy. I had driven out of the industrial area, but what I saw around me hardly inspired confidence. It looked like I was in no-man's land. Apart from a building here and there, there were few signs of development or life.

I decided to turn right at the next main road I came upon. Once I did, things started to look more promising, but the only options I saw were fast-food joints and a large chain grocery store. I wouldn't step into a fast-food joint if I were starving, and while I could probably find something edible at the grocery store, what I really wanted was either a nice restaurant or a health food store. I decided to roll the dice and gamble on finding something better.

Several minutes passed without any viable options. By this time, my low blood sugar blues were kicking in. If you were to ask my wife, she would tell you it isn't pretty when I get hangry. I looked at my watch and gauged how much time I had left. I really wanted to find something good, so knowing I had the grocery store as a plan B, I gave myself another few minutes to find something.

When my alarm signaled that time was up, I still hadn't found anything. I let out a deep sigh, resigned to the reality that I was heading back to the grocery store for a make-do meal. I made a U-turn the first chance I could, and within ten minutes, I pulled into the parking lot and trotted into the store. Five minutes later, I was heading back to my car carrying a sandwich, bottled water, and some fruit.

As I neared my car, I reached into my pocket to grab my keys. They weren't there. Figuring I had absentmindedly put them in a different pocket due to my low blood sugar, I checked my other pocket. My fingers fished around, brushing against the empty fabric. My heart beat a little faster.

You must have put the keys in your coat pocket, I told myself.

Holding my breath and saying a quick prayer, I shoved my hand into the wide-mouthed pockets of my winter coat—the kind with openings just big enough for keys to slip out unnoticed.

Did I put my keys in my coat pocket and they fell out? I wondered. It was possible. They weren't secure like my pants pockets.

With a strong dose of OCD, I shoved my hands back into my pant pockets, fumbling around for the keys, convinced they had to be there—that my fingers were just missing them. I pulled the innards of my pockets out as if that would somehow make a difference. I patted my back pockets, rummaged through my coat pockets again, then back to my pant pockets, shoving my hands in one more time, just to make sure I hadn't somehow missed them. My heart was beating hard against my chest, echoing the alarm blaring in my mind.

I walked up to my driver's side window, dreading what I was about to see, hoping—praying—it wasn't true. But sure enough, there they were, sitting innocently on the driver's seat.

My hands curled into tight fists. Less than two weeks ago, I'd done the very same thing—locked myself out of my car. It cost me eighty dollars to have some guy take sixty seconds to unlock my car using a cheap-looking gadget. With my income as low as it was, that eighty dollars should've gone toward essentials like food, not wasted on a stroke of bad luck.

If you've ever seen a child throw a tantrum at the grocery store, then you have an idea of what happened next. I literally stamped my feet and could've given Muhammad Ali a run for his money with the way I was swinging my fists in the air. I was lucky no one was there to witness my outburst; otherwise, they probably would've called the cops.

After a few minutes, I calmed myself down, realizing my victim mentality wasn't going to solve anything. *What am I going to do?* I repeated that question out of desperation three or four times, pacing back and forth beside my car. When my angst cooled, I shifted into problem-solving mode.

That's when the voice made a suggestion. That mysterious, telepathic messenger has always whispered words of wisdom at opportune moments—not out loud, but as thoughts that surface in my mind with a clarity that feels unmistakably distinct from my own. This time, it asked me a simple question: *What about setting an intention?*

Oh my God—why didn't I think of that? Everything the facilitator said about success and the power of intention came flooding back to me. Curious if it would work, I decided to test it as an experiment. What did I have to lose?

I glanced at the time—forty-five minutes left before the start of the seminar. I stood in the parking lot, visualizing what I wanted. Speaking out loud, I formulated my plan.

"Okay," I said. "Here's my intention: I want to get into my car for free without damaging it, have time to eat my lunch, and get back to the seminar with five minutes to spare!"

I swung around 360 degrees, taking stock of what was near me. The grocery store was in a commercial district, just off a busy four-lane road with a low concrete median dividing the lanes. Four car dealerships sat within striking range—three across the highway and one on my side, down the road.

I wonder if any of those dealerships would have that tool to get into a locked car? I mused.

I decided to start with the dealerships across the way. I kicked it into gear and dashed across the street.

"Hi!" I exclaimed to the guy sitting behind the reception counter of the closest dealership. "Hey, I've got a favor to ask you." I explained my situation and asked if he had that tool locksmiths use to get into locked cars.

"You mean a jimmy?" he asked.

"Is that the thing they stick down the side of the window?"

"Yeah, that's called a jimmy."

"Got it," I said. "Do you have one of those?"

"We do," he said, "but we keep it locked up, and the manager has the key. Unfortunately, he's not in right now."

I thanked him and started to walk away. As soon as I did, the voice chimed in, pointing out that I could have asked the guy if he would call the manager to have him come down and unlock the safe. That was definitely outside my comfort zone. My ego stepped in with its own words of wisdom.

If you ask him to do that, you'll put him on the spot and make him feel uncomfortable. He'll think you're a nuisance. Is that what you want?

The voice wasn't going to let my ego push him over. He informed me that this was one of those moments the facilitator referenced when discussing the intention formula—where anything less than 100 percent commitment left room for failure. The question boiled down to how committed I was to doing what was necessary to succeed.

I took a deep breath, let out a sigh, and turned back before reaching the door. The guy looked up with a questioning glance.

"Hey, I know this is a lot to ask," I said, "but would you be willing to call the manager to see if he'd come in and unlock the jimmy?"

He hesitated. I could tell he wasn't comfortable with the idea, but he also didn't want to appear unwilling to help.

"You know what, I'll give him a call to see." He disappeared into the back to make the call. Whether he actually made the call, I'll never know. I paced around the black-and-white tiled showroom, proud of myself for having the courage to ask. It didn't take long to get my answer.

"Sir," he called to get my attention. "I can't get ahold of him."

"Okay," I said. I thanked him for his help and turned to leave.

"Sorry about that," he added, then wished me luck as I hurried out and set my sights on the next dealership just down the road. I jogged over, getting there in no time. I gave the next guy my spiel, and his response was exactly the same.

"We have a jimmy, but it's locked up, and the manager is the only person who has a key. He doesn't work on Sundays."

Having built up some courage from the first dealership, I asked if he'd be willing to call the manager to come down and unlock it. I got the same hesitation.

"Uhhh . . . I can tell you right now, he's not going to want to come in on his day off."

Feeling this was a dead end, I thanked him anyway and stepped back outside.

In the pursuit of our dreams or a seemingly impossible goal, there comes a point when we must decide whether to stay comfortable with what we know or step outside our comfort zone to get what we want. It's a moment that defines not just our character, but our outcome. I was about to have one of those moments.

The air felt cool and moist as I stood outside the dealership. Things weren't looking great, but I wasn't prepared to give up yet. I stopped to take stock of my situation. Looking at my watch, I was dismayed to see that I only had twenty-five minutes left.

I eyed the dealership sprawled across the other side of the road from where I stood. I decided to give it one more try. I waited for an opening in the traffic, then sprinted across. Once inside, I hurried into the showroom and spotted a nicely dressed salesman standing by the water cooler.

"Hi," I panted, catching my breath. I explained my situation and asked if they had a "jimmy" I could use to unlock my car.

"I'm sorry, buddy, but we don't have a jimmy."

"Okay, thanks," I said, trying to hide my disappointment, and made my way outside.

I felt like Bill Murray's character in the movie *Groundhog Day,* one of my all-time favorite movies. The story centers on Bill Murray's character—a self-serving, arrogant man who gets stuck reliving the same day over and over again until he learns to become a better person. I was getting the same result over and over again.

I felt frustrated, deflated, and my hunger pangs were like a pack of wolves encircling their prey, growling menacingly, and baring their teeth. My low blood sugar was making my failure that much harder to bear. I had been able to keep it at bay with my task at hand, but it wouldn't be long before I snapped if I didn't take care of that need.

It was time to admit defeat. I patted myself on the back for trying, though it felt like an empty consolation prize. My next task, aside from sitting down to eat, was to call a locksmith. I spotted a 7-Eleven and headed over to borrow their Yellow Pages. Once I found the locksmith section, I called three or four businesses to find the best price. Satisfied that I had done my best at bargain shopping, I gave them my location and was told they'd be there in about twenty minutes.

I found a bench just outside the 7-Eleven and sat down to eat my sandwich while I waited for the locksmith to arrive. After a few bites and a moment of feeling sorry for myself, the voice manifested again.

What about your intention? it asked, like a teacher bringing a student's attention back to the assignment.

Cranky and frustrated, I snapped back. *What do you mean, what about my intention?* I asked, incredulous that this voice—whoever or whatever it was—was giving me a hard time. *I did the best I could!*

It didn't buy my story and wouldn't let me off the hook. The voice insisted I keep trying.

My frustration boiled over.

"What do you expect me to do?" I exclaimed out loud, raising my voice as if I were arguing with a real person.

I was looking down at the sandwich on my lap when something compelled me to look up. My eyes rested on what was across the street. There, staring back at me was the fourth dealership. I had completely forgotten about it.

The voice encouraged me to run over to it.

My stubborn, self-justifying ego jumped in, rattling off excuses for not bothering to try. *The other dealerships couldn't help you,* it whined. *Why would this one be any different? Besides, the locksmith is on the way. They'll be really pissed if you cancel—they'll probably charge you for the cancellation. You tried your best, and now you need to finish the rest of your lunch. You're only going to feel worse if you don't eat right this minute.*

But the voice persisted, gently but firmly nudging me to get up. Despite all my ego's convincing excuses, I knew the voice was right. I couldn't ignore it—I had to at least try.

I threw everything into my plastic bag and ran back across the busy street.

I walked into the dealership and was greeted by a young guy with a cheery smile sitting behind the reception desk. I told him a nutshell version of my story, and without skipping a beat, he said, "Yes, we have one. Let me run and get it, and I'd be happy to help you out."

I was stunned and elated, mesmerized by the latest development in the chain of events that got me to this moment. I had one more task to do. While the guy went into the back to get the tool, I pulled out my phone and called the locksmith. I braced for an ordeal, but they shrugged it off and assured me it was okay. They weren't going to charge me either.

When the young man came out with the jimmy, we hurried over to my car. This time, I was happy it only took him sixty seconds to unlock my car with his cheap-looking gadget.

My intention was to get into my car for free, but at that point, I was so appreciative of his kindness that I pulled out my wallet as he was putting the jimmy back into its case. When he saw that I was about to pay him, he put up his hand to stop me.

"No, please. You don't need to pay me."

"Are you sure? You're a godsend," I told him. "I feel extremely grateful for your help."

"No, you're good, really." He was adamant that I not pay him. I thanked him profusely, then watched him jog back to the dealership.

My whole body buzzed as if currents of energy were running through me, charged with something otherworldly. I hopped into my car and finished my lunch in quiet reflection.

My ordeal felt oddly similar to the Hero's Journey as outlined by mythologist Joseph Campbell—a narrative arc that appears in myths, literature, and even movies across cultures.

At its core, it follows a character who receives a call to adventure that takes them outside their familiar world and into the unknown. Along the way, they encounter trials, mentors, and tests that force them to grow. Ultimately, the hero returns transformed, bringing back some form of insight, healing, or reward.

It's not just a storytelling device—it's a map of transformation, a mirror to our own inner journeys. The Hero's Journey unfolds in a series of stages, each one marking a distinct chapter in the hero's evolution—beginning with the call to adventure, followed by refusal, mentorship, trials, the reward, and finally, the return.

As I looked back on the day's events, I realized I had just lived out a modern version of Campbell's Hero's Journey. The call to adventure came when I chose to leave the safety and predictability of the seminar site in search of better food. I ventured into unfamiliar streets, guided only by instinct and hunger, without a map or GPS. That small decision pulled me out of the known and set me on a course filled with uncertainty, frustration, and unexpected obstacles.

The refusal of the call crept in through hesitation and second-guessing—when I questioned whether I should keep going, settle for less, or just turn back. But I kept driving. The turning point—the threshold—came when I locked my keys in the car, stranding myself in a strange place with the clock ticking. From that moment on, I was no longer in control, and the journey demanded more from me.

The mentor arrived not as a person, but as the voice—my inner compass—urging me to set an intention rather than give in to defeat. Each dealership became a trial, a test of whether I would act on faith or abandon my purpose. The ordeal came outside the 7-Eleven, sandwich in hand, ego deflated, convinced I had done all I could. But the voice returned, persistent and calm, reminding me to stay committed.

The reward came at the fourth dealership, where a stranger offered help freely and without hesitation. It was more than a solution—it was validation. Something greater had been guiding me all along.

My ordeal wasn't a coincidence. It felt orchestrated, as if Spirit had designed a test—not to challenge me, but to reveal what was possible when I truly committed to my intention. Had I stopped at any point, convinced myself it was pointless, or let my pride keep me from asking for help, I would never have known how close I was to success. But something greater had guided me to push past those limits, to surrender doubt, and to trust in the unseen forces at play.

The reality of what had just happened settled deep into my bones. Intention wasn't just an idea—it was a force, a current that carried me forward when my own willpower faltered. When I arrived back at the seminar, I walked through the door with minutes to spare. But I wasn't the same person who had walked out over an hour ago. I had experienced something profound, something undeniable—a quiet partnership with the Universe. A reminder that when you set an intention with unwavering commitment, the Universe doesn't just listen—it responds.

32

The 25-Pound Feather

If you're a spiritual seeker like me, I highly recommend a movie that came out in 1999 called *The Matrix*, starring Keanu Reeves, Carrie-Anne Moss, and Laurence Fishburne. It's a mind-bending cinematic sci-fi masterpiece with metaphysical undertones that strongly imply some fascinating—and rather unsettling—ideas about the nature of reality.

At the heart of the storyline is a striking exposé suggesting that what we perceive as the real world may be an elaborate illusion, that human perception is merely that, a perception, one that can be manipulated by an external source, and that truth and reality are subjective and possibly hidden unless you wake up from the deception propagated by your denial.

The movie was so captivating that I sat on the edge of my seat, mesmerized by its creative genius, gripping plot, and special effects that were ahead of their time. There's one major downside: It's violent. But the graphic confrontations are depicted in a stylized, choreographed, and symbolic way, unlike the gratuitous brutality you'd find in Quentin Tarantino films.

My inner fifteen-year-old thought the inclusion of martial arts with the fighting was super cool, but for some of you, it might be too much. You can always watch a clip or two on YouTube to see if it piques your interest.

Spoiler alert: I'll be sharing key details from the movie in this story.

The premise of *The Matrix* is that AI and human beings go to war, much like in the Terminator series with Arnold Schwarzenegger. AI ultimately prevails, sending survivors fleeing to deep underground caves to hide and live. Meanwhile, on the surface, to create the bioelectric power they need to keep themselves running, the machines harvest human embryos and grow them in small pods to use as sources of energy—like batteries. Hundreds of thousands of human beings are literally plugged into gigantic generators.

To control humanity and minimize complications, the machines create a highly sophisticated, computer-generated program called the Matrix. It's a simulation that every human mind is plugged into from birth, used as a tool to keep humans docile and unaware that their bodies are actually trapped in pods being used as a source of energy.

The virtual reality is so convincing, people think they're living in the "real" world when actually they're living inside this artificial construct, completely unaware that their perceived reality is nothing more than an illusion.

I was completely floored by the film's originality, creative brilliance, and its questioning and exploration of the nature of existence, human potential, and the fundamentals of free will. Some of the dialogue between the characters in the movie espouses spiritual dogma about fate, destiny, and cause and effect—fascinating concepts that resonated deeply with me.

From a young age, I've had extraordinary experiences that made me realize there's more to life than most people in our society acknowledge. These events compelled me to question the nature of reality.

What is reality, exactly? I'd ask myself. *Who or what defines the laws of what's possible?*

The subtle ideologies woven throughout the movie mirrored my own questioning and inspired me to think more deeply about them.

I was awed and mesmerized by the movie's complex exploration of spiritual concepts. The parallels drawn between the Matrix in the movie and the reality we think we know here on Earth made my mind reel in an intoxicating spin. I had to watch the film many times to fully grasp these concepts, as they challenge the hard, cold facts we hold dear about gravity, time, and the purpose of life.

If you think about it, life here really is, in a way, a simulation. I believe we are eternal souls inhabiting a temporary physical body. I think it's highly plausible that before we incarnate into life on Earth, we go to a repository that houses every kind of earthly experience imaginable. We pick and choose what we want to experience in life beforehand, with the sole purpose of learning and evolving, knowing that free will is like a wild card that makes it more interesting and unpredictable.

The main storyline centers around a prophecy that foretells the coming of an individual born within the Matrix, who will "wake up" to the truth and use his powers to save humanity from their imprisonment. This individual, named Neo, is rescued and freed from the Matrix by a small group of people led by a wise man named Morpheus. Morpheus has also escaped the Matrix, believes in the prophecy, and has dedicated his life to finding "The One."

Morpheus believes Neo is The One, and he and his followers nurse Neo back to health while they explain humanity's plight. Some of those who escape the Matrix choose to help save others by plugging back in temporarily.

Because powerful AI agents with superhuman strength patrol the Matrix in search of escapees who plug back in, Morpheus and his team train Neo in martial arts so he can defend himself if he encounters them.

They also help him understand the Matrix and how it operates. One way Morpheus and his team do this is by creating a simulation of the Matrix—a software-based virtual reality outside the Matrix but identical in nature—so Neo can practice his skills and better grasp the nature of the Matrix through personal experience.

There's a powerful scene in the movie when Morpheus challenges Neo to a sparring match in the simulation to test his martial arts skills.[2] After you see them plug in, while lying in reclined chairs that look like they came straight out of a dental office, the next scene reveals the two of them standing in a vast room designed to resemble an old-world Japanese dojo. The backdrop is exquisite: a thirty-foot ceiling, walls and windows made of latticed rice paper, bamboo-trimmed wraparound balconies, and large wooden beams.

"This is a sparring program similar to the programmed reality of the Matrix," Morpheus explains to Neo as they stand facing each other, garbed in typical loose-fitting kung fu attire. "It has the same basic rules," he continues. "Rules like gravity. What you must learn is that these rules are no different than the rules of a computer system. Some of them can be bent. Others can be broken."

The two begin to fight, each exchanging rapid blows, until Morpheus gains the upper hand and sends Neo crashing face-first to the padded floor with a thud and a groan.

"How did I beat you?" Morpheus asks.

Neo struggles to catch his breath as he slowly peels himself off the mat and onto his knees. "You're too fast," he responds.

Morpheus stands a few feet away and asks, "Do you believe that my being stronger or faster has anything to do with my muscles in this place?" He nods toward the ceiling, referring to the simulation they're in. Neo shakes his head, struggling to come to terms with the truth.

---

2 https://youtu.be/fhrNgXJ__n8?si=5O_SGu1EavA0FhbI.

Morpheus then leans in toward him and asks a profound question with electrifying implications. "You think that's air you're breathing now?"

Neo is stunned into silence, his mind reeling as he tries to grasp the full weight of what Morpheus is saying.

I sat there riveted, hanging on to every word Morpheus spoke. I too began asking existential questions about my reality. Were we all living in an illusion like the Matrix, unaware of the bigger truth? Was our universe one reality in one dimension simultaneously co-existing with millions of others? Can we bend or break the rules of this reality? If so, how?

His words resonated deeply because I believe science hasn't gotten it right when it comes to understanding what's possible. Through my own personal growth and my work with others, I've seen time and again how we often deny our potential for greatness through negative thoughts, feelings, and beliefs—something I know personally all too well.

Under the current understanding of physics, many scientists believe nothing can travel faster than the speed of light and that we can't fly without an external power source. I say that's hogwash.

How can they be so naive? I wonder. I believe it's not a matter of if, but when. I believe there will come a time when we realize those gospels of truth about reality are not hard facts set in stone. I believe it's possible for us to transport ourselves through space with our thoughts, like we see people do in science fiction movies--we just haven't figured out how yet.

Experts once believed it was physically impossible for humans to run a mile in under four minutes. Runners worldwide tried for years. They came within seconds, but no one succeeded, which only reinforced the belief that what the scientists were saying was true.

Then in 1954, a British runner by the name of Roger Bannister broke the four-minute barrier by six-tenths of a second. That's about as much time as it takes for a person to blink twice quickly. What's amazing is that once he broke the barrier, other runners quickly followed suit.

As of now, the record for the mile is an impressive 3:43.13, set by Hicham El Guerrouj of Morocco. Roger Bannister not only broke the four-minute mile, but he also smashed a deeply rooted paradigm—one that had created false limitations. What other false paradigms are we holding on to—and how deep does that rabbit hole go?

Have I flown or levitated? No. Have I traveled faster than the speed of light? I was a quick-footed, record-setting competitive runner in my younger years, but no, I haven't run—or traveled—that fast. But I have glimpsed into the rabbit hole of altered reality more than once. I've felt my soul leave my body, I've consciously been in two realities from different centuries at the same time, and I've walked on fire.

The experience I'm about to describe left me dumbfounded— much like how Neo must have felt in the dojo when Morpheus spoke those potent words about how rules like gravity can be bent or broken.

It happened one afternoon at the gym as I was starting my weightlifting routine. I walked over to the waist-high rack holding numerous pairs of dumbbells, picked up a twenty-five-pounder to warm up with, and walked over to a padded horizontal weight bench to do some curls. I set the dumbbell on the bench while I slipped on my workout gloves.

Curls are exercises that strengthen your biceps, the main muscle in your arm. To do them, you start with your arm straight, weight in hand and elbow at your side. Then, you bend your elbow to lift the weight toward your shoulder.

When I was ready, I picked up the dumbbell in my right hand and got into position to do a set of ten warm-up reps. I placed my left knee and my left hand on the bench, bent over so that my right arm hung toward the floor on the right side, gripping the weight in my hand.

Twenty-five pounds wasn't a lot of weight for me, but it did require a certain amount of effort to lift. I applied what I thought was the right amount as I started the movement. To my astonishment, the dumbbell—with my hand still holding it—flew up and hit me in the face, narrowly missing my eye.

It felt like a scene from a Looney Tunes cartoon—only in real life, it was more surreal than funny.

The dumbbell hit me so hard it cut my skin, and I started to bleed. I grabbed a paper towel from a nearby dispenser, folded it up, and pressed it over my wound.

A weight room attendant happened to walk by and saw me bleeding. He instructed me to sit on the bench while he ran to the nearby office to get a bandage and an ice pack, and to notify the manager on duty. They soon returned together.

The weight room attendant unwrapped the bandage, placed it over my cut, and handed me the ice pack while the manager stood by, assessing the situation.

First, he asked if I was okay.

"I'm fine," I said. I was a bit bewildered and mystified, but I was okay.

"How did this happen?" he asked. It was an unusual circumstance, and the look on his face made it obvious he was trying to figure out how the dumbbell hit me in the face.

"I'm not sure," I replied. "I started to do a curl, and the dumbbell suddenly flew up into my face."

The manager looked at me askew, like he was questioning whether I was on drugs. There was a long pause as he stood there, unsure of what else to say. Once he was satisfied that I was okay, he quipped brusquely, "Just don't do it again."

He nodded his approval to the weight room attendant, then promptly turned and walked away.

I thanked the employee for his help and sat on the workout bench to mull over what had just happened. The dumbbell felt as heavy as twenty-five pounds the entire time I held it—from the moment I picked it up off the rack and carried it to my spot until the moment I took hold of it to begin my exercise. But once I initiated the movement, it felt as light as a feather.

That day in the gym, I had an encounter with the unexpected, and in that brief moment, like Neo in the dojo, I experienced something that transcended the rules of our reality. The laws of physics, gravity, and even human potential must be more flexible than we lead ourselves to believe. Who's to say what's possible?

As I was working on a draft of this story, I had a *Twilight Zone* moment of serendipity that made me pause. Earlier, when I searched online for the current world record in the mile, I didn't check when it was set. Later, out of curiosity, I looked it up again and discovered something uncanny—the release date of *The Matrix* and the current record for the mile both happened in the same year, just months apart.

This strange "coincidence" felt like the Universe was whispering a reminder—a quiet confirmation that magick isn't just an abstract concept but a living force, woven into the architecture of reality itself. Or perhaps the truth is even deeper than that—perhaps reality doesn't just hold consciousness . . . perhaps it *is* consciousness.

Like in the movie, we too exist within a matrix. What rules can be bent or broken—and by how much? Maybe our greatest limitations aren't imposed by an external source but written on a whiteboard, ready for us to erase and rewrite with our free will. History shows us that the boundaries we accept are often illusions maintained by the stories we've come to believe.

I'm reminded again of Morpheus's piercing words to Neo: "You think that's air you're breathing now?" I realize it's just a movie, but where do the ideas come from that inspire these stories? Is the leap from imagination to reality as distant as we think? Did you know that science fiction—especially shows like *Star Trek*—has inspired a surprising number of real-world breakthroughs in medicine, technology, and even spaceflight?

Speaking of illusions, there's a powerful quote from Richard Bach, author of the book *Illusions*, that reads, "Argue for your limitations, and sure enough, they're yours."

Ultimately, the instant we stop arguing for what we think to be true—like experts—and expand our awareness of what's possible, we give truth a chance to reveal itself. Just like how twenty-five pounds can be as light as a feather.

33

Healing Back Pain

The plywood flooring beneath the cheap polyester carpet of my apartment felt like concrete under my shoulder and hip bone as I lay curled up in a fetal position. I wasn't lying down because I wanted to. I was there because of two large cardboard boxes, my stubbornness, a casual dismissal of my better judgment, and a debilitating back spasm.

Back issues weren't new to me. I had been living with chronic pain on and off for most of my life, starting with an injury I sustained as a teen during basketball practice. The spasms would come and go as they pleased—sometimes it would be a couple of years before they showed up again. Whenever they did, they made my life miserable.

Over the years, I learned the warning signs of their approach, like the coming of a storm: a growing tightness in my lower back followed by sharp, sudden twinges that came out of nowhere—catching me off guard and hinting at something worse to come.

If the tightness in my lower back persisted for more than a couple of days, it would spread to other parts of my body, crawling up my spine to my neck, upsetting muscles along the way and restricting their ability to function. If it got to that point, things a healthy person takes for granted—like bending over, carrying anything over fifteen pounds, or even moving faster than a walk—became diffi-cult, if not impossible. The tension was like a boa constrictor. It slowly, sinisterly wrapped itself around my upper torso, squeezing the joy out of my life.

Searching for a solution to the problem was an exercise in futility. No one seemed to have the answer. Many of the things I tried addressed the symptoms but not the cause. Sometimes a treatment helped the first time but not the next, and some were a complete waste of time and money. In almost every case, my relief was temporary, lasting only hours before my body reverted to its tormented state. The combination of helplessness and limited financial resources with no health insurance was a source of deep frustration.

If I couldn't find a way to unlock the grip the tension had on my body, I would eventually go into what I called an "acute" stage. The pressures in my body caused by the tension created so much torque, they tweaked my upper torso, forcing it to tilt to one side just above my pelvis like the Leaning Tower of Pisa. It looked and felt unnatural.

I considered myself somewhat fortunate because my predica-ment didn't involve sharp, teeth-gritting pain on a constant basis. But the unwavering, nagging discomfort wasn't much of a conso-lation. It was like a gigantic leech attached to my back. Instead of sucking my blood, it siphoned away my energy, leaving me feeling physically and psychically drained.

Another demoralizing aspect of being in an acute stage was the fear. The fear of pain. It was an unwelcome squatter in my mind, gnawing at my peace and filling me with dread. My body felt so out of whack that it felt as though if I made the wrong move—and I never knew when or what that was—it would elicit a lightning bolt of unbearable pain.

This latest episode with my back had lasted much longer than ever before, instilling a deep concern that I might be facing a new normal. Nothing I tried made a difference. I felt resigned to the fact that I would have to live with a chronic condition for the rest of my life.

But life doesn't stop because of pain—which brings me back to how I wound up lying on the floor of my apartment, gritting my teeth while curled up in a fetal position.

As a creative introvert, my home is my sacred space, where I retreat to rejuvenate. Living in a calm, visually appealing environment is important to me. I'm the kind of person who will spend all day and night unpacking boxes after a move so I can feel settled in my new home as quickly as possible. I like being organized and believe in the adage, "clear space, clear mind." A little bit of clutter is okay, but I like it when everything has its place.

My apartment had an open floor plan, and where the dining table was supposed to be sat two oversized boxes in plain view—an unwelcome eyesore in my otherwise tidy space. Inside them were the parts for my new table, waiting to be assembled. The visual discord nagged at my sense of aesthetics and inner harmony. Even though I was experiencing back problems, I couldn't stand for those boxes to be there any longer.

I knew the kneeling, bending over, and squatting necessary to put the dining set together would be a challenge for my back, but I wasn't about to pay someone for something I could do, and I waved away any concerns with a convincing dose of willful disregard.

I'll be okay, I told myself. *Nothing a hot pack can't fix*, I recklessly mused. I rationalized that the effort was worth a bit of extra tightness in my body.

Sixty minutes later, after tightening the last screw, I struggled to get back on my feet. As I rubbed my lower back to ease the tightness, I stood by the bar-height table, admiring its simple, clean lines. I'm a do-it-yourselfer and derive a lot of joy from fixing things or putting things together. I was also, in that moment, enjoying the reestablished harmony in my home. The effort taxed my body, but

I felt confident the tension would eventually ease up now that I was done.

The suddenness and virulence of the attack took me by surprise.

One moment I was standing, and the next, a savage violence gripped my mid-torso, sending shock waves to my brain. I screamed in agony and dropped to the floor like a marionette suddenly without strings.

The sheer intensity of it shook me to the core, reaching into the marrow of my bones. I lay frightfully still in a cold sweat, groaning through my clamped jaw as the brutal force of the pain washed over me.

A flurry of f-bombs and other choice words spilled from my clenched jaw in a bitter stream. The sudden intrusion felt like a violation. I wanted to cry out of self-pity, but the tears wouldn't come. I was too angry.

My victim mindset shifted its attention to the one thing I blamed for my difficult situation—God.

Why are you doing this to me? I bemoaned inwardly. *I just want to live a normal life, do normal things that a person who doesn't have back issues could do. Is that too much to ask?* Silence met my rant, leaving me to wallow in the unfairness.

I hate feeling powerless. There were numerous frightful incidents when I felt that way as a child. And now, as an adult, I still struggled with the scars—residues of fear, humiliation, betrayal, abandonment, and the inability to stop or control what was happening. The horror of the scars was ingrained in my psyche. I spent a decade in therapy to heal the trauma, and yet, here I was, still dealing with the intensity of the feelings associated with them.

My primal instinct kicked in with the only response it knew to confront my inadequacy—rage. It rose like a tsunami. Logically, I knew unleashing my rage wasn't the answer. But its alluring appeal seduced the part of me hungry for power and protection. In the blink of an eye, my rage turned into a mountain lion. I was backed into an uncompromising corner by an unfair circumstance. I was not going down quietly.

I stayed lying on my side and closed my eyes. I clenched my jaw and formed a fist with my right hand. My fingers and thumb squeezed so tightly, my arm shook. I grimaced in battle readiness. In my mind, I faced God, baring my teeth and growling menacingly as a show of force.

I wanted to hurt Him with all my pent-up fury. I dared Him to come closer. Then I tore into Him with razor-sharp claws, slashing away in a wild frenzy. I gave the rage my voice, screaming with threats, hurling angry words I won't repeat here. In my imagination, rage knew no bounds. Its power was atomic. Its unquenchable appetite for revenge ripped God to shreds. My rage transformed from a mountain lion into an uncontrollable monster lusting for release. It threw rapid-fire punches at His face and blasted His being with bolts of lightning, and I envisioned His bloodied body engulfed in flames from the fires of hell, searing every ounce of His soul in unimaginable pain.

When that didn't satiate my lust, when my rage realized that punishing God wasn't going to relieve its feelings of impotence and pain, it turned to someone else—me.

Childhood victims of abuse often develop toxic self-criticism. The result is an internalized voice that harshly and unfairly judges and blames the innocent victim. This was true for me. My rage decided I was the one responsible for its suffering. Its inability to find redemption through power led to blame. It became my fault. I had caused this predicament, so I became the target of its fury.

Anger is considered by many in psychology to be a secondary emotion. Its presence usually means there's hurt or fear hiding underneath that we're not willing to feel. The adult, rational part of me knew that, knew rage would never bring me solace. But logic was no match for the unchecked intensity of the wounded part of me still reeling from abuse. All my rational mind could do was watch it play out its ritual of desecration, like a person in the throes of an earthquake, helpless to stop it from destroying everything in sight.

When I eventually calmed down, I examined what my rage was really about. I realized that underneath my anger was fear. I was worried about my future well-being, both financial and physical, and how it would affect the quality of my life.

In the past, my bouts with chronic back pain lasted anywhere from a couple of days to a couple of weeks. Eventually, my back would feel better, and I could resume a normal life. This latest episode felt different. Six weeks had come and gone, and my back pain was still impeding my life. At my job as a massage therapist, there were many days I had to lie on the floor between massage appointments, wondering how I was going to make it through the day. Something about this experience felt more permanent, like a bone had shifted in my body and wasn't going back into place.

I tried every trick I knew to help myself—stretches, hot packs, ice packs, massage therapy, gentle chiropractic adjustments, reiki, positive affirmations, reframing, gratitude, yelling, even ice cream. Nothing worked to get me back to normal.

Was I really going to have to resign myself to a mediocre life? As my mind spiraled down that stream of thinking, I wasn't sure I could stomach it. I didn't want to have to. *I would rather die than live like that*, I told myself.

Once I had calmed down, the growing discomfort in my hip and shoulder from lying on the unforgiving floor brought my awareness back to the present, reminding me that I needed to find a solution to my immediate dilemma. Do I dare risk another spasm by shifting my weight, or do I grit my teeth and bear the ache, lying still a while longer in the hope that everything calms down?

I couldn't tell what my body would do if I moved. I scanned it with my mind and began slowly unclenching the tension I found— in my jaw, my face, my shoulders, and my back—softening my breath and relaxing my posture while gauging the likelihood of another spasm.

I tested my condition by moving ever so slightly. When no other wave came, a deep, involuntary sigh blew past my lips. The worst of it appeared to be over. I took a few slow, deep breaths to calm my nerves. Then I held my breath, gritted my teeth, and slowly shifted my body weight. My muscles felt sore and achy, but no spasms ensued. Another long, deep sigh.

I gazed up at the underside of the table and then past its legs to across the expanse of my living room to the large window and the sunlight streaming in.

What am I going to do to fix my back? (*And my life?*) I mused.

The answer came unexpectedly, as softly as a whisper in my mind. *Read the book.*

The book? The book! I had forgotten about it.

I had bought a book the day before because it felt like I was given signs by Spirit to do so. But I hadn't started reading it yet. I reached over and massaged the muscles in my lower back and butt, trying to work out some of the remnants of the spasm. When I determined it was safe to get up off the floor, I hobbled over to the kitchen and popped a large hot pack into the microwave. Then I made my way to my desk, where the book was lying, and picked it up.

HEALING BACK PAIN in bold capital letters marked the top of the cover, with a subtitle underneath that read *The Mind-Body Connection*. In all caps at the bottom, more copy stated: "WITHOUT DRUGS, WITHOUT SURGERY, WITHOUT EXERCISE, BACK PAIN CAN BE STOPPED FOREVER." The book was written by Dr. John E. Sarno.

When I heard the ding of the microwave notifying me that the hot pack was ready, I grabbed it along with the book and headed for my bedroom. I propped up my pillows, strategically placed my hot pack, and carefully slid into bed. I wasn't much of a reader, but I was intrigued by the title, and because I felt

Spirit had guided me to the book, I was determined to give it my undivided attention.

The first time I heard about the book was from a client. I was a massage therapist at an upscale sports and social club, and during my brief conversation with him, he told me about his experience with back pain and how this book helped him. What he had to share sounded interesting, but I convinced myself a book wasn't going to solve my problem, so I didn't bother to check it out.

Within the same week, however, I happened upon an article in a magazine about a celebrity who had been helped with his chronic back pain by the same doctor. Then, the next day, as I was on a lunch break at the club, a colleague of mine I hadn't seen in a while walked by. He was finishing up his workout and stopped to catch up for a few minutes. When I told him I was having back issues, he recommended I read a book entitled *Healing Back Pain*.

"Interesting you mention that book," I said. "This is the third time I've heard about it this week."

"Must be a sign," my friend replied. "It's a game changer," he added.

Whenever something starts showing up in my life repeatedly within a short span of time—whether it's the name of a person, book, or idea—I take note because it's usually a sign from Spirit telling me I need to pay attention, that whatever the sign is pointing to is important for my life journey. In that moment, I decided I was going to get my hands on a copy. After my last client of the day, I walked over to a used bookstore nearby and bought a copy.

With book in hand, I lay in bed and began to read. I was quickly mesmerized by its contents. Some of the concepts made sense and aligned with my beliefs, but just as many of them were difficult to accept because they challenged the very nature of widely accepted beliefs about the body—not just regarding back pain, but disease and other debilitating physical ailments, some of which I had bought into.

I was absolutely dumbfounded to learn that this doctor's technique had an 88 percent success rate treating patients with severe chronic back pain. And they weren't just any kind of patient. These were people the medical community had given up on. But it wasn't the success rate that was the most astonishing—it was what he did to get those results. This doctor's treatment protocol involved one thing and only one thing—*talking!* You read that right. This doctor was able to help the most severe cases of chronic back pain by educating them in workshops he facilitated about what was really going on—that essentially, their problem wasn't physical in nature—it was psychological.

I couldn't believe what I was reading.

The gist of Dr. Sarno's findings is that back pain is not caused by structural issues within the body like the medical establishment claims—not slipped discs, not pinched nerves, not bone spurs. He determined that many ailments are caused by unconscious rage and that physical therapy, massage, surgery, drugs, or special exercises only propagate the idea that the issue is a physical one. He coined the term for the problem *tension myositis syndrome* (TMS for short). The concept was a hard pill to swallow, especially since I was a massage therapist.

On page 82, I came across a list of what Dr. Sarno calls "Daily Reminders." They are affirmations he encourages his patients to read and reflect on for fifteen minutes each day. I read each statement on the page several times, pausing to reflect quietly on each one before moving on to the next—statements like

"The TMS is a harmless condition caused by my repressed emotions."

"I intend to be in control, not my subconscious mind."

"I must think psychological at all times, not physical."

After mulling over the affirmations, I felt the need to use the bathroom, which raised my concerns about whether moving would initiate another spasm.

Whenever I'm in an acute stage, I can comfortably sit in a chair or lie down in a bed once I'm situated and don't have to move. I almost feel normal again because the muscles responsible for holding up my torqued body don't have to work so hard, hence less discomfort.

That respite was both a lie and short-lived. When it came time to get up, I would have to grit my teeth and steel my mind as sharp pain radiated out from my lower back, stoking my fear of triggering another mind-bending spasm. The full brunt of my discomfort would reappear once I was vertical.

I set the book down and carefully maneuvered out of bed and onto my feet.

Once I was standing, I took a couple of small steps, monitoring the response from my back closely. I immediately noticed a remarkable difference in my body. I wasn't leaning to my left like I had been before getting into bed.

This can't be true, I thought. I was no longer in an acute stage!

I was standing straight and tall, and my body felt more normal than it had in weeks. Not believing what I was experiencing, I braced for pain and took a couple more steps to see if I was making it all up in my head.

WTF is going on?! My body still felt tight, but there was a remarkable difference in how it felt compared to how it had felt for the past month and a half.

I stood there and soaked in the transformation. I struggled to comprehend how the dramatic shift in my body could have occurred after reading a book and focusing on a list of affirmations. It felt like a miracle. Provocative implications about the influence our thoughts have on reality swirled around in my head. It was both sobering and intoxicating.

As I continued to read the book from cover to cover, I learned about the personality and character traits of people who are more susceptible to suffering from the condition Dr. Sarno describes—people who worry or have a tendency to feel anxious, perfectionists, people pleasers, and those with high standards, strong wills, and ambitious natures, to name a few. I realized in that moment that I was one of them.

I wondered if I could have benefited from his teachings even though I hadn't attended one of his workshops.

Some of the tenets Dr. Sarno espouses go against common sense and everything I believed. These included "There's nothing wrong with your back," and "Since your back is basically normal, there is nothing to fear."

He asserts that physical activity is not dangerous. He goes so far as to encourage people to stop doing body-focused therapy and special exercises and to resume whatever physical activity they fear doing.

I wanted to believe him. Still unsure I could trust what was happening, I walked around the bedroom, tentatively testing and prodding the limits of what I thought my body could do by slowly moving in ways that previously I'd been too scared to try.

Within minutes, I was prancing around like a child, jumping and twirling through the air. A couple of thoughts ran through my mind as I did this. Part of me applauded my bravery while another part of me bellowed that I would be so sorry later. That part of me definitely had reasons to be concerned. I was moving my body as if nothing was wrong, but I still felt the usual warning signs threatening serious consequences for my behavior—twitches of spasm, severe tightness, muscle ache, and increased sensitivity.

Part of the paradigm shift I experienced was realizing that those threats were essentially bluffs. Once I understood the underlying psychological nature of what was going on, that my pain was a strategy my brain was using, I could counter it with my awareness and belief. Once the brain realized its ploy wasn't going to work, the threats would dissipate.

Feeling empowered, I snubbed my nose at the warnings and continued my escapade around the room. I repeated out loud a number of the daily reminders from the book, like war cries, imagining myself pointing my finger at the part of me responsible for manifesting the pain and letting it know I had its number.

"You're no longer in charge!" I cried. "I don't need you to distract me from my emotions. I'm dealing with them. This is a psychological issue, not a physical one!"

My confidence grew exponentially, as did the joy of my relief. Had I finally found the answer to my lifelong struggle with back pain? Was hope no longer just an abstract, unattainable feel-good state of mind? The answer was a resounding *yes*! Dr. Sarno's book changed my life. It showed me I wasn't as powerless as I thought. I didn't have to live a mediocre life dictated by my back pain.

Over the years, since that fateful day, the old strategies my brain used to deal with stress continue to manifest periodically as back issues. The difference now is that I have an awareness of what is going on and can utilize the concepts Dr. Sarno wrote about to quell the need for the pain. Instead of weeks or months, it takes minutes, hours, or a couple of days at the most to get back to normal. I learned that I can have a healthy back without drugs, surgery, or special exercises—just as his book promises.

Thank you, Dr. Sarno!

I was saddened to hear that Dr. Sarno died in 2017. But his legacy lives on. People with chronic back pain and other physical ailments continue to radically transform their lives by embracing the wisdom of his work.

Daily Reminders*

1. The pain is due to TMS, not to a structural abnormality.

2. The direct reason for the pain is mild oxygen deprivation.

3. TMS is a harmless condition, caused by my repressed emotions.

4. The principal emotion is my repressed anger.

5. TMS exists only to distract my attention from the emotions.

6. Since my back is basically normal there is nothing to fear.

7. Therefore, physical activity is not dangerous.

8. And I must resume all normal physical activity.

9. I will not be concerned or intimidated by the pain.

10. I will shift my attention from the pain to emotional issues.

11. I intend to be in control—not my subconscious mind.

12. I must think psychological at all times, not physical.

*You can find additional affirmations, posted by people who have benefited from Dr. Sarno's work, on the internet.

34

The Mystical Moth

The cool evening breeze of a San Diego spring whispered gently past the balcony of my humble second-story apartment. A drab parking lot stretched out below, but from my chair, all I could see was a horizon framed by palm trees, their fronds swaying beneath an expanse of a dreamy, picturesque sky dotted with billowy, white clouds.

I was newly single, and with the breakup came the loss of the comfortable home I'd once shared with my girlfriend. Without the benefit of a dual income, I couldn't afford that luxury. I ended up moving into a modest one-bedroom apartment—a far cry from what I'd been used to. I was the one who ended the relationship, but this was a consequence I wasn't exactly thrilled about.

I briefly closed my eyes and took a deep breath, consciously choosing to appreciate what I still had. With a refreshing drink in hand, I watched the palm leaves dance, mesmerized by their graceful movements as the breeze played through them like invisible fingers. It was a perfect evening in the Southern California city I called home. Little did I know it was about to be transformed by a profound, magickal experience.

As twilight surrendered to night, I slowly made my way to my desk at the opposite end of the living room, pausing to light the candles scattered along the way. The flames flickered softly, casting a golden glow that stretched and wavered across the walls. The room felt cocooned in stillness, wrapping me in an intimate quiet, its corners softened by the tender flicker of light.

It was dark, but the night was young, and I savored having it all to myself—no interruptions, no obligations, no demands. I enjoyed dabbling in graphic design, and that day, a friend had asked me to create a business card. The quiet hours felt sacred, offering the perfect space to lose myself in the creative zone.

I powered up my desktop and quickly slipped into the delight of inspiration. As an intuitive and modern-day shaman, I was adept at tuning into the subtle energies around me, but nothing could have prepared me for what was about to unfold.

At about eleven o'clock that night, a movement in the corner of my right eye caught my attention. I turned to look toward the front door and saw the silhouette of my cat, Neo.

Named after the hero in my favorite movie *The Matrix*, Neo was found in the parking lot of my ex's condo more than a decade ago. Small enough to fit in the palm of my hand, she had to be fed by hand with a syringe. We initially thought she was a boy, but by the time the vet set us straight, she already knew her name.

Neo sat upright the moment she realized she had my attention, poised like a regal feline fixing me with an intent gaze. She let out her distinctive warble—a trilling sound she made when she needed something. This time, she was signaling that she wanted to go outside. Neo was an indoor-outdoor cat, and while I usually let her roam freely, I didn't like her being outside so late at night.

I looked back at my monitor and ignored her, hoping she'd lose interest. I should have known better. Her warbles only grew louder and more insistent, disrupting my concentration and grating on my nerves. Whoever said, "Dogs have owners and cats have slaves," got it right. Neo had her little paws wrapped around me, and she knew it.

To maintain my sanity—and with a dramatic sigh to let her know I wasn't happy—I gave in and sauntered over to the door. I muttered my disapproval under my breath, but she didn't care. She darted into the night without a second glance. Like a worried parent, I peered out after her, cocking my head to one side to listen for any sounds of danger or concern. Convinced that nothing was amiss, I began to close the door.

Just then, something near my foot caught my eye. I leaned in for a closer look and noticed a moth lying motionless on the doorsill.

What a strange place for a moth, I mused, giving it only a passing thought before closing the door and heading back to my desk.

About twenty minutes later, I felt an urge to check on Neo. The moment I opened the door, she bolted inside, brushing past my legs as if being chased by a pack of dogs, and vanished down the dark hallway toward my bedroom.

"Hey, take it easy!" I called after her.

As I turned back to close the door, I noticed the moth was still lying on the doorsill. This time, curiosity took hold, and I knelt down for a closer look. The dim porch light did little to illuminate the area, so I switched on a nearby lamp. That's when I saw why the moth hadn't moved—its lower body was partially smooshed against the doorsill. To my dismay, I realized it was still alive.

The peaceful night vanished, replaced by a sudden surge of urgency. I leaped up, rushed to the kitchen for a paper towel, then hurried back and knelt beside the injured creature. After a brief moment to assess how to lift it without causing more harm, I gently used the towel to pry the moth from the sill.

I held the moth reverently in the palm of one hand, cupping my other hand a few inches above its fragile body. As a seasoned energy worker, I focused on creating a cocoon of healing energy around the wounded creature. In soft, prayerful tones, I spoke to it, gently expressing how sorry I was for its pain. All I wanted was to comfort it, to make its final moments on earth feel filled with warmth, peace, and love.

As I cradled the moth, something within me shifted. My heart expanded, and a surge of love flowed through me, dissolving the distance between thought and feeling—an embrace of pure, unfiltered connection, alive in my hands.

A warmth spread through me, starting in my chest and radiating out to my fingertips. It felt as if I had tapped into something far greater than myself—a cosmic thread connecting me to this tiny creature, to the Universe, to everything. I gazed at the moth with the tender awe of a parent watching their angelic baby sleep. As I studied it more closely, I was surprised to find stunning, intricate details.

Where my mind had once dismissed the moth as an ordinary, plain-Jane creature, my heart now saw it as it was—truly magnificent. Its wings, adorned with delicate gold and black designs, seemed to shimmer with quiet beauty. Moved by the sanctity of the moment, I decided to honor the moth by taking its picture. I gently placed it, resting on the paper towel, on my desk and reached for my phone. As I opened the camera app and focused on the moth, time seemed to slow.

The camera took a moment to focus. When it did, what I saw stole my breath—a luminous image had appeared on the moth's back, like a sacred revelation from Spirit. I moved the camera away and looked at the moth with my naked eye.

There, beaming from its back, with a surreal brilliance as if it were lit, was the image of a robed figure, its heart chakra aglow with a soft, fiery light. The figure's arms were raised as if offering a blessing (see photo on next page).

The world fell away, and all I could feel was the pulse of divinity in the air. My mind grappled to understand what was happening. Had that image been there the whole time and I just didn't see it, or did it only appear once I decided to take the photo?

If you're religiously inclined, you might see the figure as resembling Jesus. But for me, as a modern-day shaman, it looked like the image of a shamanic holy man—a symbol of wisdom and connection beyond the boundaries of religion.

As I studied the image, I was astonished to realize that the robed figure wasn't a natural pattern on the moth, nor were the details a random design—it had formed from the way the moth had been crushed. The glowing heart chakra, sadly, was the moth's insides that had oozed out. In its last moments, this creature became an exalted creation, a marvel revealed in the most extraordinary way, an affirmation of the sacredness in all things.

Dante, the fourteenth-century Italian poet and philosopher, once said, "Nature is the art of God."

Here in front of me was proof—a humble moth elevated to the stature of breathtaking by the masterful stroke of Spirit.

I felt an overwhelming sense of gratitude. It was a spectacular, one-of-a-kind moment, and I felt honored to have comforted the moth and to have received such a parting gift. It was a reminder that within the ordinary lies the potential for the extraordinary. Miracles can happen at any moment if we're open to receiving them.

It struck me that I could have easily missed this celestial wonder entirely. It didn't manifest despite my actions—it happened because of them. Had I ignored the moth, disposed of it without a second glance, or skipped taking its picture, this profound experience might never have unfolded. Both choice and action were essential ingredients for this encounter to occur.

It made me wonder: How many other miracles go unnoticed—not because they don't exist, but because we aren't paying close enough attention or following the nudges that lead us to them? The stark contrast between what had happened and what could have been—had I looked away—was sobering.

As the moth lay still in my hand, I sat in quiet reflection, its fragile body cradled like a sacred relic. The room felt different now—alive with an unseen current as if the veil between the ordinary and the divine had thinned. Maybe the Universe was telling me something—revealing a truth hidden in plain sight.

Maybe miracles aren't rare. Maybe they're woven into the fabric of everyday life, tucked within small choices, quiet moments, and overlooked corners. Maybe we don't find them by seeking the extraordinary—instead, we find them when we're fully present and willing to see the ordinary with new eyes.

I was reminded of a powerful lesson—that the key to love is kindness. When we extend ourselves with care—to a person, an animal, even an injured moth—we invite the flow of love. In that space, there's no room for judgment or apathy. What the mind dismisses as insignificant, love transforms into something precious—a glimmering pearl of beauty.

In the end, the moth wasn't just a fragile creature clinging to life. It was a messenger—showing me that the sacred isn't confined to temples or rituals. It lives in the fragile wing of an injured insect, in the quiet ache of compassion, and in the simple, transformative act of choosing to care.

Maybe that's the real magick—not waiting for miracles but becoming the kind of person who notices them.

35

Night of Divination

Rays of golden sunlight broke through the moody spring skies of Portland, the city I called home. Their majestic gleams and the fresh blossoms blooming everywhere brought a welcome sign that the long, dreary Oregon winter was nearing its end. The air still held a chill as my best friend, Mandy, and I made our way on foot to our favorite new age bookstore in the trendy Northwest section of town. Side by side, we strolled down the half dozen blocks from my car, the scent of rain and magnolia hanging in the air as we caught up on our latest news.

Mandy was an attractive, charismatic blonde with a lot of cute quirks and mannerisms that would either make me smile or laugh out loud. She was the epitome of the "dumb blonde" stereotype—but in the most endearing, hilarious way. I used to joke that I could've made millions if I'd written down all the things she said—classic "true blonde" gems that either made me burst out laughing or roll my eyes in amused disbelief.

But there was nothing funny or cute about what she was about to tell me.

"I'm going to move to San Diego," she proclaimed. "Why don't you come with me?"

"You're what?!" I blurted, stunned. It was the first time I'd heard anything about her plans. In that instant, the thought of my life without her hit hard and left me reeling. We had been through so much together—as former lovers and now friends.

Fate had brought us together years ago in a playful, synchronistic way that felt like something straight out of a romantic Hollywood script.

We knew we weren't destined to be together—she wanted kids and I didn't—but every time we tried to end things, we'd always find our way back. When I finally made the hard decision to end our romantic involvement for good, I knew in my heart I was committed to making it work as friends.

Despite the challenges of that transition, our friendship had become one of the most meaningful parts of my life, and the thought of not having her close felt like a chasm of loneliness opening beneath me. We'd moved to Portland together from Eugene two years earlier, and I felt like we were just settling into a good rhythm.

"Yeah," she continued, "things aren't working out the way I had hoped they would. Besides, my brother lives near San Diego, and I want to be closer to him."

My mood soured as I struggled to come to grips with her news. We were like an old married couple, minus the sex and the wedding ring. If we didn't see each other every day, we were at least on the phone. What we didn't have physically, we had emotionally.

"You can't move," I exclaimed in a whiny, poor-me voice.

"Oh, Keno Eno," she said consolingly. *Keno Eno* was one of the quirky-cute terms of endearment she used for me. "Come with me," she reiterated.

Mandy's invitation to move to San Diego held a lot of appeal. I loved California. I had so many fond memories from several summers in Marin County as a kid and countless visits to the Bay Area throughout my life. But I had never been to The Sunshine City. San Diego sounded like a dreamy place from everything I'd heard, but I also knew it was prohibitively expensive. I liked the idea of relocating there, and I certainly hated the thought of Mandy moving away, but I didn't see a major change like that happening in my cards anytime soon.

Spirit, however, had other plans. What began as Mandy's dream slowly became mine.

One of her friends—a massage therapist, like me—had moved to San Diego not long before Mandy's announcement. Over the next two months, she shared with me her friend's glowing reports about how great San Diego was. During that time, my own life started to shift in unexpected ways—several things unraveled, quietly severing my ties to Portland and making the idea of moving to San Diego feel increasingly possible.

Starting a new life from scratch in an expensive city was a big deal, but after quite a lot of thought, I eventually made the decision to move. I didn't see it as anything more than a practical decision—following a friend, starting an adventure, and chasing possibilities—but looking back, it's clear something grander was in motion.

Ironically, after I made my plans, Mandy met a love interest in Portland, and bailed at the last minute on moving south. As much as it pained me to pick up and leave without her, the wheels of change were turning and there was nothing to stop them. It became obvious, at that point, that part of Mandy's role in my life was to be a catalyst for me to move to San Diego. She would eventually move there too, continuing not only to be my bestie but a catalyst for my growth.

So, in the summer of 2008, after living in Oregon for twenty-four years, I sold most of my things, packed the rest in a U-Haul, and with Mandy's help, I made the two-day trek with my Jeep and cat in tow. I didn't have a place or a job lined up, and I only knew two people—Mandy's brother and her friend—who were both barely acquaintances. It was a tough first few months, but with Spirit's help, I eventually found both a job and a place to live.

That winter, I felt the urge to dabble in developing my psychic abilities. I still hadn't made any friends and thought finding a class would also be a great way to meet like-minded folks. I decided to check out Meetup.com to see what was available and came across a group that seemed to be exactly what I was looking for. It was called The Psychic Gym.

The purpose of the group was to give people interested in psychic phenomena the opportunity to practice and hone their abilities. The host, Tom, had just started the group and was building up the membership so he could offer ongoing events and classes. Two months after I initially made contact, the first meeting was scheduled.

The night of the first class found me both excited and nervous. I had never been to a gathering like this before, and I was intrigued by what was going to happen.

The group was scheduled to meet at the back of a café in Hillcrest, a hip and happening part of San Diego. The place, with its bold-colored walls decorated with art from local artists, had the typical café vibe of coffee connoisseurs and laptop junkies. I made my way to the back, pushing aside a curtain that acted as a door to the café's activity room.

Behind the curtain lay another world—a spacious room that felt like an energetic sanctuary, lit by curiosity and quiet reverence. The chairs formed a sacred circle, and the space hummed with anticipation, like a temple disguised as a coffeehouse.

Most of the seats were taken by early arrivals. They appeared to be between the ages of twenty-five and fifty-five and a mix of both genders, but predominantly women. I promptly took a seat and waited for the class to start, politely keeping to myself as strangers in a new class often do, with the awkward silence broken occasionally by hushed whispers of friends who had come together.

Tom, a slender, middle-aged man with an unpretentious, calming demeanor, started the class by introducing himself. He went over the ground rules, creating an ambiance of support and

nonjudgment. He proceeded to lecture on some essential princi-
ples of intuition, allowed time for questions and answers, and then
facilitated a few basic exercises working with energy. None of the
information was new to me, but Tom was engaging, and the energy
in the room was captivating.

My interest piqued when he announced that the last exercise
we were going to do was called "psychometry." If you haven't read
about my amazing initial experience with psychometry, you can
read about it in the story "The Fourth Knock."

For those of you who are not familiar with psychometry, it's the
act of reading the energy of objects to garner information about the
object's history and/or the people that have touched or owned the
object.

Just like leaving fingerprints behind, we leave energetic imprints
of our energy on things we touch, wear, or have around us. The
same goes for the people we interact with. Our energy mingles with
anyone we interact with, see, or even think about.

It had been years since I last tried psychometry. After the trau-
matic experience I had with it as a young, naive college student,
I wasn't interested in ever trying it again. More than twenty years
later, however, there were no lingering concerns from my past about
doing the exercise—just surprise at how much time had passed.

The night was getting late, and since most of the class time had
been taken up by the ground rules, lecture, and other activities, we
only had a few minutes to pair up with another person.

I found myself facing a smartly dressed, middle-aged Asian
woman who was new to psychic development.

She handed me one of her bracelets and waited patiently for me
to start.

I took a couple of deep breaths and calmed my mind. After
being a competitive runner and a massage therapist for many years,
this was something I could settle into pretty quickly.

I was able to intuit a couple of things about my classmate, but there was nothing spectacular about my foray back into psychometry. I walked away from the experience unimpressed with my results.

Tom cautioned us not to get too attached to outcomes and encouraged us to be patient with the process. Even though my experience was nothing to write home about, I enjoyed the evening and decided to attend future group meetings.

At the end of the night, before everyone disbanded, Tom made a couple of announcements. One was about an upcoming event hosted by another Meetup group called "Night of Divination." It was an unstructured opportunity for people of all abilities to gather and practice their psychic skills. I made a note of it and planned to go.

Our days are often filled with mundane moments, and we live through them thinking that nothing special is happening and that nothing special will happen. Sometimes that's the case, but sometimes it isn't. There are those days that seem ordinary but end up being forever etched into our minds and hearts because they turn out to be anything but ordinary.

This story is about one of those days—a seemingly normal one that evolved into an evening of magickal surprises and ecstatic serendipity.

My day started like any other—a couple of cups of freshly brewed hot chocolate while working at my desk, a few clients at my private office, some quick errands, a trip to the gym, and the Night of Divination event I had been looking forward to for the past week.

Despite my different activities throughout the day, one constant weighed heavily on my mind—I was single. For the most part, I was at peace with that. But in the quiet moments, my heart ached for a deep connection with another soul. It had been a long time, and I was starting to wonder if it would ever happen. I wasn't getting any younger, and as weeks blurred into months, and months into years, I began to question whether life had destined me to be a lone crusader.

On this day, I was keenly aware of my aloneness, but I did my best to focus on other things as the day progressed into the night.

It was a typical winter's evening in downtown San Diego. The air had a slight chill, a scattering of people strolled past shops and cafés, and parking spaces were sparse.

Though psychic development had fascinated me for years, I'd never actively pursued it. Going to intuition classes was a new venture for me, and this was my first event with this particular group. As I made my way there, I wasn't quite sure what to expect.

One thing I did know for sure, however, was that I was late. To make matters worse, the meeting was held at an apartment I'd never been to before, and it was proving difficult to find.

Being late and lost are far from any place I like to be. My irritation grew rapidly, like a band of screeching monkeys gone rogue, rattling the bars of my brain. I took a few deep breaths and tried to pacify them with peaceful mantras, but they ignored every mental banana I tossed their way. Finally, after some detective-like sleuthing, I stood in front of the door where I needed to be. I took a deep breath to calm my frazzled nerves and knocked.

I was greeted by a group of people engaged in conversation in a large, pleasant living room. Their heads turned toward me as I entered. I apologized for being late, and as I stepped inside, I scanned my surroundings. The apartment was a spacious L-shaped loft with numerous nooks and crannies filled with pockets of people. Rich earth tones and aesthetically pleasing décor created a soothing ambiance that resonated with my own taste.

Because I was late, I had just missed the opening introductions. When I arrived, people were getting up and pairing off to practice psychic readings for the rest of the night. I needed a moment to catch my breath and get my bearings, so I meandered back through the apartment to find the kitchen and a glass of water. The space was full of people of all ages and backgrounds milling about, their voices creating a chaotic chorus of chatter. My eyes rested on a few faces as I navigated through the crowd, but one stood out, holding my gaze a moment longer than the rest.

Her dark skin, raven-black hair, and luminous eyes seemed to radiate a soft glow, capturing my attention amid all the clatter and boisterous energy of the room. It was only for a moment, but as I continued on, I could feel that moment etch itself into my mind like a still shot from a movie. Then, as if I had woken too soon from a fleeting dream, all traces of her quickly dissolved into the swirl of the crowd as I focused on finding my way to the kitchen.

Back in the kitchen, I grabbed a glass of tap water and sat on the bench of an empty table for six. As I was taking a moment to ground myself, Tom from The Psychic Gym emerged from the crowd. He greeted me with a hello and then sat down across the table from me. The next thing out of his mouth surprised me. He looked me in the eye with a sly smile and, in an I-know-something-about-you-that-you-don't-know tone, said, "I want you to read for me."

I was taken aback. Feeling unprepared and completely unsure of myself, I replied, "I don't think I can."

He gently persisted and encouraged me to give it a try. Feeling self-conscious, I reluctantly agreed. He fished something out of his pocket and handed it to me. I took a few deep breaths and tried to ground myself. I closed my eyes and began our session. By this time, several other people had joined us at the table and watched me with rapt anticipation.

I was relieved when information about Tom started floating into my mind, but it felt jumbled and haphazard. I tried to make sense of it, but all I could do was stumble over my thoughts with my words. Tom stopped me and encouraged me to relax.

Unbeknownst to me, Tom was about to say something that would dramatically affect my life. It was a Luke Skywalker–Obi-Wan Kenobi Jedi mentor moment that would open me to the Force like never before.

"Keno, stop judging what you're sensing," he said in a hypnotic tone. "Trust that you have the ability—and trust what your intuition is saying."

It wasn't just the words he spoke that landed. It was the way he spoke them—the steady calm in his voice, the unwavering compassion that cut through my self-doubt like sunlight through fog. In that moment, it was as if he reached into the dark and flipped on a light inside me. The door I hadn't even realized was closed suddenly opened.

And with it, the information began to flow—clear, purposeful, and alive with meaning.

The energy around the table shifted. People leaned in, eyes wide, catching the current of something unseen yet undeniably real.

Until then, I had forgotten that I could intuit things about people at will. It was a profound reawakening. In Star Wars terms, it was the moment I realized the Force had never left me. I had only forgotten how to listen.

When the session ended, he smiled warmly, nodded in approval, and said, "I'd like you to read for a friend of mine."

"Oh?" I responded. "When did you want me to do that?"

"Right now," he replied. "She's here somewhere. Let me go get her."

He rose with quiet determination and disappeared into the crowd.

Moments later, he returned with a woman by his side. After a brief introduction, she handed me an object, and I wrapped my fingers gently around it, letting it rest in my palm.

This time, the connection was instant. The energy moved through me like a current, and words came effortlessly. I found myself going deeper than I had with Tom—touching on things more intimate, more revealing.

By the time the session reached its natural end, a wave of fatigue washed over me. I hadn't realized just how much energy I was expending. I thanked Tom and his friend and returned the congratulatory high fives from those who were watching.

As I stood there, I glanced at the sea of people crowded into the apartment and inadvertently zeroed in on the mystery woman I had seen on my way in. In that moment, I felt a compelling urge to read for her—as if commanded by something greater than myself. As her gaze met mine, I motioned to her with my hands and silently mouthed, *Would you like to practice with me?* She nodded her interest and, after grabbing some snacks and a drink, we made our way to a private table for two.

Within minutes, the air around us sizzled. Sitting there with Rashmi, I felt like I had stepped into a Bollywood movie where two souls meet, drawn together by the forces of fate. I half expected background music to rise from nowhere and a slow, steady wind to sweep through her hair—the kind you see in Indian romantic films when love arrives on cue and soulmates find each other.

Looking at Rashmi, I swore I could hear the rumbles of a thunderstorm rolling in, its fervent winds and tendrils of lightning stoking the fire between us.

The room fell away as our eyes met, then broke away, only to find each other again. The warmth of her sweet smile and deep, dark, soulful eyes wrapped me in rapture. I was convinced that if we touched, we might have electrocuted each other.

Rashmi was considerably younger than me, but I couldn't deny the chemistry between us. It was becoming clear to me that I was in the presence of a kindred soul. But what kind? The kind you have a wonderful interaction with and then part ways, never to see each other again, or the one you take home to bed for an erotic fling, who maybe stays a while, or the soulmate you live with for the rest of your life? All I could tell in her presence was that my heart began to melt from the heat of her gaze.

After a few smiles and just as many giggles, we decided to start practicing. I did my best to focus as I started to read her energy.

"I sense the presence of a young man," I said. "He feels like a lover from your past. Am I right when I say you're still interested in him?"

I was dismayed and a little confused when she confirmed my intuition—because it sure felt like she was sending me some good vibrations.

"You've been reaching out to him," I continued. "But he keeps putting you off, ghosting you. That's because he's not in a place emotionally to reconnect with you."

As she pondered what I had just shared, I wrestled with my integrity. Part of me wanted to honor her feelings for this guy and show restraint, and part of me wanted to leap up, take her in my arms, and press my lips to hers in a passionate embrace. I thought I saw sparks flying between us, but now I wasn't sure.

When I was done, Rashmi thanked me, sat up in her chair, then closed her eyes to go within to prepare for my reading. She was new to this, and I could tell she was nervous. With a little encouragement from me, she started sharing her impressions.

At one point, she hesitantly confided in me that she saw something about me but didn't think she should mention it. She sounded rather cryptic—and out of curiosity and support, I encouraged her not to censor what she was getting and to take the risk of sharing it.

Imagine my surprise when she told me she saw me having sex.

I burst out laughing and said, "I hope that's a premonition that's actually going to come true soon—because it's been way too long."

Heads turned to see what the ruckus was as our deep, unfiltered laughter echoed through the apartment. As it softened into a shared smile, I couldn't help but wonder if the vision Rashmi saw was of the two of us in an erotic embrace.

Her reading ended just as the event was beginning to wind down. We lingered, slowly gathering our coats, neither of us ready for the night to end. I wanted to tell her what I was feeling—how the alchemy between us had ignited both passion and possibility—but shyness, and a fear of coming across as too forward, kept the words from coming out.

As we made our way to the front door to thank the host, I struggled with the ache of holding back, unsure whether to share my not-so-innocent thoughts and feelings. We weren't holding hands, but it felt like we might as well have been. There was no denying—something otherworldly had us tethered.

I asked where she'd parked and told her I'd walk her to her car.

The distance to her vehicle was short—way too short. I had hoped it was at least five hundred miles away. I was feeling buzzed from my interaction with Tom and his friend, along with the high school giddiness I hadn't felt in a long time. I wanted to revel in it with her all night.

As we stood by her car, we expressed our wonderment about the evening's events and then gave each other a hug. Her body felt good as it pressed up against mine in an embrace that seemed to hold unspoken implications. I didn't want the night to end—not without her—but I lacked the courage in the moment to voice my desires.

I looked into her big, beautiful eyes one last time, wished her a good night, and turned away to walk into the late hours without her. I hugged my sides tight from the cold and made my way back to my car, savoring the incredible events of the night.

The next day, I emailed Rashmi. I expressed my delight and awe in the charm and passion of our meeting and asked her if she enjoyed it too. I also expressed an interest in seeing her again. Her playful reply put a smile on my face.

Rashmi and I shared some good times together moving forward, but our connection was to end much sooner than I was ready for. Her decision to part ways took me by surprise. And so, just like that, she left mysteriously, in the same way she came.

I was reminded that life is full of impermanence—that expectations may go unmet, and things don't always unfold the way I wish they would. Not every spark of magick, no matter how brilliant, is meant to outlast its moment or be captured in stone.

That night with Rashmi was a profound, heartwarming gift—a testament to the power of soul connections that will remain etched in my memory. And the added bonus? I got to bask in it all over again as I wrote this story.

As for my psychic development? My reading with Tom initiated a chain reaction that would plant the seeds for the many experiences I was to have in my not-so-distant future.

One of those experiences actually happened the very next day, following the Night of Divination. I called one of my besties, Bella, who lived in Portland, and told her the exciting news about my experience. We combed over all the details like treasure hunters marveling at a long-lost find.

At one point, she caught me off guard with a request. "How about you read for me?" she asked.

"Uhhhhhh . . . I can't," I stammered. "I don't have any objects of yours to read from."

"Try anyway," she said in her typical, confident, empowered manner.

Bella was all about being a force for good in the world, and she believed in me. She wasn't about to let me shy away from a challenge. I suddenly remembered that I had a photo of her saved on my computer's hard drive. Feeling unsure of my ability—but comfortable enough to try with Bella—I pulled it up and looked at it while we stayed on the phone.

Much to my amazement, images and insights began to flow. If

the door had been opened the previous night, it was now blown off its hinges.

Interested in seeing how far the rabbit hole went, I began actively reading for volunteers, both within and outside the Meetup groups. What I learned from those practice sessions was that I didn't need an object or to see a picture of someone to read them. I could just think of that person and connect with their energy, even if I had never met them. I could hop on a call or write an email to tell them the things I was intuiting.

That discovery changed everything. It was as if the Universe had handed me a key to an unseen realm—and I had finally dared to turn the lock. No longer tethered to objects, photos, or proximity, I realized I could access intuitive insight through intention alone. My reality expanded, and with it, my sense of purpose deepened. What began as a night of innocent practice became the catalyst for something greater—an awakening to a path I hadn't known was available to me.

In the space between logic and mystery, I was reminded of something: The quiet knowing that the veil between worlds is thinner than we think, and that some invitations, whether from someone you know, Spirit, or a stranger's eyes across a crowded room, are never just coincidence—they hold within them moments of cosmic magick.

The End

You may have just finished reading my book, but on Earth, as it is in the world of Spirit, there is no end. Energy can neither be created nor destroyed; it merely changes from one form to another.

Maybe some of the details of my memoir will linger in your heart and mind, creating ripples in your life that lead to healing, more wonder, and new beginnings.

If you've enjoyed reading my stories, I would love it if you wrote a review and posted it on platforms like Amazon, so that other readers of like mind can discover it for themselves. Of course, I would be ecstatic if you thought my book was good enough to share with your network, friends, and family.

Writing a book is not an easy venture, and sending my memoir out into the world, intimate details and all, is like standing naked on a street corner (I haven't tried it and don't plan to, but I think you know what I mean). I feel both proud and vulnerable.

While I can't promise I'll respond to everyone who writes, hearing how this book helped you would mean so much to me. You can write to me at: keno@kenompowers.com

I also invite you to visit my website to learn more about what I'm up to: https://kenompowers.com/

Acknowledgments

To my wife: I'm not always the easiest person to live with, despite all my many endearing qualities. I appreciate your playfulness, spiritual awareness, and intellect. You stood by me through a dark time. I might not have made it without your support. I love you.

To Vesna Tišma, my book cover designer: It was evident you were talented from the design samples I saw on your profile on 99Designs. You took my ho-hum mockup and transformed it into something beautiful beyond my imagination. This book is so much more special because of your artistic eye.

To Candace Johnson, my editor: I found you because you had edited a colleague's book, but it wasn't until we spoke that I knew we would be working together. Your guidance and encouraging words were a boon to my confidence. It was a pleasure to work with you, and I look forward to working with you on my next book.

To Gary Rosenberg, my interior book designer: I appreciated your support, input, work ethic, and above all else, your sharp wit and sense of humor.

And lastly, to you, my reader: Thank you for giving my book a chance to make a difference in your life and in the lives of others. I trust that it spoke to you in the sacred ways you needed.

About the Author

"It's not who I am underneath,
but what I do that defines me."

—BRUCE WAYNE (as Batman), *Batman Begins* (2005)

Keno Powers is a Sun-in-Scorpio, Moon-in-Libra, Capricorn-rising soul who is respectfully irreverent and deeply fond of wit, creativity, and good food. He's also a proud dog-dad to a Havapoo furbaby named Muflee, whose personality keeps life entertaining.

Known for his resourcefulness and emotional intelligence, Keno is also unapologetically human—occasionally stubborn, prone to overthinking, and actively learning what it means to offer himself the same compassion he gives others.

He wishes kids didn't have to go hungry and that everyone had a safe, comfortable place to call home. He admires people who invent things to improve our planet and the lives of others—and entrepreneurs and business leaders who share their success by paying people generously and investing back into their communities.

As an agent of transformation, Keno inspires, guides, and empowers people to cultivate a healthier relationship with money. His life's work is also focused on supporting others to pursue their dreams and aspirations. Learn more at kenompowers.com.

www.ingramcontent.com/pod-product-compliance
Lightning Source LLC
Chambersburg PA
CBHW070906130626
46555CB00001B/16